THE DAILY ADVENTUR

The Daily Adventures of

MIXERMAN

Backbeat
Books

AN IMPRINT OF HAL LEONARD CORPORATION

NEW YORK

Published in 2009 by Backbeat Books
An Imprint of Hal Leonard Corporation
7777 West Bluemound Road
Milwaukee, WI 53213

Trade Book Division Editorial Offices
19 West 21st Street, New York, NY 10010

Printed in the United States of America

Book design by Mark Lerner

Library of Congress Cataloging-in-Publication Data
Mixerman.
  The daily adventures of Mixerman.
     p. cm.
  ISBN 978-0-87930-945-9 (hardcover)
  1. Mixerman–Diaries. 2. Sound engineers–United States–Diaries. 3. Sound recording industry–United States. 4. Rock groups–United States. I. Title.
  ML429.M57A3 2009
  781.49092–dc22
  [B]
                              2008051517

www.backbeatbooks.com

Acknowledgments

Special thanks to:

Fletcher
Mercenary Audio
John Piskora
Deb Ferguson
Philip Stevenson
John Dooher
Frank & Mary Dooher
The entire Dooher Family for the use of Bungalow Island
Don Put
Peter Green
David Wozmak
Bo Sweeney
Deborah Neville
Peter Bunetta
The entire team at Hal Leonard and Backbeat Books
All my friends who make The Womb Forums possible

& Mom

Foreword by Philip Stevenson
Editing by Mom and Polly Watson

Foreword

"All literature is gossip," offered Truman Capote, in the sly, able way that only someone who has mastered his own art form is allowed to get away with. While a flip remark initially, the quote itself has become more insistently true with the passage of time. Whether it's the *New York Times*, Hunter Thompson, or Boswell's *Life of Johnson*, we're never quite sure who said what, who did what, or what really happened. Through all the complexities of reporting human existence, one thing is certain: All stories are true.

When news and entertainment decided to fully consummate their marriage sometime in the 1980s, we were faced with inconsiderable checks and balances. Like every other industry, the music business was left with few people to call it on its own excesses. Sure, entertainment had always been news—but news hadn't always been entertainment. And, while the Beatles may have been as popular for their hair as for their music in the mid-'60s, it could be asserted that, in the mid-'80s, Madonna, while popular as a singer, was idolized for, well, being popular. Tenacity, not talent, had become the *sine qua non* of the modern entertainer.

By the time the Internet exploded into everybody's living room, we had a bloom of self-appointed critics and experts, most of them dilettantes. No longer did you have to get published. You pushed a button and you were. Rants, blogs, and critiques were everywhere—right alongside porn, hobbyist newsgroups, and institutional forums for academic exchange. With the personal computer, the instant Norman Mailer was born.

Unfortunately, as is often the case of those who wallow in the blush of new technology, this new frontier of self-expression fostered mostly a dull, solipsistic bunch of drivel. People initially enchanted by the Web were rapidly disillusioned at how boring all that browsing could actually be. Every once in a while though, you get lucky. Enter Mixerman.

On July 27, 2002, the mysterious music insider, who had already gained a reputation for dispensing sound technical advice via Usenet, started chronicling the day-to-day goings-on of a recording he was making for a large record company. It was a little slice of the rock and roll dream—a young band promised stardom, a big budget, and a name producer. However, instead of the story we'd all heard about getting to the top, riding in limos, and being chased by throngs of screaming fans, this was something different. It had all gone terribly wrong. Not only had the wheels fallen off, but, as one delved further, one started to see the truth illuminated: This immethodical circus was not the exception. Perhaps it was the rule. Perhaps it always had been.

Industry professionals immediately identified with the empirical details, and the uninitiated were equally drawn in by this rubbernecking view of making records. There was clattering speculation as to the who, when, and where of it, but everyone knew Mixerman was not a poseur. To those who knew him personally, he was an established, respected professional. To those who didn't, it was clear he was no Trojan horse.

By its fourth week, the diary was getting 25,000 hits a day and drawing attention from every stripe of the music business, as well as other bloggers, Internet junkies, and insiders. It was a phenomenon.

Being suspicious by nature, I got there a little late. Why the hell should I read what I already knew? When I did, I realized it wasn't the usual safe Dennis Miller shill in the guise of rebellion. It was actually great. Dryly funny and, while the style was cocky, it completely lacked the shrill egoism to be some kind of boorish self-advertisement. Rather, one pictures, like any good diarist, Mixerman—a person thrust into an aesthetic situation that seemed too hard not to document. Is it satire? Perhaps. But Daumier and Lewis Carroll were satirists too—arming their point of view with the truth rather than spastically mocking their audience with rude invention.

The diary went on in fits and spurts, winding its way into subplots and then returning to form again. Abruptly, it ended on December 10, 2002, the final chapter never published.

In this book, for the first time, we now have the completed diary as God and Mixerman himself intended. The final chapter is here, too, for new readers, as well as the more than 140,000 Web readers who may have lost a night's sleep here or there, wondering what became of their all-too-human, less-than-gifted cast of characters.

All stories are true. This one is no exception. Only the names have been changed to protect the guilty. Of course, it doesn't really matter. The old saw is that truth is stranger than fiction, but the best fiction distills the truth down to its most fiercely compelling attributes.

This is a book of both humor and truth, something rare, and independent of fact or fiction. Music of conviction and personality will always go on, but in this artistic end of days, where Jimi Hendrix is sold as nostalgia rather than art, and rock and roll, once rebellious, is so establishment that there's a Les Paul in every doctor's and lawyer's closet; the music that a lot of us grew up on has been so mollified we can barely recognize it.

Rock and roll is dead. Consider this its autopsy.

– Philip Stevenson

THE DAILY ADVENTURES OF MIXERMAN

The Supreme Negotiators

LOS ANGELES

POSTED: JULY 27, 10:33 A.M.

On Monday, July 29, I begin a new project. I will be recording an album of a band for a very famous producer. The band is relatively unknown other than within the record industry—an industry which, for the most part, is currently filled with the bitter losers of the biggest bidding war in the history of the music business.

I am an acquaintance of the producer—although "acquaintance" likely exaggerates the depth of our relationship. I did record for him once, but only for two hours, and I'm not entirely confident he'd even remember that. I can assure you, he would have never thought to hire me if it weren't for the band.

You see, I know the band. Or perhaps I should say I know half the band. Regardless, the band members are fans of my work.

The bands are often fans of my work. Hell, they don't know any better. They listen with the innocence of a person who enjoys music and musicality. They are still, to some extent, pure as listeners. They do not have the baggage of needing a hit affecting their judgment.

Yet.

If I could describe what I know of the band in just two words, those words would have to be *supreme negotiators*. The label wanted them to use one of a short list of producers. From what I understand, there were two names on said list. The band members, understanding the ways of the world, pointed out to the label that it was really their choice as to what producer they hired. After all, *they* were the ones who would ultimately pay the producer's advance and royalties. Hell, they'd be paying him a balloon payment for their sales before they made a dime in royalties, setting them even further in debt. Of course, the record company pointed out that it was the label's up-front money that would allow the record to be made in the first place.

Just in case that wasn't enough of a reality dose, the label also explained that, although it paid over two million dollars for the right to have them, it would be perfectly content if the only purpose for spending that money were to prevent the other "children" from having them. Ouch! The band looked at the short list and made the obvious choice.

The first name on the list.

As I said, the band members are supreme negotiators, and while they lost their first big negotiation where the making of their album was concerned, they had an alternate plan. They would get an ally in the room. That's where I come in. They insisted in their negotiation that I record the album. Oh, yeah. You can imagine how that went over. Mixer who? Mixer what? The label, not wanting to seem completely unyielding, and firmly believing that the tracking engineer has little power in the direction of the album (heh, heh), agreed, so long as the producer was cool with it.

As it turns out, the producer is familiar with my work, which I suppose isn't so hard to believe. After all, we *are* acquaintances. Countless times we have passed each other in the halls on the way to and from the loo. Perhaps that was the clincher, I don't know. Regardless, the producer agreed to meet with me and ultimately agreed to the band's terms. Now the band has its ally.

Of course, the band is overlooking the fact that in the next three years, the producer will probably record in the neighborhood of twelve albums, while the band is God knows where, playing the same fifteen songs every night, wondering why they would ever write such trash. And if I were to connect the dots for you, the producer could offer me a hell of a lot more work in the coming years than the band could. But yes, despite this, I am surely the band's ally.

And so I have decided that in the coming months, I will be documenting my daily adventures in recording an L.A. bidding-war band with a famous producer. Romance novels have been written on the basis of less, so why not? It's entirely possible this documentation will be complete come Tuesday. You never know, I could be fired. But for now, I'm hired, and we start Monday. Each morning, I will supply you with documentation of the past day's events. The identities of those involved will not be revealed, so as to protect the not-so-innocent.

Knowing the band (or at least half of it) and having some knowledge of how the producer operates, I expect it could be an interesting read. Add in the cast of characters that work for the label, who are not without their own fame, and we have the makings of a veritable soap opera. Or it could be the most uneventful album I've ever made.

But, somehow, I doubt that.

– Mixerman

DAY 1

Uh-Oh . . .

POSTED: JULY 30, 12:01 A.M.

According to most of the world, the crack of dawn would be just about the time the sun peeks above the eastern horizon. In studio terms, however, the crack of dawn is approximately 10 A.M., and this is precisely the time that I arrived at the studio today. I can assure you that in the world of record making, 10 A.M. would be considered a downright obscene time in which to start a session. But today was setup day, and an early start was absolutely critical. Although, in retrospect, I wish I had shown up at noon.

In setting up a session I have two main goals. First, I want to make certain that the session can move forward without a hitch. The more organized the session, the more readily available instruments and microphones are, the faster the session can move. Second, I take great pains to be sure that everyone is as comfortable as possible, including me. A little extra time, care, and effort in the setup can go a long way toward these goals—hence the early start.

Upon my arrival, I headed immediately to the recording room, which, from this point forward, will be referred to as merely "the room." The room was, as expected, in complete disarray with instrument and recording cases strewn about. It is a very large room, approximately forty feet wide, fifty feet long, and with twenty-five-foot ceilings. There are also several decent-size isolation booths[1] attached to the room, two of which flank the control room.

The cases contained all manner of instruments—amplifiers, drums, and general recording gear—that were to be used for this session. The cases were to be removed from the room and stacked against the enormously long wall lining the hall. The gear within the cases was to be set up in assigned locations—assignments that I had planned out well in advance and supplied to the studio via fax.

Among the stacks of cases stood a not particularly handsome young lad, whom I assumed (correctly) was the drummer. He was methodically assembling his drums smack-dab in the middle of the room. The way I figured it, this was likely more positive than had he not been there at all, but certainly less positive than had he actually been setting up his drums in the correct spot, which in this case, was *not* in the middle of the room.

As I watched him, another young lad entered the room carrying a load of cables and some microphones. He was a tall, lanky kid, laden with acne, with but a single eyebrow running across both eyes, neglecting the usual break above the nose. He wore the fairly typical nondescript studio garb of a washed-out pair of jeans, no belt, and a severely faded T-shirt, bearing the name of the studio upon it. Saving his pathetic ensemble were a beautiful necklace made from beads of rosewood and a rare '70s-era stainless steel Rolex Explorer watch. I can only assume the watch was some sort of hand-me-down-style graduation gift given to him to celebrate his completion of a two-year course in audio engineering—a course in which I'm quite certain he learned nothing of any real value. Still, I suspect he had a good upbringing, partly for the watch and partly because he immediately stopped to acknowledge me.

"Hey, I'm Lance," the lad said, holding out his pinky finger, as his arms were too full to offer his entire hand.

"Hey, I'm Mixerman," I replied, helping relieve him of some of the cables. "Are you my assistant?"

"Yeah, that's right."

"You didn't happen to get my fax with the instructions and the locations of the players, did you?"

"Yeah, thanks."

Thanks? *Thanks???*

I looked around the room, half wondering if I were on *Candid Camera*, as I noticed that there were no mics[2] set up, and there were no headphone boxes, no music stands, no A/C strips.[3] Nothing was set up, save a rug and some drums—in the wrong place, no less. I had taken several hours of my time putting together instructions to have all of these things set up, or at least nearly set up, before I had arrived. I had marked a to-scale map of the room, notating where each member of the band should reside, taking into account the acoustics of the room and the sight lines.

Thanks? He thanks me for my fax that he has thus far ignored?

"Did you happen to get the diagram of where I wanted the players to be placed?" I asked.

7

"Yeah, I got it. But no one ever puts drums where you wanted them."

MOTHERFUCKER!

I hate to say it, but under normal circumstances, I would have just fired his ass. This session will be costing the label, and ultimately the band, thousands of dollars per day, and it's my job to make sure the session flows smoothly. If the session is *not* running smoothly, I will get the blame. Not my assistant.

Unfortunately, the producer spends a significant amount of the year in this room. It could prove problematic if the producer found out that I went off half-cocked and fired his favorite assistant. My every instinct said that I was on shaky ground to begin with on this session, so for the moment, I chose the diplomatic route. I calmly and carefully explained to Lance that I would like the drums set up where I had originally planned, regardless of what anyone else had done prior to my arrival.

"Let's just set them up over there, okay?" I quipped.

"Okay, whatever you want. All I know is this is where the producer likes them."

I stared at Lance, unable to respond partly for fear that I might say something that I would regret, partly because I never actually saw a person with one eyebrow, and mostly because I had not yet consulted the producer with my setup plan. This was a fact that I was now painfully aware of given Lance's comment.

I chose to abruptly drop this line for a moment and focus my attention on the drummer. For the most part, his drums were set up, as he was obviously making some final adjustments. Not wanting to disturb him, and in an effort to keep the session progressing in some manner, I leaned down next to his snare drum to investigate the spacing in which I had to thread a mic. Typically, this procedure is a relatively safe exercise. Today, it was an exercise fraught with danger, as the drummer suddenly and inexplicably began whaling on the snare drum.

Fuck! That hurt.

Startled would be an understatement, here. Were I a cat, I would have been on the ceiling holding on for dear life. To make matters worse, I stood up so quickly I hit my head and my shoulder on his cymbals, just barely retaining my balance enough to grab his drumstick in mid-strike as I steadied myself with my hand on his snare drum. All in all, this was a dangerous maneuver, for had I not managed to grab the drumstick, he would have likely cracked several bones in my hand with the pending whack.

A well-timed snare hit could do untold amounts of damage to my hearing. It could end my career. At the very least it could shorten it significantly. One should NEVER play the drums when the engineer is standing next to him, certainly not without fair warning. This is Recording Etiquette 101. It's a rule. Perhaps an unwritten rule, until now, but a rule just the same. I, of course, explained all of this to the drummer. I suppose I made some sort of impression upon the guy, because the next time I entered the room, he stopped playing.

Very good, I thought to myself, easily trainable. Still, it was unnecessary for him to stop playing if I walked into harm's way, but I saved that discussion for another time, as I didn't want to confuse the issue.

"Thanks for stopping," I praised, "but I want to hear what the drums sound like in the room, so you can play now." And he did just that.

For the briefest of moments, I thought that the drummer was actually playing a practical joke on me. I say this because I can only categorize the sounds emanating before me as some of the most god-awful drum sounds I've ever heard. Ever! Believe me when I tell you, I've heard some awfully bad-sounding drums. I mean, these drum sounds weren't bad in a cool sort of way. These drum sounds were bad in every way imaginable.

Perhaps it was the drums, I thought to myself, if only to stave off the actual truth of the matter from my fragile brain.

"I think these drums are probably better for playing live," I said aloud.

This was a standard line that I, and just about every other recordist in the history of the world, uses when a drummer's kit[4] sounds like shit. While I generally prefer to be as straightforward as possible with people, this little white lie is sometimes necessary and works far more effectively than copping to the drummer on the first day of a session that his drum set sucks — live or otherwise. Believe me — if the drum set sucks in the studio, it sucks live too.

"What would you think about playing a nice set of rental drums that are designed specifically for recording?" I asked him, as admittedly it is very difficult to stop telling white lies once you've started.

The drummer sat there following my inquiry, with nothing more than a blank stare upon his face, as if I had asked him this question in Chinese, which I'm assuming he doesn't understand. I know I don't. I considered waving my hand in front of his face, but chose rather to rephrase my question into a statement.

"I think we should probably rent some recording drums," I stated, a little more slowly this time, as emphatically and with as much conviction as one can muster while using words like *think* and *probably*.

"Okay," he snapped quickly with this odd little smile that I could only assume was his best impersonation of Jim Carrey in the movie *Dumb & Dumber*.

By 10:30 A.M. the drums were in the wrong spot, my assistant was anything but assistive, and my confidence over my planned placement of the instruments had been shattered. Oh, joy. A call to the producer was in order.

In our phone conversation, the producer and I discussed a variety of topics germane to the setup for the recording. For the most part, he gave me carte blanche to place the players where I saw fit, so long as the sight lines were good for everyone. We also discussed a few sonic and directional concepts for the record, picked a song to start out with, and broached the subject of the rental budget, which, as it turns out, is quite sizeable.

"Get what we need to keep the session moving, regardless of cost," the producer said. Sizeable, indeed! Unlimited, more like!

All in all, it was a very positive conversation, until the producer dropped a bomb on me, coming in the form of both confession and request.

"One last thing before you go," he said. "You might already know this, but Lance is my nephew, and I want him to get some actual hands-on experience recording. If you wouldn't mind, any time you can let Lance take the reins and get some time behind the console, I'd really appreciate it."

Great! I thought to myself, as my mind flashed into the future to the record-release party where I was ceremoniously given my copy of the manufactured CD. I imagined myself sipping champagne and guffawing with the band, as I came to find out that there had been one million preorders for the album, an unprecedented event for a new band—hell, an unprecedented event for an established one. We toasted the huge success of a record that wasn't even for sale yet. Then I watched myself opening up the CD much like Charlie opened up his chocolate bar in search of the golden ticket in *Willy Wonka & the Chocolate Factory*. I remember being vaguely conscious of the bandmates each nervously and expeditiously excusing themselves from my presence, as I made my move to open the CD. Momentarily ignoring their peculiar exits, I opened the booklet to gaze proudly upon my name as the recordist of such a successful work, only to find in bold print the following text:

ENGINEERED BY LANCE NEPHEW
ADDITIONAL ENGINEERING BY MIXERMAN

Of course, that particular dream sequence was ludicrous on more than one level. Such an obviously overblown scenario would likely be the least of my problems, as my assistant was supposed to be my ally, watching my back for possible mistakes or potential problems. Not a relation to the producer!

"Sure, no problem," I gulped.

Despite the distressing news of the nepotism and the fucked-up dream sequence in which I was deprived of a well-earned credit, I had established my needed authority to set up the session as I saw fit. At the moment, this was all the ammunition I needed.

I found Lance and explained to him that I'd had a long conversation with the producer and that I would like to set up the room as I had originally laid out in my fax. Then I asked Lance, as politely as I could possibly phrase such an inquiry, "Are you planning to set up the mics in the near future?"

Without so much as a grunt, he rolled his eyes, picked up my setup sheet, and exited the room as I remained wondering what the fuck he thought his gig was.

By this point in my day, the rental drums had arrived, and I had managed to sample a few of the kits. I finally settled on a vintage Ludwig kit, which seemed the most appropriate for the song we were starting with. The producer had expressed a desire to use a few different drum sounds on this album, so I had the rental company leave a couple of other kits as well. I also kept about ten extra snare drums. It's very expensive to keep this amount of drums on hand, but I just couldn't get the phrase "get what we need to keep the session moving, regardless of cost" out of my head.

I asked the drum tech from the rental company to set up the drums in the area that I had originally selected. He obliged and proceeded to fine-tune the drums. Being a seasoned pro, the tech asked my permission to play while I was in the room, which I happily granted. The drums sounded great! I was elated. Relieved, even.

Then the drummer took a turn. He adjusted some positions of the toms and cymbals to his liking, settled into his throne (drum stool), and unceremoniously commenced playing the drums. My feelings of elation instantly turned to dejection. This drum kit, which I have actually recorded with great success on numerous occasions with drummers of every ilk—a kit which had sounded fantastic just moments prior—now sounded like absolute dog shit.[5]

As I listened to the wretched tones bombard me, I confirmed what I could only have defined prior to that moment as a super-strong suspicion. The drummer sucked.

To be perfectly honest, I should have known this coming in. I think that perhaps I did, but was trying to convince myself otherwise. The drummer didn't sound very good on the demos. But drums rarely do sound good on demos. I'd seen the band live once, but that was with a different drummer. The fact of the matter is, I didn't know this drummer. My relationship with the band was with the lead singer and the bass player. I was surprised that they would accept playing with such a lousy drummer.

Regardless of my feelings on the quality of musicianship sitting before me, I resigned myself to setting up the mics, which were still trickling in at a snail's pace. After some prodding, I finally got Lance to get all the mics in the room, and I proceeded to set them up around the kit.

Aside from the actual instrument in the room, mic placement is probably one of the more important steps to a good recording. Where a mic is placed can make a huge difference in what it picks up. Even what appears by eye to be the tiniest of movements of mic position can cause a dramatic improvement or degradation in sound by ear. In the initial placement of mics, I am merely making an educated guess as to where I think they will sound best. I must go through the listening process in order to determine where they will ultimately end up. To some extent, that's a hit-or-miss process.

With mics in their initial placement, I had Lance get the drummer behind the kit, as I made my way to the control room, where I had the most mind-numbing communication that I've ever experienced with a man. And no, I am not a chauvinist. But if

14

you're a woman, you must realize by now your propensity toward largely complex and seemingly illogical thought processes, making you capable of inflicting unusually cruel amounts of distress upon the relatively simple mind of a man. Personally, I'd take that as a compliment.

"Play, please," I said over the talkback, which is much akin to a walkie-talkie, allowing the players in the recording room to hear me when I hit a button.

"What?" the drummer yelled, as if he couldn't hear me.

"Can you hear me?" I asked. It's quite possible that he couldn't hear me, although the talkback volume was way up, and I could hear a momentary feedback, which told me that my voice was probably pretty loud in the room. As if this wasn't enough to convince me, I recalled having heard Lance communicating earlier to me in this manner.

"YEAH, I CAN HEAR YOU FINE!" he responded, yelling as if I couldn't hear *him*.

"I want to hear the drums in here. Could you play?"

"What song do you want me to play?" At which point I told him the name of the song that the producer had requested we start with.

"Okay!" he replied. Ten seconds went by.

"Are you going to play?"

"Do you want me to play now?"

"That would be helpful."

"Which drum do you want me to play?"

"The whole kit!"

"Oh, okay!" He started playing and then stopped after barely a measure went by.

"How long do you want me to play for?" he asked.

"Until I ask you to stop."

"Okay!"

He started playing again and then stopped after a whole two measures this time.

"What?" he yelled out.

"I didn't say anything!"

"Oh, I thought you yelled to stop."

"No. I want you to play for a while."

"Okay!" Ten seconds of absolute silence went by.

"*Play!*" I yelled. The drummer jumped in his seat, and immediately started playing again. As I listened, I realized that he was playing the wrong song.

"Stop!" I yelled in the talkback, but he didn't stop. "*Stop!*" I yelled louder and closer to the talkback mic. "STOP!!!!!!" I yelled at the top of my lungs directly into the talkback mic.

"What?" he replied with a stupid-assed look on his face.

"Yes, could you play the song we discussed?" I was close to exasperation.

"You want me to play it now?"

No, I want you to play it tomorrow!

"YES!!!"

"Okay!"

These brilliant exchanges went on for the entire day. This guy was easily the dumbest schmuck that I've ever had to deal with, and I've dealt with some serious idiots. I swear to you this drummer is only one notch above being a retard, and I've come to find out through the course of the day that he is the butt of the band's constant jokes and haranguing. At one point, I began calling him Cotton, and the bass player asked me why I called him that.

"'Cause he's dumber than cotton," I said dryly.

I guess he thought that was funny, because he fell off his chair and ran to tell the singer. To me, however, the name Cotton doesn't really do the drummer justice. Personally, I much prefer what I've been calling him out of earshot and between exchanges on the talkback.

Dumb Ass.

After about six hours of changing drums, moving mics, trying out compressors—which are tools that engineers use to even out an overly dynamic volume differential of an instrument—and *anything* else that I could do to somehow make Dumb Ass's drums sound acceptable, I finally got a sound that I thought was fairly decent considering what I had to work with.

By this point in the day, the other players had been at the studio for some time, and they had been setting up their instruments and their playing areas. Lance Nephew was on "vibe" detail and had been busy hanging my tapestries, arranging lava lamps, candelabras, candles on plates, string lights, and Magic 8 Balls (of which I have three varieties). He also took it upon himself to place the studio's wool Oriental throw rugs throughout the room, a service for which I was most grateful. For the moment, Lance was doing what he was supposed to and wasn't causing me too much grief.

With drum sounds relatively complete, I could focus on the other instruments. I rented a bass head and cab,[6] because I wasn't particularly enamored with the rig[7] the bass player was using. I rented a few guitar amps for the sake of variety, and the producer had several amps of his own that were delivered along with a large assortment of percussion instruments and guitars. I set up a wall of guitar amps in the large iso booth so that the guitar player could plug into a variety of amps, depending on the song. All in all, I would say there were about fifty guitars in the room, some rented, some newly acquired by the guitar player, some belonging to the producer. I rented a few of these big twelve-banger guitar holders, and we got the cases out of the room.

I set up the bass cab (the speakers) in another decent-size iso booth, and placed the bass player's head (the amplifier) in the room with the drums so that he could stand next to Dumb Ass while they were playing. Bass players usually like to stand near the drummer, as these two instruments supply the groove of a song. I set up large baffles[8] to cut the players off from the drums and to give the band members their own kind of space. Each player had his own little "Apartment," or "Living Room" garnished with his choice of furniture, gear, and assorted vibe paraphernalia.

After about ten hours, the room was finally completely set up, the players had been placed, and their instruments were accessible to them. All the empty cases, racks, and extraneous gear were piled up in the hall. The room was beautiful. It was a sight to behold!

I got a bass sound and a few guitar amp sounds. I had mics throughout the room so that I could readily hear each band member, and they could readily hear each other in their headphones. Each Apartment got a set of headphones and small mixers, where each player could set up his own little eight-fader mix for himself (very handy). We ordered dinner, which is a complete story in and of itself that I'll reserve for another time, and I set up the vibe in the control room.

Post-dinner, we were ready for the producer. So I called him and left a message telling him same. But the producer never made an appearance, even though he had expressed a desire to make some takes tonight. I guess he was too busy.

Not wanting to sit around doing nothing, I had the band play down the first song a couple of times, as I laid it to tape and made a few adjustments. All in all, I'd say the test recording sounded okay, but quite honestly, Dumb Ass really sucks balls as a drummer. He has no feel, no time, no talent, is stupider than fuck, and has an incredible knack for making great drums sound like ass.

Other than that . . .

– Mixerman

DAY 2

Dandy Day

POSTED: JULY 31, 1:23 A.M.

Today gives the term "dandy" new meaning. That's because today was definitely a dandy.

About thirty minutes before the crack of dawn, I received a call from the producer. Apparently, he had mysteriously been stricken with a great idea. He wanted to use a PA system[9] to amplify the drums in the room, so as to get a really "big and fat drum room sound." He referenced another producer who was a friend of his that swears by this. He then proceeded to tell me that he'd had his personal assistant (a relative, I'm sure) hire a sound reinforcement guy to come to the studio and set up the system.

After dropping the little PA bomb on me, he decided to ask me how everything sounded.

What's it matter? It's all going to change now! I thought to myself.

Regardless, since I wasn't 100 percent happy with the drum sound, thanks to Dumb Ass's less than stellar coordination of multiple limbs hitting skins, I decided to fill the producer in on my disappointment with his drumming skills.

"I think the PA is a good idea. The drummer could use some help," I said in an exaggerated, half-laughing way so as to get my point across.

"He could? I'm surprised to hear that," replied the producer.

Surprised? Didn't he do rehearsals with this band? How can this be a surprise to him?

"I thought he was a really good drummer," the producer continued.

As if I wasn't fucked before!

I intimated that I thought the PA system was a good idea, and, in an attempt to perform some damage control, I told him that the PA would probably solve the small problems that I was having with his drumming.

"When will you be coming in?" I asked innocently.

"I'll probably be there by late afternoon—early eveningish, to listen to sounds."

"Great, see you then," I replied as the producer abruptly hung up the phone.

I drove to the studio for a noon start. When I arrived, I saw the sound reinforcement company's truck in the parking lot and Dumb Ass sitting on the patio smoking a cigarette. Dumb Ass informed me that he always likes to get to the studio early. Oh, joy! I decided that I'd make a beeline for the room, since that was where Dumb Ass was not.

Normally, I would expect to see the room exactly as I had left it the night before. Expecting this would be as usual as expecting summer to be hot, birds to fly, dogs to bark, or any manner of everyday occurrences that have few exceptions. Unfortunately, today was one of those exceptions.

Rather than walking into a well-organized, fully prepared recording session that I had spent ten hours of my time preparing, I was greeted by a half-dismantled, unorganized clusterfuck. You see, when I arrived at the room, the microphones that were only fourteen hours prior to this tightly locked down and surrounding the drums—microphones that I had spent hours painstakingly positioning in order to somehow gain even the slightest edge on the poor drum tones I must somehow present in a flattering manner—were now completely removed from the drums in an arbitrary and seemingly random fashion. At first, I was stunned.

As I said yesterday, mic placement is the single most important part of recording, aside from *what* you are recording and the room you are recording in. Lance had made movements of centimeters (per my direction), as I listened in order to get the mic to pick up what I wanted it to "hear." To move the recordist's mics is the cardinal sin which anyone who has spent more than a day in a studio knows you never commit under any circumstances—certainly not without first consulting the person who *placed* the mics.

As I stared upon the disastrous scene before me, I became consumed with anger—anger so great that I could not accurately describe in words the extent of it. In fact, there is really no way that I could accurately describe the magnitude of the microphones having been removed from the drums, as certainly no one in the history of the world has died from such an event. Still, I'll try my best to put this into perspective.

If you have ever spent hours laboring over anything at all, in the hopes that you will derive some fruits from that labor, even if those fruits are merely the self-satisfaction of accomplishment; if you have ever created anything that in and of itself is intended to have no permanence, but by its nature serves as a painstakingly critical first step toward the accomplishment and free flowing of a creative endeavor; if you have ever created anything, even as mundane and unimportant as a jigsaw puzzle or a sand castle, or even a domino trail, only to have it destroyed in one fell swoop by an idiot with no consideration toward common sense or human decency, then you have a firm grasp on the aggravation and pure unadulterated hatred of mankind that I was feeling at that particular moment. Put another way, I was about to fucking lose it!

Knee-deep in the carnage before me stood a disheveled Mountain Man sporting a full-on Grizzly Adams do, wearing a torn tank top, shorts, hiking boots, and a trucker's baseball cap with a perfectly straight brim—a fashion faux pas of the highest order in some circles. He was casually plugging a whole new set of microphones into a live PA console parked, no less, in the middle of the singer's Apartment, destroying every bit of vibe that I had worked so hard to achieve. This, of course, was the least of my problems.

"What are you doing?" I asked, practically shaking, half thankful I didn't have a gun, half wishful that I did.

"Oh, hey," the Mountain Man replied obliviously. "Just setting up my mics for the PA."

Getting slightly distressed I asked, "Why did you move my mics? You moved my mics! Where's Lance?"

"Who?" he asked.

"Lance—where's Lance—who let you in?"

"I don't know, one of the staff or something," he answered. "I hope you don't mind, but I had to move the mics to get my mics in on the drums," he continued. "Ah, you're a pro. You know how this works."

I stood there for a moment in absolute disbelief at what this Mountain Man had just said to me. My mouth hung wide open. Were there a fly in the room, it would have likely flown right in. I would guess that I looked more stupid than Dumb Ass looks on a regular occasion. For a moment, I understood what it was like to have an out-of-body experience. My consciousness was floating above me, looking at myself and the room, wondering how this could possibly happen. I watched myself gazing vacantly at the drums with a feeling of helplessness, much like one feels when he's lost something important to him. Thoughts of physical violence as a means toward retribution entered my mind, but I quickly dispensed with such ideas, for both the studio and the ridge of a volcano are two of the last places one wants to get into a physical altercation.

"Excuse me," I retorted, as I made a quick exit from the room for fear that I might say or do something that I could regret. In retrospect, I can think of plenty of things that I wish I'd said, but one always comes up with the best comeback material after the fact.

At that point, I had pretty much decided that it was time to meet the studio traffic manager. Unfortunately, I was way too pissed at that particular moment to express myself clearly and without sounding like a raging lunatic. I decided it would be best for me to take a drive, which is what we do instead of take walks here in La La Land. Dumb Ass offered to come along, an offer that I turned down flat.

After allowing myself the opportunity to calm down, I returned to the studio complex and headed directly to the office. It was time to introduce myself to the traffic manager, Magnolia, whom I've never actually met. While I have worked at this particular facility before, it has been many years, and Magnolia has only recently accepted the position as traffic manager. Oddly, despite the fact that we have many mutual friends, circumstance has prevented our paths from ever crossing. But then, circumstance is like that.

Magnolia seemed happy to meet me as she immediately wanted to kibitz, a skill that seems to be a requirement for becoming a studio manager. Personally, I desired to get right into the circumstances of the disaster but couldn't do so effectively with all of the kibitzing going on. I grudgingly exchanged some niceties, but I quickly and awkwardly segued into the disaster in the recording room.

"All of my mics were torn down from the drums," I stated.

"Wow, I'm surprised to hear that," she replied to my complaint.

Surprised? I've lost hours of work and she's surprised? How about appalled? I would have been happy with appalled. Appalled would have been a reaction that I could live with. She gives me surprised?

Motherfucker!

Upon investigation into the matter, Magnolia informed me that Lance still hadn't arrived yet, so a runner had let the Mountain Man into the room. She apologized and promised to speak with the runner, but she attempted to remove some of the blame from herself and her staff by pointing out that the Mountain Man should have known better. In some small way she was right—he should have known better. But certainly one of the purposes of an assistant and a studio staff is to prevent the clueless, under the guise of being professional, from infiltrating a session and moving the microphones! Doesn't she know that?

By now, I had come to accept the fact that I couldn't change what had happened and that my only recourse was to prevent it from happening again. I told Magnolia that in no uncertain terms was anyone allowed in the room without myself or (gulp) Lance being present. I'm not 100 percent convinced that had Lance been there, this disaster would have been thwarted, but at least I could have held him accountable. Perhaps then I could have hired someone *not* related to the producer to assist me!

Having resigned myself to getting drum sounds again and convincing myself that I probably would have had to approach the drums completely differently anyway with the addition of a PA system, and having temporarily shelved my hatred of the entire world for how it happened to affect me, I was able to face the situation at hand in my usual happy-go-lucky manner.

The first step in the healing process, since I was probably the only one in need of healing, was to introduce myself (officially) to our beloved Mountain Man/sound reinforcement specialist.

"Mixerman," I announced.

"Buck," the Mountain Man replied, as he held out his hand momentarily and then sneezed into it.

"Charmed, I'm sure," I quipped sarcastically, neglecting to accept his hand as he was now wiping it on the rear of his pants.

"You know, you moved mics that I had spent hours setting in place. In general, that's considered really bad form."

He seemed unfazed by my admonishment as he continued to patch cables into the monstrosity that sat obtrusively in the middle of the singer's Living Room.

"Uh, do you think we could move this beast?" I said as I placed my hand on the console.

"Oh, I thought that would be the best place for it," he said after briefly glancing up to see what I was referring to.

"Well, it's right in the middle of where the singer is going to be for takes."

"You're not going to keep those vocals are you?"

"That's somewhat irrelevant," I replied, as I was beginning to lose my patience with his obtuse nature.

I can't for the life of me understand why I ask a question when what is really called for is a statement—note to self: Consult with shrink about this.

"I'd like to move the console to here," I proclaimed as I held out my hands, as if they were on the sides of an imaginary console and walked to an unobtrusive corner of the room.

"But I won't be able to see," he replied, bewildered.

"Why do you need to see?" I responded, even *more* bewildered, "You're not even going to be here once we get audio passing."

"Oh, I thought you would need me to be operating the board."

What???? I almost choked on my own saliva I was so taken aback by the absurdity of this statement. What was he talking about? Why would we need someone to operate the board? This wasn't some live mix gig. This was a PA to be used to boost the level of sound of the kik[10] and the snare drums in the room. It was for an effect. "Set and forget" is what I do in a case like this. And if I do make changes, it's between songs, and those adjustments can be made by me and/or Lance, depending on the situation.

"No, we definitely won't be in need of that!" I replied bluntly.

Lance had finally arrived, nary an apology for his extreme tardiness. He seemed raring to go. Yeah, right! After some coaxing on my part, I convinced Lance to help Buck move the live board to the corner of the room, out of vibe's way.

I took a moment to go through Buck's mic collection in the hopes that I could avoid having two sets of mic stands and two sets of clunky microphones on each and every drum. In reality, I didn't need a second set of mics at all. It would have been just as easy, if not easier, for me to use the same set of mics for the recording as for the PA, which I won't get into the technical details of here. But there were valid arguments for using two sets of mics, although at the moment I can't think of one. Buck had a plethora of clip-on mics in his arsenal. I managed to convince him to use those instead.

Since all of the mics had been removed and since there was now a PA in the room, I decided to reapproach my own mic selections for the purposes of the drum recording. Upon completion, I gave Lance my new and improved list of mics and asked him to set them up instead of what we had set up yesterday. Lance sat down to examine the list, which leads me to suspect that Lance's father may have berated him one too many times for walking while reading, an act I would have much preferred. But I guess that's not how Lance operates.

In the twenty-four hours that I've been around Lance, I've not once seen him make what could be construed as an accelerated motion of any part of his body. The guy would *never* be mistakenly shot by police officers thinking that he was somehow "going for a weapon." Since this operation would likely take awhile, I decided to go out and eat lunch with the band. Of course, even my lunch was ruined, what with the presence of Dumb Ass.

I realize that I may seem a bit harsh with Dumb Ass, but honestly, I'm nice to the guy, particularly compared to the rest of the band. In fact, they've taken to calling him Cotton to his face. Certainly, Cotton can frustrate me endlessly to the point that I either want to choke the living shit out of him or just give up on life in general. But I do remain calm, I never put him down to his face, and I'm always extremely careful to let go of the talkback button when I call him Dumb Ass. He is the definition of a boy that only a mother can love. I am thoroughly convinced that, were Cotton and the Pope in a room together, it would only be a matter of minutes before the Pope would begin insulting him. There's just no way around blatantly stating your disdain for him. I mean, if the Pope can't refrain, you certainly can't expect me to, right?

As if Dumb Ass's incessant idiocy isn't enough, the guy has this whole retard act. I mean, he'll *act* like a retard. I would greatly appreciate for someone, anyone, to tell me why a retard would *act* like a retard. I posed this in the form of a question to the singer, but he kept repeating the question as if attempting to decipher the answer to some complex, deep philosophical question. "Yes, why *would* a retard act like a retard?" "Why would a *retard* act like a *retard*?" "Why would a retard *act* like a retard?"

Ya got me!

After returning from lunch, I watched as Lance was putting the finishing touches on his mic setup in a manner that one might imagine Michelangelo touching up the ceiling of the Sistine Chapel. Dumb Ass was kibitzing with Buck, getting along like one would expect two retards to get along. I placed my mics on the drums, went through the painful exercise of getting Dumb Ass to actually play the drums when I wanted him to—as opposed to when I didn't want him to—and got Buck to get the PA pumping (like I needed him for that). After a couple hours of tinkering with subtle mic movements, I got the drums to sound okay again.

You have to understand, okay drum sounds are not what I'm going for here. With a great drummer, drum sounds take all of ten minutes. With a shitty drummer, if you actually give a shit about your craft, drum sounds can take hours. I suppose one could argue that I'm earning my money. Admittedly, sometimes the recordist's job is to take a less-than-stellar source[11] and make it acceptable. This is what I'm spending my time doing thus far, so in this case, that *is* my job. But personally, I prefer the other side of the coin, which is to stay out of the way of what is inherently great or, in other words, to do everything in my power not to fuck things up. To me, that's a far more valuable service than the first, as anyone can stomp the snot out of drums with compressors in order to make a crappy drummer seem slightly consistent, which I am already doing to arrive at just "okay."

At this point, I wasn't sure if my new drum sound was better than last night's, so I recorded a little bit and compared. While the PA was slightly different, it didn't really improve Dumb Ass's sound very much. At this point, I had come to the realization that there was no way for me to avoid reality anymore. He just sucks! How can drums sound good when the guy just plain sucks? The answer is, they can't. I was dejected and needed a producer because I was out of answers. The drum sounds were fine. It was the drum playing that was fucking things up to this point, and until the producer could come to that conclusion himself, there was little more that I could do on this front. The fact that the producer perceives him as a good drummer is not a good sign. I can't help but wonder if I'll make it past tomorrow.

I dismissed Buck, and he exchanged numbers with Dumb Ass. I believe I overheard that Buck thought Dumb Ass was a really good drummer. [Sigh]. Is it just me? Have I lost my ability to judge drummers? Perhaps I've set my standards too high. If this guy's actually a good drummer (and he's not!), then I'm toast.

It was dinnertime again. When I have a less eventful daily log, I'll be sure to fill you in on how such a benign thing as ordering dinner can turn into a fucking fiasco of epic proportions. Finally, we ate our dinner and still no producer. I had the band play the first song again, this time with the PA drums, and I recorded it. The band enjoyed the new sound. Dumb Ass thought it was the most rad drum sound he'd ever gotten. Funny, it's one of the more pedestrian drum sounds I've ever gotten. I suppose it's true. . . .

Perception is reality.

– Mixerman

DAY 3

Operation Control
(& Will He Show?)

POSTED: JULY 31, 11:38 P.M.

Today, I decided I was going to take *some* control of my life. It is typical for me to constantly evaluate how I am contributing to the well-being or degradation of a session. By not taking control of the assistant and the studio — and in some respects Dumb Ass — I have come to the self-critical conclusion that I have contributed to the degradation of this session. At the very least, I have not been improving upon the situation and therefore I needed to make a tactical change in how I was handling myself. Of course, not having a producer show up has not helped matters. Still, considering the fact that we haven't even made a take yet, the damage should be easily rectified.

Take control was the plan of the day. Thus, the name of my plan: Operation Control.

The first thing I did today after drinking a cup of coffee, taking a poo . . . Okay, forget about all that! The first thing I did today was to call the producer and ask him if he'd be coming in today.

"Yeah, man. Definitely. Sorry about the delays. Drama. You know how it is. How's the PA working out?" he asked.

"It's fine. I recorded one take with the PA and one without, and you can be the judge."

"Great, you're the best! I'll see you later today." And with that he hung up the phone.

I wasn't quite sure how to take "later today." Regardless, I chose to be optimistic and assume that I would have a producer later today.

Now I needed to implement Operation Control. First up on the agenda was Lance Nephew. Phase One of Operation Control began, unwittingly on my part, last night.

Phase One: Train Lance to be a worthwhile assistant.

At the conclusion of yesterday's session, ahem, I explained to Lance what I meant when I used the term "start time," expressing very plainly that if we call the session to start at 10 A.M., then I wanted him there at 9:30 A.M. Among other duties, he was to double-check all the documentation from the day before (he was a bit confused by this one, as he still hasn't documented one thing); fire up the "tube" equipment,[12] which takes time to warm up; make sure the Apartment environments are neat and clean; organize notes, messages, and receipts; remove obvious trash; and untangle cables, lines, etc. Some of this was being done by the cleaning staff, but Lance was not without his own obligations. I explained to Lance that his job was to help me keep a session running smoothly and quickly, and I asked him if he was going to be able to do this. He assured me that he would.

Lance was only thirty minutes late this morning, which was incredibly encouraging considering that, to date, he has not been less than an hour late. As encouraged as I was, this wasn't good enough. So I decided that he needed to meet the wrath of me. After all, an important Intelligence Operation cannot always be implemented without the use of some force. In a nutshell, I tore Lance a new asshole—a tactic I reserve for when all else fails.

Lance was shocked, nay, flabbergasted at the way I laid into him. But at least I think he's starting to get the picture now. No more Mr. Nice Guy! I was either going to have an assistant I can use, or one of us was going to go. At this point, I didn't care which one of us went—although I was hopeful it wouldn't come down to that. Lance wasn't a bad kid by any stretch of the imagination. Phase One would have to remain a work in progress. I moved on to Phase Two.

Phase Two: Put the studio on notice.

I went to the traffic manager's office, exchanged daily niceties, and allowed Magnolia her mandatory kibitzing time, which I found quite painful as I abhor kibitzing when I'm in the middle of a mission. I then reiterated to her that ours was a "closed session." Only the band, the producer, Lance, and I were permitted in the room. She agreed to my terms. I also explained to her that I wouldn't tolerate Lance's being late any longer, and that I wanted him there before the session started, regardless of nepotistic relationships that may exist. She was noticeably taken aback by my bluntness on this matter. She quickly regained her composure and assured me that it wouldn't happen again. I was reasonably sure she "got it" now. Phase Two of the plan was complete. Back to Phase One.

I took Lance into the room, grabbed a clipboard with a pad of paper, and demonstrated how one documents the settings on a guitar amp. I drew a little circle for each of the knobs on the guitar amp, and I drew a line, like the hands of a clock in each of the circles, which indicated where the knob was set on the amp. It was kind of like kindergarten class, but this was an important step in implementing Phase One.

I explained to Lance that on every song, and even every take, if we're switching instruments and amp settings, he was to write down the guitar that was used, the amp that was used, the settings of the amp, the pickups, tone and volume control settings on the guitar, pedals used with their appropriate settings, mics used, snare drum used, kik used, bass used, head settings, compressor settings, mic pre-gain settings, EQ settings, tempo, etc. I suggested he make some templates and photocopies of those templates, so he didn't have to constantly redraw the guitar amp knobs every time we changed the settings on the guitar.

I showed Lance how to use a pencil, as opposed to a red Sharpie marker, on a label directly on the two-inch tape[13] box, much like the marker that he used to sloppily write what I believe said "Test Drums & Test Drums II"—even *he* wasn't quite sure if that's what it actually said. I explained to him the importance of using details in order to prevent assured confusion later on down the road. I counseled him on the importance of trying to use neatness in his documentation, so that we could read what he had documented at a later date. There is one studio in town that actually runs its future assistant engineers through a course in penmanship. Obviously, this wasn't that studio. It was then time for Phase Three.

Phase Three: Teach Dumb Ass to play drums like a man.

I took a listen to Test Drums and Test Drums II, as Lance was affixing labels to the two-inch box and writing a novelette on the origins and purpose of each take.

In listening to the takes, I determined that I would need to make some more adjustments with the PA, but more importantly, with Dumb Ass. He hit the toms like a pussy but would whale on the hat[14] as if he imagined it was the guy who raped his sister. I gave him the short lesson on hitting his drums and then had him practice while I made my adjustments with the PA.

The sound improved tremendously. The toms were singing in the room a little better. In fact, the drums were starting to sound pretty good overall. I gave him some more encouragement—yes, I *do* encourage Dumb Ass—and recorded "Test Drums III," labeled as such by my newly inspired literary scholar of an assistant, with a three-page dissertation written on a label designed for, at most, a sentence or two. (Sigh.) Should I tell Lance he's gone too far? Or should I just send the runner out to buy a quality magnifying glass on the band's dime?

Dumb Ass's drums were actually halfway decent, although the guy has this very odd loping feel. It's like riding a galloping horse with its push-pull motion. I see Alsihad in my future.

Alsihad (pronounced AL · see · hod) is my own personal name for what is currently the most widely used computer program for recording in the industry. I created my own name for the platform, partially because I don't think the real name fits the product, and partially because I wouldn't want to be responsible for even one sale of the product.

For years, albums were recorded to tape. To date, many rock albums are still recorded to tape. But many albums are recorded to computers. In order to record to a computer, one needs both software and hardware aside from the computer itself. The hardware converts sound into the digital format of 1s and 0s. The software is the platform in which an operator can manipulate the sound. Alsihad is both the software and the hardware. Some people in this industry feel that Alsihad sounds fine, and some people in this industry feel that it sounds awful. Some people don't think it really matters, since all records end up in the digital format of a CD anyway. I'm in the camp that thinks it sounds awful.

Regardless of my feelings on the issue, when a drummer comes in and has such poor timing as is prevalent in Dumb Ass's playing, Alsihad is typically the first choice to fix the timing anomalies. At that moment, I didn't see Alsihad in the room, and this was just fine by me.

When the singer and the bass player entered the control room, they immediately noticed the improvements on the drum sound. I requested that they go back in with the guitar player and play down the song, which they readily obliged. It was late afternoon, and the producer still hadn't made an entrance. As they played down the take, I remember having these unusually insecure thoughts come through my head.

This drummer sucks, regardless of how I improved his tone, I thought to myself. Sure, I'm hearing an improvement, and it actually sounds pretty good to me. But perhaps I've lost perspective. Perhaps the tones still suck, but I think it's okay because of the improvements I've made. But what will the producer hear? The producer is under the impression that Dumb Ass is good, and he's heard Dumb Ass play. But it's sooooo obvious to me that Dumb Ass is not a good drummer. Will he hear that the drumming is subpar, or will he hear that the drums just don't sound good? After all, you never can tell with producers. He might not recognize something so painfully obvious. Just because someone is a successful producer doesn't mean that he has the skills to go with his success. This industry is fraught with people who have no business being near a studio. Would that be the case here? *Wait a minute!* I thought to myself, as I snapped from my trance of doubting thoughts.

I was in the midst of Operation Control. I couldn't allow insecurities to overcome me. I've been in this situation countless times before. I *must* think positively and overcome any obstacles that present themselves. It was useless to worry about the producer's reaction. I just needed to be prepared to convince him of where the problem lies. Operation Control was about taking control of the situation. Not fear.

With that little episode behind me and with a renewed sense of confidence, I decided to mic up the rest of the guitar amps and get the mics positioned so that I wouldn't have to move them every time we switched amps. The more I can avoid moving mics, the faster I can keep the session going. With the rental of several microphones, all of the amps and cabs had their own mics placed in front of them. The guitars were sounding great. I also had two EQ/compressor chains set up, which I named Chain A and Chain B.

As an engineer, two of my tools are equalization (EQ) and compression. When one uses these tools in series, they form what's called a chain. The entire chain in this case would be the following: the source (the player, the guitar used, and the amplifier used), microphone, mic preamplifier (which amplifies the microphone), EQ, compressor, and tape machine.

The treble and bass boost in your car stereo system is a simple EQ. I use much better and much more powerful EQs in the studio. I can cut or boost just about any frequency in the human range of hearing and beyond with EQ. This allows me to shape the sound of the instrument for the benefit of the recording.

A compressor allows me to reduce the dynamic range. You know the DVD of the movie that you watched at home last night? The one you had to turn up in the soft parts and down in the loud parts? That's an example of a wide dynamic range. A compressor reduces that dynamic range so that the soft parts are closer in volume to the loud parts. If you strapped a well-set compressor onto the output of your DVD player, you could put your remote control away. I have engineer friends that do just this.

A compressor, however, can alter the sound quality of the source dramatically. Learning which compressor to use, how much compression, and even when to use compression can take years to master, and the selection of which can be a somewhat hit-or-miss process.

Lance's job was to document accurately not only the settings of the entire chain, but also the settings of Chain A, while I was recording with Chain B. The reason for this is sometimes we have to go back and fix something later on in the session and for any number of reasons. If I don't have all the settings in the chain documented, we would have to redo the entire track, rather than a small section of the track.

With my guitar chains in place and Lance prepared to document everything, I was ready to go. Unfortunately, something, or shall I say someone, was missing.

The evening went pretty much as the previous evenings had— some dinner, some billiards, some foosball, some resting, and yes, some clandestine diary writing. I took the measure of calling the producer and leaving a message telling him we were 100 percent ready for him. The way I figured it, he might have been waiting for this information before he planned to make an appearance. But much to my chagrin, he didn't call back, he didn't come by. Nothing.

I was half tempted to start making takes, but thought better of it, as I couldn't be sure what the reaction to such a course might be. The band doesn't seem to mind too much at this point. They're happy to be in the studio: They were signed two years ago, and the record company has had them writing the entire time. They were just happy to finally be ready to make an album. Plus, as far as the band was concerned, we *have* been working the entire time. They are extremely happy with the tones. I'm getting along *very* well with everyone, even Dumb Ass, regardless of my disdain for him. So that's positive. In fact, all in all, it was a very positive day—mostly because I got back control of my session. I would venture to say that my first two days are a good reminder for all of us, regardless of our professions: We must run our sessions and not let our sessions run us.

With lesson in tow, all I needed now was our esteemed producer, who I have decided will no longer be referred to as "the producer," as I've named him for the purposes of this journal. His name henceforward?

Willy Show.

– Mixerman

DAY 4

Paulie Yore

POSTED: AUGUST 2, 4:17 A.M.

Lance and I arrived at the studio simultaneously today! Of course, I was fifteen minutes late. I might as well have been twenty-four hours late, because Willy didn't show again. We didn't record. I didn't even make an attempt to put the reel on the machine.

I wish I could tell you some great recording stories from today. But I can't.

Essentially, I was paid my book rate to sit around and kibitz all day. Hey, I enjoy kibitzing as much as the next guy, so long as I'm not on a mission. As much as I'm happy to be paid highly for such activities, I chose to record and mix[15] albums for a living because that's what I wanted to spend my days doing. If I just wanted to kibitz, I would have chosen kibitzing as my profession.

Sometimes, however, I feel that I'm irrational on this subject. Why should I give a shit if I'm actually recording the album or not? Every day I'm at the studio I'm getting paid. But I don't want to be recording (or in this case *not* recording) an album for months on end for lack of momentum. Been there, done that.

Discographies[16] are the name of the game in this business. The deeper and hotter your discography is, the better. The recording biz is basically a small controlled lottery. The more albums I work on in the course of a year, the more lottery tickets I have in my possession. The more lottery tickets, the more chances of a hit. Once you have a hit, you get even more lottery tickets. I just hope I didn't get the piece of paper with the black spot on it, as I have a marked aversion toward being stoned to death.

If I'm locked up spending months on this record because Willy Show never shows, then, overall, that's not a good thing for my career. The more this record costs to make and the longer it takes, the more unlikely it is that it will ever sell more than 10,000 records. For an individual, that number is decent. For a major label, that number is abysmal. The fact that this band was a bidding-war band and that they've been basically on the shelf for two years does not bode well in the first place. So yes, I want to be recording right about now.

I called Willy Show again this morning. He answered his phone, and he apologized again for his no-show. This time he decided to give me a little information teaser. He alluded to having trouble with the contract, and he was confident that it would all be worked out by this afternoon, after which he would be in to take a listen. I told him that I was looking forward to finally meeting him again, and I felt like an awkward idiot in doing so, but I'm over that.

I was considering asking Willy if he wanted me to make some takes, but the fact that he intimated a desire to listen to where we were convinced me to abandon that thought. There are plenty of producers who expect their engineers to do the nuts-and-bolts work as the producer acts more like an executive. I had a producer tell me once that my job was to make him look good. He wasn't kidding. I had to make all the decisions and take complete control of the session. In that case, the producer viewed his job as an overseer of sorts. He would come in and approve or disapprove of what we had done, and then it was my job to either move on or fix what he didn't like.

As with every high-profile producer, there were plenty of stories floating around about Willy Show. The word on the street is the guy is pretty hands-on. His not showing to the session would be, quite obviously, uncharacteristic for a hands-on-style producer. Asking him if he wanted me to make takes seemed counter to getting our relationship (can I call it that yet?) off to a good start. I know that if an engineer I hired asked me that, I'd be immediately distrustful and probably dislike the engineer.

On the other hand, I know several producers that just expect you to start making takes. But those tend to be hands-off, music-supervisor-type producers. They won't even tell you that's what they expect. I knew that Willy was going to eventually show, and we would be working on the album. I also was reasonably confident that he did *not* want me to start making takes. So that was the tack that I would continue to take.

The band seemed pretty happy by the end of yesterday. Unfortunately, after only a couple of hours of no-show Willy, their happiness swiftly eroded to discontentment. The guitar player called their management on the issue. Personally, if I were the band, I would have called my management two days ago. But that's me, and fortunately for me, I'm not in the band.

The mystery of Willy Show's nonappearance was finally revealed. Apparently, Willy's producer's contract wasn't complete.

Furthermore, Willy had made it very clear to everyone involved in this project, who didn't happen to be in the studio waiting for him, that he would not start work on the record until the contract was complete. In my travels, this is nothing short of unusual. In fact, it is not uncommon to finish a producer's agreement in the middle, or even, remarkably, post-completion of the album. But Willy was holding out for some reason.

Hmmmmmm.

It's even more unusual, on those rare occasions that the producer is threatening work stoppage (or should that be work non-startage?), for the band to be in the studio waiting until the contract is done. In the rare instances that a producer is insistent on a finished contract before commencement of the album, the session will typically be put off until such contract is completed. At the moment, thousands of dollars are being spent every day with no music being recorded. As near as I can figure it, based on the information relayed to me by the guitar player, Willy Show didn't tell the label that he wasn't going to work without a contract until this past Monday, probably simultaneous to my reeling in pain from a snare shot to the ear.

Uy-yuy-yuy!

Producer contracts sometimes take weeks—actually months— to complete. Was the label going to actually fork over all that bread to have us sit here for weeks doing nothing? It wouldn't be the first time something like this happened. I'd be lying if I said I weren't somewhat suspicious of this contract story. I couldn't help but wonder if Willy Show was finishing up another album and not admitting to it? Or was it truly a case of wanting the contract complete? Perhaps the contract issue acted as his "beard," much like a gay man's girlfriend is intended to hide his sexual preferences.

I can't say the band was very happy about this news. They weren't. Neither was I for that matter. Their management told them that the contract was almost complete, and there were only one or two more negotiating points of contention. Apparently, the contract would likely be done by tomorrow, which begged the question, Why am I here right now?

Then there's the issue of my nonrefundable three weeks of work deposit to hold the time. I haven't even gotten that money yet. Fuck that! If they cancel or postpone this session, the label will only want to pay me for the days I've worked. With independent labels (indies) and international labels, I will do *no* work without a deposit. With major labels (majors), I've never gotten a deposit before I actually started a gig. So I hadn't given it much thought.

In receiving this information, I placed a call to my manager, who acts for me just as a band's manager acts for it. She promised me that she would get me my deposit "pronto." For as much money as labels go throwing around like it's disposable, they sure don't like giving it up.

I spent time with the boys in the band today, and I'm starting to get a good idea of their personalities. As I said earlier, the bass player and the singer I've worked with before. I mixed a record for them when they were in another band that was ultimately dropped. Unfortunately, mixing with people for seven days doesn't provide much time for developing super-tight personal relationships, and I wonder if I, perhaps, had overestimated just how well I knew these guys. Regardless, I wasn't there because I was buds with the band. I was there because they liked how I approached music and engineering. That's nice, but I wish they would have told me about Dumb Ass before I took the gig.

I continue to marvel at the depth of Dumb Ass's stupidity. Today he was running around the studio naked. I didn't even ask why. That would just encourage him. I just pretended like it wasn't happening. Don't feed the retards, I always say. All the band members have a certain distaste for Dumb Ass. He is probably the diversion that actually unifies this band. He's the scapegoat. I think if it weren't for the "pile on Dumb Ass" game that they have so regularly engaged in, this band would be broken up by now. I say that based on my recent determination that the singer and the guitar player really can't stand each other.

The two of them have been writing this album for two years now, and the label has been ruthlessly—with no concern for the band's general mental well-being or confidence—rejecting their demos outright and insisting that they keep writing. The label wanted hits. Remember, they were a bidding-war band. That means that when they were being bid on, the labels all thought their music was great at *that* time! So why two years of writing? That's like torture. Come to think of it, so is this session so far.

I also discovered that the band has gone through two A&R reps[17] (now on their third), both of whom hated the band, mostly because they were a president's signing. Frankly, I wonder if this band might be a pain in the balls for the label. I could see that side of them in today's conversations—many conversations of which I was only half privy to. It seems that there is a serious history of problems in this band's marriage. As if that weren't enough, it also seems that publishing, which deals with how the writer's portion of the money is paid, is a *major* point of contention among the band members. I've been down this road before.

I'm starting to suspect that the singer is a megalomaniac, but I *know* the guitar player is completely tweaked. I can't cite anything too specific yet. Actually, I suppose saying that I *know* the guitar player is tweaked is a bit strong. Rather, I'll call it a super-strong vibe—a premonition based on years of experience dealing with people who can't hold down a job. Let's put it this way: I would vote for the guitar player to be "most likely to mow down a crowd with a machine gun" in the band. I think he's unstable, and I'm almost positive this guy is seriously depressed. I'm not a shrink, although after years of recording bands I might qualify for an honorary degree. All I know is that the dude doesn't seem very happy most of the time. He mopes, and he never seems to get excited about anything. We're going to be making a record for Christ's sake! Every new record is exciting for me. How could it not be for this guy?

Case in point, I'll record what I and the rest of the band think is a pretty killer guitar sound on our test takes, and he'll walk into the control room, listen to his part, and talk about it like his grandmother just died.

"Yeah, I guess that's okay," he'd say, followed by "I hate my life." I'd be lying if I say that didn't depress the fuck out of me. Shit, I put my best foot forward, and the tone I capture makes someone hate his life? That's certainly not good for one's ego. It's not as if he's playing poorly. He's a good guitar player. I just don't know. Perhaps he's depressed that Willy Show hasn't shown. I can only hope. In the meantime, the guitar player shall be dubbed, most appropriately, Paulie Yore.

As always, I wonder if Willy Show will come to the studio tomorrow. More importantly, will I be working on Saturday? Seeing as, to date, I can only reach Willy in the mornings, I'll have to ask him that question tomorrow. And seeing as it's almost 4 A.M., I'd better get some sleep.

As if I won't have plenty of time to rest during the day.

– Mixerman

DAY 5

The Question

POSTED: AUGUST 2, 10:51 P.M.

I called Willy Show late this morning. As usual, he asked how I was doing. Why, I'm fantastic, Willy. I love sitting around all day waiting for you to never show, and how are you? This is what I wanted to say to him. For obvious reasons, I chose the more diplomatic route.

"Er, I'm fine," I replied, "but the natives are getting restless."

"I'm sure they are. I'm sorry about that. I'm pretty sure I'll be there this afternoon," he replied.

Ahem.

Days two, three, and four, he basically assures me he's going to be there. Today, he's just pretty sure? Is this some kind of sick joke? Can you place bets in Vegas on whether producers will show to recording sessions? Because I was ready to bet a bundle on today's outcome.

"Great, it'll be great to finally work with you again!" I replied as I reeled silently at my own response. I wanted to kick myself, not only for being a dork for having said this to him on four separate occasions in as many days, but also for using the word *great* twice in a sentence.

Upon completion of our morning niceties, it was time for me to ask the most important question of the week—The Mother of All Session Questions—the question that's been in the back of my mind ever since this project began and to date I haven't dared to ask and for good reason! I don't know Willy Show from Adam. So at my first opportunity, and without the use of a remotely clever segue, I took a deep breath, and I blurted out my question.

"Will we be working Saturday?"

My sanity and well-being as a person hinged on the answer to this very important question. In my experience, sessions that run six-day weeks go downhill at an alarming rate. One day of rest is just not adequate time for people to recharge their batteries after six twelve-hour-plus days of trying to record an album, something that to this point we have not done at all. I realize that the practice of working six days is commonplace in this business, and many others, as well. But I also know from experience that sessions with weekends off are generally more fun (ahem), less stressful, and, most important of all, more efficient than the dreadful six-day work week.

The phenomenon of losing the forest for the trees in the creation of a production is reduced drastically by taking two days off a week. The people involved in making records five days a week are generally more rested and happier than they would be if working six days. I've been on projects that we have worked both ways. Even the most seasoned engineer and producer are better able to judge takes, sounds—hell, just about everything—when they are well rested.

Sure the first week of a six-day-per-week project isn't usually too bad. But by the middle of the second week, people start to become testy. Starbucks runs become more frequent. Red Bull[18] becomes a staple rather than a refreshing mid-afternoon boost. By the third week at the six-day pace, most people have no business even being in the studio. Why do people torture themselves so? I contend, (and this could never be proven for obvious reasons) that if I were to take the same band with the identical set of circumstances in parallel universes, and one band worked five days per week and the other identical band worked six days per week, the band that worked five days would actually finish the album sooner, even having spent less actual time in the studio.

As much as I dreaded the answer to my question about working on Saturdays, I was at the very least relieved to have finished asking it. Now I just needed to hear his answer.

Please let it be five days, please let it be five days, I thought to myself in the 500 milliseconds it took Willy Show to respond. That's half a second to those unfamiliar with metric conversions. To be honest, my greatest fear was that Willy would be a seven-day kind of producer. There's no way I could do that. I'd be dead.

"I don't usually work Saturdays or Sundays . . ." he started.

Yes! I pumped my fist like I had just scored the game-winning, sudden-death, overtime goal in game seven of the Stanley Cup finals. No matter how fucked this project is or becomes, I can handle it if I'm not working Saturdays. That means a good night's rest on both Saturday night *and* Sunday night! This is huge! My excitement knew no bounds as I jumped for joy at the news.

". . . but I think we need to work this Saturday," he finished.

"Okay," I replied. "That's cool. Whatever you want to do," I replied in an upbeat manner as my heart sank.

He proceeded to tell me that if all goes well, he'd see me today. With that, our phone call was complete.

Although I was elated with the news of a five-day work week, I was mildly bummed at the prospect of working this Saturday. I could only come up with two viable scenarios. Either I was going to sit there all day Saturday and Willy Show was going to live up to his name, or Willy actually *would* show, and we'd be working long hours for day six. Either way, this sucked. Disheartened, I got myself ready for my day and went to the studio.

I've been setting our start times later and later. Yesterday, I didn't even go to the studio until 2 P.M. I figured if the producer wasn't showing until late afternoon (as you recall he didn't show at all, as if anyone could forget that little fact), why should I go in at 10 A.M.? Regardless of what time I come in, I've been staying close to twelve hours a day. I don't know what the hell I'm doing waiting there for such a long-ass day. But any time I think that I should just split at hour nine or ten, another part of me thinks that if I *do* go, that will end up being the time that Willy Show finally decides to make his first appearance. So I wait—not wanting to risk missing the big entrance. And who could forget Lance Nephew's way of keeping me longer than I really thought I needed to be there, just by his mere presence as a relation to the producer. Although, I *have* come up with ways to manipulate Lance's sense of time, particularly as it relates to the beginning of the day.

With a planned 2 P.M. start, I told Lance that our start time for today was 1 P.M., and I told Dumb Ass our start time was 3 P.M. That worked great! According to Magnolia, Lance arrived at 1:30

P.M., half an hour early. Dumb Ass, at 2:30 P.M., was half an hour late, although he thought he was half an hour early, but still asked if he was late. Perfect! This would be my new method of making schedules work. It should be good for a while, until Lance figures out that he's always half an hour early or that I'm always half an hour late, at which point he'll likely start to come half an hour late to the start time I call for. Confused yet? Read it three times fast. But when he does that, I'll switch it up on him, and then he'll be really late again. He'll never know whether I'm giving him the real time or the fake time in order to get him there early. What can I say? When you're not recording for twelve hours a day, you have time to come up with these sorts of schemes.

The singer, the bass player, and I all arrived around 2 P.M. They told me that we'd definitely be recording either today, tomorrow, or Monday. Apparently, they had just gotten out of meetings with their management and attorney trying to wrap up the producer's agreement with Willy. There was only one sticking point, and that was being sorted out today. I surmised from my conversation that the band's been dealing with this all week; it's just that Willy kept saying he was going to come in, even though the contract wasn't done. It has become quite obvious that this was not, in fact, the case.

In anticipation of actually recording, Dumb Ass was asking me today about Alsihad. Actually, he asks me every day about Alsihad. He's scared to death of having himself edited. You'll recall that Alsihad is my fabricated name for a very common brand of recording software and hardware that uses a computer for editing takes. It is a very intricate program, and it requires a trained expert to operate it, which I call an Alsihah. Alsihah is actually the name of a Shriners' Lodge in Georgia, and Alsihad is a derivative of that word. There's no actual reason for my using that word, other than I liked the ring of it, and it was emblazoned on my friend Fletcher's fez.

Regardless, it seems that Dumb Ass doesn't want to have his drums edited, as he thinks it destroys the feel of the drumming. I couldn't help but think to myself that the feel of an unnatural galloping motion — much like the one caused from slowing down the beginning of the measure and then speeding up the end of the measure — is a feel best left for destruction. As I've intimated, I'm not a big fan of Alsihad myself, but I wasn't quite sure how his drum takes were going to be kept without some serious editing.

I pointed out to Dumb Ass that currently, Alsihad was nowhere in sight. But that fact didn't seem to calm him.

"Do you think Willy will use Alsihad on my drums?" Dumb Ass asked.

"I have no idea," I replied.

"Is Willy big on using Alsihad?" Dumb Ass asked a few moments later.

"Uh, I've never worked with the guy, so that would be pure speculation on my part," I replied.

We went around and around this subject. It was ridiculous. He kept coming up with different ways of asking me the same fucking question that I had no way of answering. I tried telling him not to think about it, but that was useless. So I told him that he needed to play the takes like they were performances, and if he laid down a good performance, he wouldn't need to be edited. That too was ineffective.

At this point, I was doing anything I could to get away from Dumb Ass. I even went into the lounge to play video games with Paulie Yore. That was about as much fun as visiting the urologist for a prostate massage session, but it was still better than trying to explain for the zillionth time to Dumb Ass that I DON'T KNOW THE FUCKING PRODUCER, hence, I couldn't predict what Willy Show would want to do about his drum takes.

At one point, I decided to take a moment to talk to Yore about Dumb Ass's insecurities. I couldn't figure out why the hell he would be so worried about being edited. These days it seems that most drummers *want* to be put into Alsihad.

"I think Cotton is worried about being edited in Alsihad." I explained to Yore.

"Fuck him. Cotton's lucky to even be in this band, so he should just shut the fuck up and do what he's told," Yore stated without hesitation. Nice.

I sat there for a while in silent and stunned disbelief as I attempted to hurl ninety-nine-mile-per-hour Randy Johnson fastballs past Barry Bonds in a virtual baseball game. I knew the band liked to razz Dumb Ass, but this was a whole new level of disdain that I was unaware of. Shit, do any of these guys like each other? I didn't even know how to react. I suddenly realized that Dumb Ass has an inferiority complex, and it's because of the band. Determining to what degree their dismantling of his confidence was degrading his performance was impossible to tell. That's like trying to figure out whether the chicken or the egg came first. Was he this bad before the band started laying into him, or was he halfway decent, and the band was bringing him down several notches with this attitude?

As I marveled at Barry Bonds' home run number 126 on the season flying out of the park off the most dominant pitcher in baseball, it struck me that Dumb Ass might also be nervous. This was his first record, whereas the others, including Yore, have all made records before. It was clear that I was going to have to talk to Dumb Ass and try to build him up. Acting upon this revelation would have to wait though. I had a call.

It was my manager. She had news. It was five in the afternoon, and she had just gotten off the phone with the band's management. I was free to go home for the day!

Halle-fucking-lujah!

Willy would be coming in at 11 A.M. on Monday morning to start work on the album. My manager said that everything was cool, the contract was complete, and Willy was ready to start work after the weekend. At first I was skeptical, but my manager offered irrefutable proof. My deposit was being couriered to my house as we spoke.

Yes! I thought to myself.

Labels don't give you a three-week deposit when there is some question as to the status of making the album. *That* is the reason that I had not gotten it before today. Willy *is* going to show on Monday, and we are finally going to start making this album. I could feel it. I sent the band and Lance home for the weekend, and I sent myself home too. My week of purgatory was over. No longer would I have to push the same large boulder up the same hill over and over again.

Of course, being that I was going home in Friday rush hour in L.A., it took me close to two hours to drive what takes me approximately thirty-five minutes late at night. But that just seems to be par for the course.

Now doesn't it?

– Mixerman

DAY 6

Chocolate Muffins & Razor Blades

POSTED: AUGUST 5, 11:48 P.M. — WEEK 2

Today started like any other day on this project. I was brimming with anticipation as to whether I was going to be recording an album with the world-renowned record producer Willy Show. I could hardly contain myself. Not wanting to be late, I left myself extra time to get to the studio. This was the big day.

I didn't even tell Lance a false time on Friday. I just told him that his uncle was coming in, so he'd better not be late. Damn! I don't think I've ever seen anybody turn that red. You see, I hadn't let on to Lance that I knew about his familial relationship with Willy. After seeing his reaction, I'm glad I kept that to myself for so long.

I arrived at the studio half an hour early, and to my surprise, Lance was a mere five minutes later than I was. I congratulated him, telling him that by the end of this project, he was going to be a good assistant. He thought that was funny, but I was quite serious.

I asked Lance to put up the reel with "Test Drums" on it and to cue up the current drum take. I checked out how the tracks sounded and made sure that I liked the static mix of the instruments. I casually played with the balances, put them back to my marks, and decided to go get a muffin.

One thing that's great about the better studios in L.A. is that they supply you with a plethora of food. On any given day we could have muffins, bagels, croissants, fruit, or even veggie trays. At this particular studio, there were almost always muffins. I love the muffins, especially the chocolate muffins. But for some inexplicable reason, the runner only buys one chocolate muffin per day for the basket (he also only buys one onion bagel, which is even more dumbfounding to me). The longer I wait to go to the muffin basket, the more likely I'll have to eat a bran muffin — something that I was not in need of at that particular moment.

Today, I figured I'd get myself to the muffin basket early and guarantee myself the lone chocolate muffin. When I arrived at the muffin room, lo and behold, before me stood Willy Show himself! And he was eating a muffin. This had to be kismet! Fate! Willy Show liked muffins too! And he liked chocolate muffins. . . .

MOTHERFUCKER!!!

Willy Show was eating *my* chocolate muffin! Was this any way to start off our relationship?

As usual, I chose the path of minimal confrontation. I smiled and greeted Willy. He hugged me as if we were old buddies. That's what producers do here in L.A., they hug you. It was great. So we talked for a minute, and he asked how I was. I told him I was doing well, and that I was glad to spend the weekend with the family, yadda, yadda, yadda.

The band arrived one by one, and eventually we made our way to the studio. First, we went into the studio, where Willy checked out the setup. He commented how he'd never placed the drums where I had them (yes, I seem to have heard that before), and he commented on how great the vibe was. He liked the setup, complimenting it as musician-friendly. I was elated to have him comment positively on the vibe, as that's my pride and joy. I want the room to be so comfortable that guys are dying to get back in and play. I was very happy that he noticed the hard work that went into that detail.

After some kibitzing in the room, we made our way into the control room. Willy sat down, and we continued to shoot the shit for a while, until Willy asked if he could hear some drums. So I played him the last take we did. He listened for a verse and a chorus of the song, and he turned to stop the machine.

This was the moment of truth. To be honest, it sounded okay to me. But I hate just "okay." Okay might as well be shit. That's because I am at all times attempting to achieve the level of "magical," which I can assure you is many levels above okay. But the hard and cruel fact of the matter is that magical comes from the player, not from me.

"It's too room-oriented," he said with his finger still on the stop button, as if the tape could stop any more than it already had.

Okay, so what does that mean? He wanted a PA in the room. The way I figured it, that meant he wanted the sound to have a bigger-than-life room sound.

"I can make it less room-oriented within the balances," I said, as I made some fader adjustments.

"No," said Willy thoughtfully. "I don't know if the PA is right. Did you do a take without the PA?"

I had Lance put up Drum Take I, which I made a week ago with a totally different set of mics. He stopped the tape after less than thirty seconds.

"This is much closer to what I'm looking for," he said.

I couldn't help but laugh to myself. He liked my first instinct, without the PA. A sound, mind you, that took me hours to dial in for lack of a good drummer, and a sound that is now gone. Now he was going to want me to take hours to get that sound back again. Hilarious!

"Well, then, I guess we should go back to that setup," I replied enthusiastically.

Willy concurred, left me his cell phone number and split. I went to work.

I spent about three hours with Dumb Ass and Lance trying to re-create this sound. First Lance had to reset the mics that had been long ago pulled down. That took about half an hour, even with my help and haranguing.

After hearing the drums on the mics and fine-tuning the placements, I realized the heads were dead. Drum heads have only so much life in them before they're dead. In the studio, we typically prefer to replace drum heads often. Some producers prefer to change them daily. Some producers prefer to never change them, but if Willy liked the sound from the first day, then it would seem to follow that he liked the sound of new heads.

I called for the rental company drum tech to come down and change out the snare and tom heads. I guess between going for two drum sounds with tweaks, and the marathon drumming sessions that the non-drummers of the band were participating in throughout the week, we'd managed to kill the heads.

Finally, I managed to get reasonably close to the original drum sound. I had the band play the song down, and I made a take. I called Willy and told him I got it. He returned to the studio within twenty minutes.

Willy listened again and then stopped the tape.

"Yeah, it's good," he said as he rubbed his chin in thought.

Man! That was easy. But doesn't he hear the shitty-ass drumming? Perhaps he knows that it's going to have to be edited. Hey, the guy's a pro. He can tell the difference between a shitty sound and a shitty drummer, right?

"But let me compare it to something," he continued.

Uh-oh, I thought to myself. I've been down this road before.

We spent the next six hours comparing our drum sound to the drum sounds of mastered CDs which, for the most part, contained very pleasing songs that had no bearing whatsoever on this band or the song we were about to cut. We were comparing apples to oranges. None of the CDs was anything that Willy had produced, so it wasn't like he was knowledgeable about what was done to achieve the sound. Not only that, but many of the drums seemed to be doctored with samples.[19]

I pointed this out to Willy, backing up my claim with the fact that some of our comparisons were being made to songs mixed by Sir Arthur Conan Mixallot. Sir Arthur is well known for triggering samples on drums. This is all well and good, but the fact of the matter is, we were *not* using triggered samples. This made for wholly unfair comparisons. Unless we were planning to put in samples ourselves, it was unrealistic for me to match drum sounds to those mixes. Willy seemed unfazed. He felt I could get that sound regardless.

Throughout the day, I felt like a hamster on a treadmill. I was going around in circles. One of the CDs had tons of low end,[20] another had *no* low end. How the fuck was I supposed to match a sound between two completely different sonic landscapes?

Willy liked the kik from one CD, and the snare from another CD, and the cymbals from yet another. The CDs were mostly insanely bright[21] and loud.[22] So I rented several sets of Pultec EQP1a EQs, which I consider to be my not-so-secret weapon to help me brighten the drums. Pultecs are forty-year-old tube EQs, that are very expensive as they are highly coveted and in limited supply. I like them because I can add a lot of high end without adding a lot of distortion, which is not the case with many, many EQs on the market.

I spent many hours A/B-ing[23] CDs and trying to make Dumb Ass's drums sound like a conglomeration of what I suspect were some of Willy's favorite recordings. This process can be extremely fatiguing. So much so that it becomes difficult to tell what the hell you're listening to after a while. One can become extremely confused and frustrated throughout this process, and the only weapon to combat these maladies are breaks, of which I took many. After much hoop jumping, I finally came up with a drum sound that I thought might satisfy Willy, who was making my life miserable at this particular juncture.

He listened. He liked it! Halle-fucking-lujah!

The only obstacle that remained was for Willy to do a car check (the process of checking a recording in the car), which he did without incident. Just like that (nine hours later), we were moving on.

We spent about another hour changing out guitars and amps and trying to find a combination that he liked for the song. We ended up back on the original combo that I had arrived at with Yore, who seemed to have no reaction to any of the sounds, and at times seemed bored to be participating in the making of his own album.

"Yeah, whatever," Paulie Yore said, as if he had lost something important to him. "It sounds good enough to me," he would say as he hung his head and slunk out of the room.

Listening to Yore in a studio was as treacherous as listening to the Sirens as you sailed a boat through a rocky cove. Needless to say, I did my very best to avoid buying into his most unenthusiastic comments, as I moved on to some bass adjustments before we began making takes.

By the time we actually were making takes, I was thoroughly exhausted, yet pleased that after more than a week, we were actually recording the album. As I sat, nearly dozing off in the middle of the second take (which sucked ass), I was awakened by what I considered at the time to be an odd event. Willy reached toward the console and turned down the music.

"So you been having fun all week with these putzes?" he inquired from out of the blue.

What kind of play was that? He knows the band requested that I be on the session.

I chuckled rather uncomfortably.

What did he expect to gain from this question? He obviously was interested in my reaction. I couldn't for the life of me figure out what he was looking for, and I had only a split second to give him one.

"They haven't been too bad," I replied shortly after my chuckle, looking away from Willy, but quickly darting my eyes to see his reaction, as he turned up the music again.

After I said it, I figured this was the best answer I could give. I wasn't acknowledging that I thought they were putzes, but I wasn't denying it either. Until I could determine his angle, noncommittal was the name of the game.

As take after take after take went by, I pondered what had just transpired. The more I thought about it, the more I realized Willy was right. These guys *are* putzes. I get along reasonably well with all of them, but if I had a day off, I wouldn't call *any* of them to go hang out. Dumb Ass drives me up a wall. Shit, he drives everyone up a wall. Paulie Yore is either full-on depressed or a total asshole. I don't think that guy actually likes anyone. The singer has proven himself to be a class-A jerk. He is the most self-centered, inconsiderate prick to walk the earth, which is somewhat inexplicable to me, because he wasn't this way the first time that I worked with him. The bass player is generally a fine guy when we're hanging out alone, but this group of personalities has brought out the worst in him. These days he seems to derive his greatest pleasure from fanning the flames of the singer's favorite pastime—the pushing of other band member reaction buttons. A bad combination, to be sure. This band clearly fits the definition of "dysfunctional."

As if that weren't enough, there was constant bickering over "Monopoly money," which songs would make the album, and who owned what share of which songs. "Monopoly money" is my term for money that doesn't exist yet. The money, for example, that *would* be made if an album *should* sell two million albums. Money that does not currently exist is the single most destructive entity in this business. For the most part, these kinds of arguments are preposterous, but no bandmate wanted to have another make more money than he. At the same time, nobody in the band wanted to split everything equally, in case his song happened to be the one that became a hit. "Happened to" being the operative phrase here.

Near as I could figure it, Willy wasn't making a play; he was expressing what I should have discovered by now on my own. He knew they were putzes, where I had been temporarily blinded by my relationship with two of them and their communal desire to have me in the room as some sort of counterbalance. On top of all that, I'm sure that my brain was somehow attempting to prevent me from actually hating the band I was recording—a condition you generally want to avoid at all costs. In one sentence, Willy had destroyed the protective bubble I was keeping myself in, and I was now on a project in which I hated the band and could actually express that. Once again, I was fucked.

Regardless of my revelation, we filled several reels with takes. He just let them play the song over and over and over again, sitting practically motionless in front of the speakers. As I sat next to him, I couldn't help but think that Willy must be trying to figure out what the fuck he was going to do. Somewhere around the sixth take, he asked me to solo the drums. He was shaking his head in disgust. "This just doesn't sound right," he confided, never looking me in the eye but rather staring blankly ahead.

I've been waiting for the opportunity to tell Willy what I thought of this drummer for the better part of a week. To this point, I have done little toward this front, mostly because it's pointless to debate over something that you cannot prove right then and there. If one person is arguing from the perspective of speculation, then I contend the other is a fool to try and persuade. I now had Willy in the room with the shitty drumming of Dumb Ass blasting out the speakers, and if Willy still was not convinced, I could now at least prove it to him. Without hesitation, I replied.

"Cotton sucks."

"Cotton?" he asked as he turned to look at me.

"That's my pet name for the drummer," I explained.

"Why Cotton?" he inquired.

"Because he's dumber than cotton," I said dryly.

That *must* be a funny line because Willy practically fell off his chair just like the bass player had after I said it. When he regained his balance, he sat perched on the edge of his chair, and he laid his head in his arms on the console with his body pulsating from silent laughter almost inappropriately, as my line really didn't warrant such a reaction. Just as the band was completing its fifth take, I, too, found myself laughing, as laughter is oftentimes infectious. Fortunately, I was able to regain my composure.

"I'm going to tell them to make another take," I announced.

Willy sat motionless with his head down as I asked the band to play another take. Lance rolled tape at my cue, and I rolled the clik track.[24] Willy had finally regained his composure. He sat up in order to wipe away tears from his face.

Personally, I don't get it. I mean, I thought it was mildly amusing, but this seemed to be an overreaction. Perhaps he was vulnerable—much like one is when he or she is extremely upset. Perhaps the drumming had depressed him so much that he was susceptible to even the mildest of humor, sending him into a tizzy. I can't quite figure it out.

Regardless, to me, humor is the single most important part of a session. I'm like the class clown of a session. I dance, play practical jokes, fuck around constantly, make up names for people (I know, big surprise), and I'm an incessant smart-ass. I'll do anything to keep the people involved, happy, and entertained. The more miserable the circumstance, the more I use humor as my weapon. I had achieved what I needed most to achieve today. I got Willy to laugh. More importantly, I got him to laugh uncontrollably. This was a good thing.

"You're right, Cotton sucks," Willy finally replied, still catching his breath, and still having occasional momentary tremors of laughter. "Do you know how to use a razor blade?" he continued.

"Of course," I replied. I should have stopped there, but I was curious, since he had already asked me this in our pre-gig interview.

"You asked me that before."

"Yes, that's one of the reasons you have the gig. Somehow, cut me a good drum take tomorrow," he said. And after the band finished playing the last take, he called it a night.

This isn't going to be easy.

– Mixerman

188 Ways to Kill Your Drummer

POSTED: AUGUST 7, 12:34 A.M.

Last night, as I was leaving the studio, I told Lance to burn me two CDs of all the takes, to program an ID for each section of the song as the CD was being burned—intro, verse, chorus, etc.—and to document clearly and concisely which ID was which. Then I told him to have one of the CDs couriered to my house and have the other delivered by runner to Willy's.

When I got up this morning, I was well aware of what this day would be like. Hours upon hours of tedious cutting and editing. I'm a big proponent of cutting tape, as opposed to using a computer. For starters, I like the way tape sounds better than computer programs—especially Alsihad.

As I alluded to earlier in this diary, and which I suppose I can't say enough, Alsihad is, without question, the most purchased and used Digital Audio Workstation (DAW) in the recording business. There are other manufacturers of DAWs, but none have anywhere close to the market share of Alsihad. As is typically the case with electronic equipment, computers, etc., it seems the best product rarely rises to the top. Beta players and Macintosh computers are prime examples of that phenomenon.

The advent of the DAW has changed the way recordings are made because products like Alsihad have reduced the buy-in cost to making records (albeit this is largely irrelevant in this particular case) and the editing software greatly speeds up the actual process of editing. Unfortunately, the power of editing that Alsihad provides can, and in many cases will, slow down the recording process as a whole rather than speed it up. This paradox occurs partly because people seem unable to resist using the editing power that Alsihad offers, and even the most disciplined producer, recordist, singer, or player (myself included) begins to depend on the fixing power of the computer, as opposed to the performing power of the musician.

Of course, the speeding-up or slowing-down of the process given the presence of Alsihad is a hotly contested subject. But if you tell just about any studio manager in L.A. that the session he/she is booking will be using Alsihad, their eyes will light up as if you had just announced he/she won the lottery.

Che-ching!

To make matters worse, there is some debate as to the quality of audio reproduced by Alsihad. Recording and the process of editing within Alsihad is a subject of great contention among the community of audio engineers. To me, the sonic quality of a recording is drastically degraded just by putting a recording into Alsihad. Even though there are technical ways to reduce this degradation, it is often either cost-prohibitive or, in the case of big-budget records, viewed as unnecessary fat in the constant battle to trim costs.

Unfortunately, the process of editing within Alsihad can cause the most egregious degradation of all—particularly with drums. With as many edits as were going to be necessary on this song, the quality of the recording would, without a doubt, be reduced substantially in quality. A recording that sounded "alive" and "vibrant" sonically can be reduced to "mundane" or "dead" by editing within the computer. I don't know the technical reasons why this sonic degradation occurs, and to be fair, as with all of this that I am discussing here, there are those that will argue vehemently that said degradation is imagined. But as far as I'm concerned, anyone that argues that might as well argue that the earth is flat.

This phenomenon of degradation doesn't really happen from physically cutting together pieces of tape, unless you accidentally use a magnetized blade, in which case you get a permanent "pop" on your recording. Nice! Unfortunately, the process of cutting tape together can be slow, laborious, and, to some extent, archaic. Archaic would certainly be the truth of the matter here. This wasn't simply a case of cutting three large sections of takes together to get the best performance, in which case I'd be done in about ten minutes flat. This was going to be some heavy-duty editing. There would likely be a very large number of edit points in the song, a task that even on a computer would take many hours. On a tape deck, a job like this would easily take close to an entire twelve-hour day.

As I walked out of my house, I picked up the padded envelope that contained the CD Lance made for me. I listened to the takes as I drove to the studio. The freeway was clogged, as it always is during the day in La La Land, so I wasn't endangering too many lives by writing notes on each take as I drove. About

71

halfway there, I stopped even taking notes, as I was overcome by the irony. While Dumb Ass could not maintain a consistent pulse from one beat to the next, his propensity to speed up the snare hit and slow down the kik was nothing *short* of consistent. Yes, Dumb Ass was actually consistent in his inconsistency. To make matters worse, Dumb Ass wouldn't play the form of the song the same way twice. Some verses, he was still on the ride cymbal, when clearly he should have been on the hat. I was going to have to pick a take that he played the proper arrangement on and edit from there.

I couldn't help but wonder why I was editing a drum take out of this bullshit. But at the same time, it's not like a good take would have ever been played by Dumb Ass. So I can hardly criticize Willy's decision to have them play the song down a bunch of times and try to cut something together. But perhaps it would have been better if the drummer played the takes similar to each other. It certainly would have made editing easier. But, as I've come to realize, this isn't about easy.

Even with the traffic, I managed to make it to the studio at my planned start time. Seeing as Lance wasn't in yet, I made my way to the muffin room. I had been thinking about that chocolate muffin all morning, and I wanted to make sure that I was the person who ate it today. As I made my way to the table, I could see my muffin there at the top of the muffin pile in all its glory. Knowing that Willy liked the chocolate muffin, I actually considered leaving it for him. But seeing as I was going to be editing all day, the muffin was just going to get stale anyway, so I did us both a favor and ate it. It was delicious, and I was enjoying it thoroughly. That is, until Dumb Ass walked in.

I almost choked on my muffin. (That sounds bad!) This led me to lapse into the oddest momentary daydream of Dumb Ass incorrectly performing the Heimlich maneuver on me, and in the process, badly bruising my sternum. Then I imagined Dumb Ass performing CPR on me, punching my bruised sternum as hard as he could in hopes of reviving me. By the time my mind had wandered to Dumb Ass leaning over to administer mouth-to-mouth, I was overcome by disgust, jolting myself completely out of the dream sequence.

What the fuck was he doing here? I was going to be editing all day. I didn't even want him anywhere near the studio.

Lance finally sashayed his skinny ass into the muffin room.

"You're late," I told him curtly, now in a bad mood with the presence of Dumb Ass.

Even if Dumb Ass were a cool, laid-back dude, I wouldn't want him around while I was editing his takes together. The process requires enormous amounts of concentration, and having a nervous Nellie in the waiting room, or worse yet, in the control room, asking me a lot of questions or criticizing a work in progress would only serve to hinder that process. So I decided to make a sign. I wrote on a piece of paper with a dull blue Sharpie pen, and I taped my sign to the window of the control room door.

NO DRUMMERS ALLOWED! THIS MEANS YOU!!!

"Whaaaaaaa," Dumb Ass whined in his best retard voice. "Why no drummers allowed!?" he exclaimed while stamping his foot as if he were three years old. Perhaps he thought he was Tarzan or something.

73

"That's just the way it is, my man," I replied compassionately.

"You're not going to have to edit me very much," he continued.

What? Was this guy smoking crack? Was he not listening to the way the music rocked awkwardly like the blinker of a car?

"Of course not!" I lied. "But this takes a lot of concentration, and I can't really have disturbances."

"Okay, but don't make me sound like a robot."

Better a robot than a horse, I thought to myself. The way the drums were now, were the song to ever get on the radio, entire cities of people would have to be treated immediately for seasickness.

"I won't," I replied, smiling as I closed the door gently on him.

Once I got into the room, I quickly realized that this studio wasn't the least bit prepared for tape editing. There were no extra two-inch take-up reels (I would need a bunch), no half-inch splicing tape (I needed the thin tape to do the amount of edits I would be doing); there were no speakers in the machine room; the razor blades were not demagnetized; there was barely a nub of a white grease pencil for marking tape; and I was in desperate need of a common two-by-four piece of lumber, the purpose of which I will explain momentarily. I provided Lance with a list as I spent the next hour-plus charting out the rest of Dumb Ass's takes from the CD, as Lance put together my equipment list and proceeded to demagnetize and mark blades just as I had showed him moments earlier.

Fuck! The task before me was overwhelming. I've done editing like this before, but it's been years. Editing is a groove thing. It's not difficult, but efficiency comes from the act of doing. This was ridiculous. Dumb Ass's drums pushed and pulled like the aptly named *Doctor Doolittle* creature Pushmi-pullyu. In order to fix this sort of disastrous feel, I was going to have to use little bits of audio tape from before kik drums or after snares to insert in order to manufacture drum hits that fall where they are supposed to. I reserved an entire take that I felt was less than stellar for those bits, and I had Lance label it "Equalizer."

The two-by-four I asked Lance to get was for making a time and distance template. Length of tape is the equivalent of time in a recording. The two-inch machine spins tape at a speed of thirty inches per second. Therefore, thirty inches of tape is the equivalent of one second of running time. If the tempo of the song is sixty beats per minute, which is the equivalent of one beat per second, then the length of one beat is thirty inches.

The way to determine the distance of a beat that is not so easily calculated is to physically cut a piece of tape between clicks on the clik track and to mark that distance on the two-by-four. This distance becomes my template, and I halve and quarter my template in order to mark my distances for eighth notes and sixteenth notes, respectively. With the template, I have what amounts to a measuring stick, so as to see physically whether I need more tape or less tape between drum hits.

After a couple of hours of mapping out what I thought were the best measures of the takes and Lance getting the items on my list, I was ready to start cutting tape. The question was, Do I start immediately and cut the two-inch master, or test my cuts on half-inch tape? Normally, I'd at the very least start by cutting half-inch drum mixes of the takes as a trial run of sorts to see how the song was going together. Since I was already two hours into my session, I decided against this course of action and just went for it.

I spent the next eleven hours with Lance by my side cutting tape. At first, Lance was mesmerized by the barbaric nature of slicing up tiny pieces of audio tape and pasting them together with sticky splicing tape. But he quickly forgot about that, as he had his hands full in swapping reels on the machines, documenting where every scrap of tape came from that made up the master take of the song, and, just as important, documenting where every scrap of tape was missing from the production reels.[25] All this without writing a dissertation, but furnishing enough details so it was clear where everything had gone and everything had come from.

Shortly after commencing the editing process there were reels and tape everywhere. I had two machines going; I was measuring, cutting, adding, checking, redoing, and rechecking. There were little bits of audio tape adhered all over the wall with grease markings on them telling me what they were. I was adding in scraps as time equalizers that were barely over a half inch wide. It took me over two hours just to do the intro and half a verse.

My kingdom for Alsihad!

Yes. That's right. My kingdom for Alsihad! I give! This is not a job for editing two-inch. When a drummer is as bad as this, fuck it! Who gives a shit if the sound degrades? With this many edits, it *will* degrade within Alsihad, but again, so what? Hell, with inserting little bits of "Equalizer," I was degrading the sound on two-inch anyway. The drums sound like shit regardless. Degrading the recording really doesn't matter.

I know that this revelation—or throwing in of the towel, as it were—might be slightly disappointing to Luddites everywhere

(Luddite is my pet name for those who prefer working with audio tape as opposed to computers), but there is a difference between editing the shit out of a decent drum take and doing what
you have to in order to make a shitty drum take decent. In other
words, my disdain for Alsihad does not lie in the good it can do in
making a project more efficient. Clearly, in this particular case,
the pros of using Alsihad *far* outweigh the cons. My disdain lies
in the use of Alsihad to edit what otherwise could have been a
perfectly acceptable performance. The fact of the matter is, the
recording is now under a visual microscope. But in my opinion,
music should never be judged visually.

Unfortunately, the use or nonuse of Alsihad on this project
wasn't my call. The global ramifications of Alsihad on the making of music had nothing to do with the making of this particular
record. My job was to edit the entire song on two-inch whether I
wanted to or not. I had to complete the job no matter how much
of a waste of time I thought it was. This is what Willy Show wanted, and clearly, it's his show.

I realize now that I've had a pretty cushy recording life in recent years, in that I have not had to perform this type of heavy editing. I've done some two-inch editing in that time, but no more
than five cuts in a song. In those cases, I was basically compiling
entire sections. These days, this kind of extensive editing is left to
Alsihah. In fact, I have a newfound appreciation for Alsihah.

Prior to today, my normal workday was spent sitting in a comfortable chair getting fat as I ate chocolate muffins and worked off
the calories by punching buttons and moving faders. Editing two-
inch to this extent was serious fucking work. I was standing the
entire day, sweating like a pig, with my back killing me and my

head swimming. I even sliced my finger today, an unusual event under the circumstances, and an event that I am painfully and constantly being reminded of as I type this diary entry.

At the six-hour mark of my day, Dumb Ass finally left. The singer made a brief appearance and split. The bass player and Yore relaxed in the lounge all day, drinking Johnnie Walker Red and playing video baseball (this was beginning to be a trend). Willy checked in and wasn't surprised in the least to find out that it would take me all day and possibly some of tomorrow to finish the job.

I made 188 edits today, and the feel of the drums still sucks ass.

It's just that now the drums are in time.

– Mixerman

DAY 8

A Fatty Day

POSTED: AUGUST 8, 12:49 A.M.

Lance was sitting at the table on the patio with Dumb Ass smoking a cigarette as I pulled into the lot. Lance was there before me today, most likely due to the fact that last night I told him I'd be starting at 9 A.M. It was now 10:30 A.M. Lance didn't dare complain. It was Dumb Ass who commented on how late I was. I smiled and told Lance to follow me.

Dumb Ass tried to gain admittance to the studio, but I told him that the "no drummers allowed" sign I had made yesterday was still in full effect and that he'd have to wait. I guess he thought I was kidding, because he came in anyway and sat down in *my* chair between the speakers. There wasn't much I could do about that. Technically, this was his session. Regardless, that was my chair, and I had work to do before Willy came in.

"Excuse me," I said. Convinced that he had actually made a point other than the one on the top of his head and further convinced that I wasn't going to force the issue, Dumb Ass got up and moved to the couch in the back of the room.

By the end of yesterday's editing session, it was almost impossible for me to accurately judge the big picture of my editing job. I had to wait until today to hear how my edit job had worked. I dimmed the lights and closed the machine room door, which houses the multitrack[26] machines, so that I wouldn't have to listen to the incessant thwap, thwap, thwap of 188 edits passing the entire run length of three minutes, forty-five seconds. I prefer to listen to takes with the lights dim. I've found that there is something about reducing the amount of stimulation on your eyes that makes your listening more acute.

It was just as I had expected. There was no feel to the drums. It doesn't really matter that the kiks hit the one and the snares hit the two. Feel comes from everything in between. Feel comes from the way the rhythm makes you "feel"—hence the term. A drumbeat should make your body move by pure reflex. There should be an infectious physical reaction from the drums.

How could this actually be a surprise to me? I must have spent too much time convincing myself this morning that I might be pleasantly surprised with the results of yesterday's marathon editing session. The cold, hard reality had set in. I spent twelve hours editing these drums with the single goal of making them, at the very least, acceptable, but at the very most, they sucked ass.

I called Willy's cell phone to make sure he was coming in. He asked me how the drums were, and I told him they were in time now, but that they still sucked. There was no point in trying to sugarcoat it. I didn't want Willy coming into the studio expecting a killer drum track. He told me that he'd be in shortly and he hung up.

Willy came in at around eleven and immediately hugged everyone. My first notion was that Willy must not like dim lights, because after the morning hugs, he turned them all the way up. Willy was asking how everyone was, and we participated in the exchange of morning niceties as he reached into his leather satchel that he has thus far carried with him, pulled out a huge baggie of green, and proceeded to roll a fatty. It was eleven in the morning, and Willy was smoking a fatty.

"Breakfast of Champions," he stated as he smiled contentedly, holding his breath.

He pointed at Lance to dim the lights again. I understood now that it wasn't that Willy disliked dim lights. Willy couldn't roll a fatty in the dark.

He offered me the fatty, which I declined. Not because I don't smoke fatties, but rather, I don't smoke fatties if there is any chance in hell I'm going to have to cut tape. Combining the use of wickedly sharp instruments with substances designed to alter and dull the senses was an activity I preferred to avoid. Besides, my finger, which I probably should have gotten stitches for, was still throbbing with pain.

Willy offered his fatty to the others in the room, and Yore accepted without hesitation.

So far, Yore is the big partier in the crew. He's keeping his empty bottles of Johnnie Walker and Maker's Mark as trophies from his drinking sessions. The empties are currently stacked on top of the refrigerator in the lounge, and his collection is already nothing short of impressive. The bass player also participates in the drinking sessions, but I get the feeling that he drinks nowhere near the amount of alcohol that Yore drinks.

After Yore took a hit, the singer was the next to partake, as he walked over to take the fatty and proceeded to draw from it.

Willy asked me if the edited take was up. I nodded, and he proceeded to listen to the edited take. I sat there listening to the take, thinking to myself, This just isn't right. Willy stopped the tape machine when the take was done.

"It's not right," he said. "You're right about what you said on the phone," he continued.

I sat there slightly uncomfortable, trying not to show it. Willy made that comment while Dumb Ass was in the room, and I was just waiting for Dumb Ass to ask what I had said. Thankfully, he didn't even ask, but he *did* speak.

"I sound like a robot!" Dumb Ass pouted, actually sounding like a robot. Everyone pretty much ignored him.

We all sat there dejected, staring straight ahead. We were on our eighth day on this project, and we still hadn't recorded a usable note. As if that weren't enough, and as if the band, Willy, and I weren't sitting there wondering what else could go wrong, things got worse. The runner delivered a phone message, which he handed directly to Willy. I was sitting right next to him, and I could read plainly what the message said.

> To: Willy Show
> From: Jeramiah Weasel
>
> Willy, I'd like to come by. Please call.

Jeramiah is the band's newest A&R rep. He is basically a minion with a very strong opinion. I'd be surprised if he even had signing power, although I'd be willing to bet he's conned more than one band into signing a Memo Deal, which basically gives a label the right to the artist until a contract is entered into, greatly reducing a band's power of negotiation.

This band was the president's signing, and Jeramiah is a figurehead. But he certainly has the president's ear, and it would not be good for him to come over before we had something worthwhile to play for him. He isn't a dumb fellow, but he is a bit of a poseur, and he really doesn't understand much of anything about the studio. I've run into Jeramiah several times in recent years, and I've never been impressed by the dude. How he keeps getting gigs is beyond me.

Willy crumpled up the note and threw it in the trash.

"Perhaps we should trigger[27] some samples," Willy said unfazed by the note, "and then pump the samples out the PA and record the room. We can use your drum machine," he said to me, pointing to my drum machine.

"May I?" I said, picking up the fatty from the console.

Normally, I wouldn't partake this early in a session, or for that matter, this early in the day. The fact of the matter is, I was upset. This was a terrible situation. If Jeramiah comes to the session and finds out that we can't play him a note of music, he could completely shut the session down. As much as that might very well be a blessing, I'm committed for the next two months to this gig.

As if that weren't enough, we were now trying to trigger drums and somehow mask the fact that Dumb Ass sucks. At that moment, I knew there was no way to make Dumb Ass good, and it was obvious to me that I was going to have to spend an inordinate amount of time forced into relearning this particular lesson. Add in the fact that I was absolutely drained from editing all day yesterday, and for what? Perhaps if my efforts had been fruitful, I would be adequately energized. But this wasn't the case.

It was pointless to resist. Willy was obviously going to exhaust every possibility to make a usable drum track out of the mess. The way I saw it, I had no choice. By the size of Willy's baggie (that sounds bad), and the fact that he laughed so hard at my "dumb as Cotton" line two days ago (which was only one step beyond mildly amusing), I was gathering that Willy smoked fatties every day. At this point, I needed to be in his head space.

The fatty did just what it was supposed to. I finally had recognized the situation for what it actually was. Humorous.

Not pathetic, not ridiculous, not hairball. Humorous. I had been given an instant attitude adjustment. I now understood what Willy was trying to achieve. Where I had been negative and doubtful that anything could save Dumb Ass, I was positive that we could do something creative to make the edited take work.

"Who ate my chocolate muffin?" a voice came from across the room. It was Willy, half-kidding, half-serious about the muffin.

I, of course, ate the chocolate muffin the moment I walked in this morning. I wasn't proud of that fact. The muffins are huge. I could have been less of a pig and left half the muffin, but I chose to eat the entire thing. Could I really cop to such insensitivity?

"I think Cotton ate it," I said after checking the room to be sure he wasn't around.

"Why the fuck do we only get one chocolate muffin a day?" Willy said.

With that, Willy picked up the phone and summoned the runner, who was sent out for twenty chocolate muffins. That was a bit much. Even being high I don't think we ate more than seven of them between us. Willy instructed the runner that he was to never put fewer than five chocolate muffins in the basket each day.

"And five onion bagels!" I exclaimed as the runner was walking out the door of the control room. Willy nodded his head approvingly as I brought my focus back to the task at hand—the triggering of samples.

Samples are basically very short recordings. A kik drum sample is a recording of a kik drum. A trigger allows me to replace the recorded kik drum with the sampled kik drum. This gives a very consistent kik drum sound, as opposed to the very inconsistent sound that was on tape. Bad drummers play their drums with a great deal of inconsistency, both in timing and velocity. Being that I fixed the timing, it was the velocity that was now obviously lacking consistency. The trigger works by automatically playing the sample once it receives a certain threshold of audio information from a source. In this case, the source would be the track that was designated for the kik drum mic. This way, anytime Cotton hit his kik drum, the trigger would play the sample, and that is what we would hear as the kik drum.

Before we were to begin triggering samples and the like, I really needed to make a copy of the edited tape. It had way too many edits to record over. Every time we played the tape, I was worried that something was going to fuck up. I knew exactly what I wanted to transfer to.

After *much* discussion, and perhaps a little sales pitch on my part, Willy decided that, rather than go down an analog generation, we should transfer the edited drum tracks to Radar.[28] Radar is a digital multitrack recorder that I actually like the sound of. The great thing about Radar is it operates just like a tape machine. Willy was concerned about going digital, citing his disdain for the sound of Alsihad. But Willy had heard good things about the Radar, and I certainly wasn't telling him anything different. The drums had already received the benefits of analog tape; now my concern was having a master that worked. I finally convinced him to give it a try.

After the Radar arrived, I transferred the edited drums. Willy *did* like the sound of the Radar very much, and this was the best news of the day. I was in a great mood as I sparked up another fatty. Now, with Radar at my disposal, I had a chance to help move this session along. To say that we have been painfully unproductive would be an understatement. My goal was to eventually have someone else editing the drums, perhaps even in the Radar, while we continued recording takes each day. Spending an entire day editing while everyone just sat around drinking like fish wasn't good for the band. We needed momentum.

When you have a band sitting around all day, they never get into a groove. Somehow, Dumb Ass and the band must get into said groove. If Dumb Ass had some confidence and momentum, it's likely he would play better. This would make all of our lives easier and more efficient, and *this* was the key to making the session more productive. The band needed to be playing and moving forward, not sitting on their asses all day. Unfortunately, at the moment, I was alone in this thinking.

After pounding down chocolate muffins followed by lunch, we spent hours putting together samples, triggering them, playing them through the PA, and moving room mics. I had to program mutes[29] on the kik and snare because I was getting so many mistriggers.[30] Dumb Ass was just too inconsistent as a player, and with the compression, gating[31] wasn't effective. We tried all sorts of wacky tricks to make the drums work (perhaps on a day that I'm a bit less exhausted I'll go through some of those). Actually, we were having a blast fucking with the drums. But by early evening, Yore, who was toward the end of his bottle of Johnnie Walker Red, had had just about enough.

"Let's just record the other instruments on this fucking song already."

The band was obviously getting frustrated at the lack of progress, and Yore was drunk enough to remove himself from his depression and expose the more assholish side of his personality. Willy, picking up on the subtle cue, decided we should lay down music on the drums. I took about half an hour to make an analog slave[32] of the drums from Radar.

Finally, we were recording! We started with the bass, which quickly became a tedious punch-fest.[33] of recording one measure at a time. Apparently the bass player wasn't used to playing with drums that were so steady.

Uy-yuy-yuy.

Next we recorded Yore's part, which was pretty painless, regardless of the fact that he was three sheets to the wind.

Unfortunately, as has typically been the case on this session, someone was sure to bring our progress to a screeching halt. The singer, who should probably stick to singing, expressed the desire to lay down some guitar parts, too. Willy obliged, sending Yore home, and wisely exiting stage left himself. I got to hang for another two hours, wanking off recording a below-average guitar player at best, whilst the quality guitar player was at home, likely sleeping off an entire day's worth of drinking. Why does this always happen with bands?

Here the band has a very good guitar player who can effortlessly and quickly lay down the parts, and the shitty guitar player is the one laying down the majority of them. Next thing you know, Dumb Ass is going to want to sing one of the songs.

God help us if that happens.

– Mixerman

DAY 9

Old Wounds May Run Deep
But New Ones Hurt Like Hell!

POSTED: AUGUST 8, 11:05 P.M.

I woke up around 5 A.M. from my finger throbbing with pain.
I took a look at the wound, and it wasn't going to take enroll-
ment in medical school for me to determine the cut was drastically infected. Great. This wasn't a case for Neosporin. This was a
nasty-ass infection. So I showered—which proved to be a difficult
process while holding my hand in the air as if to say, "Pick me"—
got dressed, and went to the emergency room.

After waiting there for three fucking hours—apparently people with hemorrhaging wounds, kidney stones, ripped placentas,
strokes, and heart attacks have priority over people with throbbing, infected cuts oozing pus—I finally got to see a doctor. I was
half wishing that I would drop dead right there in the waiting
room to teach the triage nurse a little lesson on just how dangerous an infection could be. Of course, then I'd be dead. The doctor prescribed a strong antibiotic (or so he says) and a triplicate
form opiate mixed with Tylenol.

After over three hours in the ER, my morning was shot to hell. I took my antibiotic, took my Tylenol #3 with codeine (which I *never* take just before operating heavy machinery) and drove to the studio (oops!). Having gone to sleep at 2:30 A.M. and having woken up at 5 A.M. this morning, coupled with an entire day of smoking fatties, as you can well imagine, I was wiped out. What I needed was Starbucks.

Specifically, I needed a super-size Starbucks drip of the day. I'm not quite sure what *super-size* translates to in the bullshit foo-foo Starbucks lingo, but it's the largest cup they've got. They're pretty good at Starbucks about not fucking with you, if you venture from their seemingly proprietary size terminology—even a term as obnoxious as super-size. I guess they figure if you need that much coffee, you're probably in a shit mood anyway. In this case, they would have been right.

Equipped with my extra-large, extra-hot, extra-black coffee, I hit the button on my car phone that activates voice recognition. It's actually a cell phone that converts into a car phone. I hate fucking cell phones. Driving holding a cell phone the size of a credit card sucks. Personally, I prefer to talk on speaker phone when I'm driving.

"Call Willy," I said to the microphone above me. "Calling Willy," my phone repeated back to me.

Willy answered his phone as he always does in the early morning. He asked how I was, and he asked how the guitar part went down. I told him I was fine (not wanting to go into my morning hospital visit at that moment) and that it took two hours to record the guitar part the singer laid down. Then I told him that I thought Yore could play better after a fifth of Johnnie Walker than the singer could ever hope to do straight. Of course, that wasn't news to Willy. That's exactly why he exited stage left last night.

I was enjoying my coffee and my conversation with Willy as the codeine was starting to relieve the pain in my finger. Willy's a great guy, I was thinking to myself. I love hanging out with him.

"So what should we do today?" Willy asked.

I really wish he hadn't asked that question because at that exact moment I was taking a swig of my coffee. The question caused me to suck scalding hot coffee through my sinuses, which then percolated through my nose. Holy fucking shit! I was screaming in pain. Willy kept asking if I was all right. He thought I was in a car accident or something, and I almost was as I recklessly pulled my car over. I had scalded my sinuses. My kingdom for some cold water and a neti pot![34]

After a couple of minutes, the pain lessened, perhaps due to the codeine in my system, which was really starting to kick in. I had coffee all over my shirt and pants, and to make matters worse, there was coffee all over my car. In my pain, I had managed to drop the cup, spilling coffee in both the cockpit and shotgun positions of the car. I told Willy I was going to be a little late, since I had to go back home, change my clothes, and try to clean out my car. He understood.

Great! I'm thinking on my way to the studio in a fresh set of clothes. Now Willy's asking *me* what we should do for the day. But as I thought about it, I considered that this could quite possibly be a positive development. As much as I liked Willy, this session was going nowhere, and someone—namely me—had to step up and get things moving.

So I called Willy again. After he determined I was going to live (he was very concerned), I asked him about Dumb Ass and the ramifications of actually using the shitty drum tracks on the album. Willy explained that the band was sure that if they used another drummer on this album that Dumb Ass would leave, and they would be dropped. Under normal circumstances, I (and I think Willy) would call that paranoid thinking. But the more money a label spends on a band's first album, the more likely the band will either be shelved or dropped. Being that the band was given such a fat deal but was then forced to write for two years is a bad sign. The band obviously wanted to make sure that they finished an album. Having the drummer quit would be counter to that goal.

I'm not sure whether I agree completely with this thinking or not. First of all, I doubt Dumb Ass would quit. He may be a retard, but he's not crazy. Secondly, drummers are replaced in bands on a daily basis. It's not like anyone outside of the industry has ever heard of this band before, so the buying public certainly wouldn't be the wiser.

Still, I could understand their concern. It's quite possible the label would take any opportunity to cut their losses. The band would certainly have a better feel for that than I would. Regardless of my thoughts on the matter, Willy explained that both Yore and the singer were adamant and unified on this subject. Surprising, considering I've never seen them agree on anything to date.

There was really only one way that Dumb Ass was going to be removed from this project. Yore and the singer had to agree to it. They wrote the lion's share of the songs, and they were the ones with the power to remove Dumb Ass from the equation. The only way that Dumb Ass was going to be evicted was by demonstrating that keeping Dumb Ass was surely worse than losing him. Whether Willy had actually thought the situation out this clearly, I couldn't tell. I decided not to leave it to chance.

"I think we should record three or more songs to completion and let them hear for themselves that Dumb Ass isn't going to cut it," I said to Willy, finally answering the question that allowed me the opportunity to experience new depths of internal pain. "I also think Dumb Ass needs to play more than one song every four days to build up his confidence. Perhaps we should consider not using a clik track to see if he plays better that way."

I had more suggestions, but I decided to stop there and see how my comments were received.

"I think you're right," Willy replied.

Yes! Finally, we were going to move forward. If we could get a few songs in the bag, it would go a long way toward morale, confidence, and vibe. Best of all, it gives something for Jeramiah Weasel to bring to the president of the label.

When I arrived at the studio, Lance was in the room, setting up what looked to be a mic for a vocal overdub.[35] All the telltale signs were there. A music stand positioned as a table, a stool, and, of course, a pop screen.[36] Had Lance completely lost his mind? Did he decide to take over this session? Then the bass player walked into the room.

"Oh, good, you're here," he stated matter-of-factly. "I'm going to record a vocal on this song we're working on."

I was flabbergasted.

"But what about the singer?" I asked confused.

"I wrote this song, and I think it'd be better if I sang it," the bass player responded indignantly.

Even with the tone of voice with which he had spoken to me, I was actually considering telling him about the new plan of attack, but I think he must have been playing Mind Tricks on me, because I said nothing. I was at that moment convinced that the best thing for me to do was record a vocal. It would be up to Willy to put a stop to the nonsense.

We spent the next two hours recording vocals. The whole time I couldn't stop thinking about the shit that would be hitting the proverbial fan when our favorite megalomaniac singer walks in and sees me recording the bass player singing. But the singer didn't show up during the vocal session, and I found out later that the bass player *knew* that the singer would be a few hours late. Not knowing this myself, I tried desperately to reach Willy by phone, but to no avail.

Recording vocals with the bass player was more arduous and more torturous than recording guitars with the singer. I couldn't help but think to myself, Perhaps everyone should just shift over one musical station, pick up whatever instrument happened to be there, and then start recording the album. It would give a whole new meaning to the game musical chairs. The way I figured it, there would be a one in two chance that whoever sat on the drum throne would be a markedly better drummer than Dumb Ass. For a moment, I started to wonder if I were showing signs of my age in thinking that players in a band should actually play the instrument on which they are most proficient for the purposes of recording an album.

So much for the great plan that I had laid out earlier with Willy.

I finally finished recording several takes of vocals after having to punch just about every line on every take. The bass player, whom I have named Harmon Neenot (pronounced NEE · no) for the purposes of this diary, had no pitch, no time, no vibe, and no talent as a singer. Other than that, he was great. I started comping Harmon Neenot's vocal, which is the process of compiling one take out of several by switching between them for sections, lines and, in some cases, words. Willy *finally* walked into the studio.

He was surprised that we were recording vocals. Yes, me too!

"That's awful," said Willy, scrunching up his nose. He was referring to the noises coming from the speakers that sounded more like seals squealing in agony than to someone actually singing. Willy quickly looked around the room, realizing that Harmon might be around. Fortunately, he wasn't.

I filled Willy in on what had happened, and he told me I might as well finish the vocal comp. I guess the plan was for Harmon to hear for himself just how shitty his vocals were—a plan I feared could backfire.

When I finished the vocal, I went outside for a breath of fresh air, and the band was playing basketball. Even with my finger as bad as it was, I figured some exercise wouldn't be a bad thing. It turns out that this was a poor decision on my part, for I went up to get a rebound, and as I came down, my foot landed on the edge of Dumb Ass's foot.

MOTHERFUCKER!

My ankle bent in half. I've never been in more pain for so many different reasons in one day in my life. I was half tempted to take out insurance on myself just for the remainder of the day but feared it might be too expensive for the risk. Dumb Ass must have thought we were playing competitively or something, because he went under me while I was in the air. What a schmuck! I had sprained my ankle and very badly to boot.

The good news was that the pain in my ankle made me completely forget about my sinuses and my finger. The bad news is that my ankle was swelling up so fast it looked like someone was actually blowing it up like a balloon. Lance ran to get me some ice in a towel, which I promptly wrapped around my ankle. I shouldn't have even gotten up today, I thought to myself. Now I was sounding like Paulie Yore.

Dumb Ass and Yore both helped me hop to the lounge, where I put my foot on the table with the ice on it. Everyone decided to hang out in the lounge with me, when the singer came in looking irate aplenty. Lance, being unseasoned in the art of discretion, had foolishly spilled the beans to the singer about our yodeling sessions starring none other than Harmon Neenot, singer extraordinaire.

The singer went ballistic. Normally around now, I'd exit stage left. Unfortunately, I wasn't upwardly mobile. This was not a fight that I wanted to be present for. There wasn't a doubt in my mind that this was going to get ugly, and it did.

Yore joined the fray early on, pointing out that the singer spent two hours recording guitar parts last night. As far as Yore was concerned, he couldn't really understand the difference between singers playing guitar and bass players singing—and he had a point. Dumb Ass was still complaining that he sounded like a robot, and the entire band yelled simultaneously at him to shut the fuck up. I was half tempted to say, "Jinx," but thought better of it.

On the Richter scale, I'd say this argument registered in the neighborhood of a 7.0. Willy's way of dealing with the discord was nothing short of fascinating to me. He proceeded to spark up a fatty and pass it around the room, as the argument took odd twists and turns, which had no relevance to anything but years of baggage and the need to perhaps blow off some steam. I was starting to get the idea that Willy was like the Phil Jackson of the recording world, in that he likes to let things work out on their own. And who can argue with success?

What I found most amazing about this scene, as I sat there with my ankle throbbing, my finger throbbing, and the inside of my face throbbing, was that, as the band members continued to yell at each other with marked disdain, they were simultaneously passing the fatty to each other and partaking. Not one person turned down the fatty. When the fatty had made its way to my position, I paused momentarily. I had made the decision this morning that it would be best if I abstained from such activities as smoking fatties. But the way I figured it, the session for today was blown, my codeine (which I was in need of about now) was some distance away from my present position, there was no Lance in sight, and there was no way I was going to muster the strength to get up and hop all the way to my medicine. Not that fatties are very effective in dealing with pain, but hell, it couldn't hurt. So I, too, accepted the fatty.

When things settled down and talking wasn't doing much good anymore, Willy called the session. With Willy's declaration, everyone left, although I'm really not sure anything was resolved. Perhaps Willy felt a good night's sleep would be the healer of these wounds. I had my doubts. After everyone was gone, Willy, who obviously recognized my need for something positive in my life at this moment, invited me for sushi. My favorite!

A week ago I wondered if I was going to survive the session. But at that time, my concern was with being unjustly fired, not killed!

After a great sushi dinner we went back to the studio, hung out, smoked a fatty, and listened to music.

Now, if only we could *make* some music.

– Mixerman

DAY 10

The Albatross

POSTED: AUGUST 10, 12:27 A.M.

Willy called me at the crack of dawn. We would not be working on the album today, since he was going to have a long meeting with the band to try and deal with the rift that had formed. Willy then provided me with some history. Apparently, this was not the first rift during Willy's short tenure with the band. During the rehearsals, the band had another similar blowup. The band members hate each other. No surprise there. What I didn't know is that the money is almost gone.

For the most part, the band is under a tremendous amount of stress, because they've all been living on their advance money, and each of them was quickly running out of that money. At first, I was taken aback by this news. Two million dollars—the reported value of the deal—was a lot of jack to piss away. Of course, I don't really know the details of how that money was disbursed, nor if the budget for the record was included in that figure. Then, of course, there are any number of wacky accounting practices that go on at record companies. Regardless, the more I considered the possible costs of taxes, possible down payments on houses, musical equipment, and two years of no income in a city with one of the highest costs of living in the US, this was *not* that surprising. When I think about how much of my own money goes out the door from living in L.A., the scenario was not that hard to imagine. On top of all that, I'm sure the band never dreamed that it would be writing for two years before it would be making a record. I'm sure the band figured they'd be touring by now and making money playing.

The label was taking a "tough shit" attitude with them, which was exacerbating the situation. Allegedly, the label has been pretty shitty with them all along. Last week, Yore was telling me that their previous A&R reps (since fired) were total assholes to them. The way it was described to me, it was as if the label was psychologically torturing them. This somewhat explained the constant depression that Paulie Yore was in, although it didn't make hanging with him any more pleasurable.

It's not like the band didn't have good songs when it was signed. Quite the contrary—I've heard the songs that they had when they were signed, and in my opinion, they're great. I can even understand why this band was a bidding-war band. Labels don't give a shit anymore if there's a weak player in the band. Everyone just assumes you either fix it with a computer or get a session player on the project. The only thing that labels are interested in is a song that they can break to radio. That's it, nothing more, nothing less. Everything else can be fixed.

I'm assuming that when the label signed the band, they recognized the excellent songwriting and figured it wouldn't be too long before they got their obvious radio single out of the band.

From Yore's descriptions, the label was having them write music that was similar in characteristic to hot music of that moment. Being that what's hot is constantly changing, so too did the direction of the writing.

Willy felt that in the rehearsals they weren't a bad band. He knew the drummer was weak but probably didn't realize that this would translate so badly in the recording. I guess I could understand this. I've been fooled by drummers in really awful-sounding rehearsal spaces, so I'll give Willy the benefit of the doubt. Willy also confided that, due to Dumb Ass's limited intelligence, he wasn't capable of remembering the form changes they would make in preproduction. Willy would make a change, and Dumb Ass would immediately forget to do it. I can just imagine the conversations, with Dumb Ass thinking Willy meant the chorus when Willy said verse. Working with Dumb Ass was nothing short of maddening. The reality is that I'm *not* exaggerating when I say that Cotton is probably only moderately more intelligent than a retard. It's that bad.

Since we weren't working today—God forbid I get a three-day weekend after this debacle—Willy asked me if I could mix a song for him from another project that he's been working on. So that's what I did today. I mixed a completely different act with my leg up in the air and my ankle still two sizes too big. I had Lance running around doing everything for me, as I sat there just mixing. It was actually nice to bring a piece of music to completion and so quickly. The recording reportedly took only two days, and the mix took me only five hours.

I'd be lying if I said I wasn't getting down from this project. Setting aside all of my physical ailments (which are numerous, and each has occurred as a direct result of this project), it's torture to spend nine days working twelve-hour days to accomplish nothing save an unusable and incomplete take.

When I go into a session, I go in every day with a cheerful attitude. I put on my game face and try to keep everyone happy and amused. I want everyone to feel good and be excited about what they're doing. That's what making a record should be about. Sure, roadblocks are bound to happen, but those roadblocks serve to make life more interesting and invigorating. If only we had traveled far enough on this project to actually hit a roadblock, I'd probably be in good spirits. But really, when you consider everything, we haven't even *started* our journey. It takes me longer every day to put that game face on, which is even more depressing to me, since I view *that* as one of the most important parts of my gig.

My only salvation on this project has been this journal, as it allows me to demonstrate in real time just how destructive to music the business has become. Unfortunately, this journal has also been my albatross, as I am obsessed with writing and posting, without fail, my thoughts as they are freshest in my mind. Worse yet, I attempt to do so at a level of quality beyond my current capabilities as a writer, even at the risk of exhaustion and even at the risk of appearing ungrateful for the job—something I have been accused of and criticized for by some outspoken readers of this online journal.

The way I see it, anybody who thinks I should blindly skip through life satisfied with being unproductive so long as I'm being compensated for such activities isn't considering the negative effect that lack of accomplishment can have on the brain. The act of accomplishing nothing other than wastefulness is both exhausting and debilitating to the soul. While in the short term it may be self-serving to my financial well-being to participate in such unproductiveness, the resulting waste only serves to sicken me.

Still, I'm optimistic. Willy wants to start fresh on Monday. Perhaps the weekend off will recharge everyone's enthusiasm, and we can become what we, as humans, were put on this earth to be.

Productive.

– Mixerman

DAY 11

Win One for the Gipper

POSTED: AUGUST 13, 12:09 A.M. — WEEK 3

After three good nights of sleep and quality time with the family, I woke up this morning in far better spirits and with a renewed sense of purpose. Still, I couldn't help but be partially concerned with the potential of my day going downhill from here. For the second time since this project began, I had a conversation of some substance with Willy. The first was over sushi on Thursday night. The second, and the one to which I am referring here, was over the weekend. According to Willy, his marathon band-therapy-bitch-session had gone well. Being a producer can often require a hard-knocks degree in psychology, and Willy, no doubt, needed to make use of that degree this past Friday.

Even Willy, who has revealed himself as a man who prefers to avoid mediation unless there is clear and present danger — sometimes referred to as "waiting until just before everything goes down the shitter" — has to occasionally resort to the role of therapist in order to keep a session moving forward.

I could just picture Willy in his slippers, rolling fatties in a plush crushed-velvet chair, as the band members vented for hours their disdain for each other until they reached the point of utter exhaustion. In no small part, the inevitable *argumentus coitus interruptus* would occur from the band members' disintegrating fighting spirit, as fatties could turn even Ivan the Terrible into Gandhi given enough of the substance. Then I could imagine Willy viewing the band's temporary inability to discuss its insurmountable problems as some sort of therapeutic victory. Yet, although I criticize, I can't help but think that were Willy to actually intervene, the results would likely be nothing short of disastrous where the completion of this project is concerned. At least with his usual course of action, problems are neither solved nor aggravated in the process.

Suffice it to say, Willy was confident that we would be moving forward on Monday. I had my reservations.

Three days off on a project is an eternity. Even though I worked on Friday, it was still a break from this project. When players are in a groove, three days can destroy every ounce of momentum that had been achieved. Of course, that certainly wasn't a danger here, as we were having the opposite problem—stagnation. When stagnation sets in, three days can be as revitalizing as an unreciprocated blow job.

I was truly impressed with Willy's decision to take the time off. Many producers would have chosen to work through the weekend, citing a need to catch up. Catching up would have likely been the *worst* decision he could have made. From my experience, if we had tried to power through the weekend, this session would be over. Cooked. Done. Finito. It amazes me how many producers, both big and small in stature, don't recognize the value of rest and separation. Even a matter of one night's sleep can condense what would otherwise be a three-hour late-night task down to only minutes come morning. That's because after a long day's work of recording an album, two conflicting phenomena can occur—oversaturation and hypersensitivity.

Oversaturation causes one's brain to be incapable of discerning and evaluating subtle and even not-so-subtle differences among such things as timing, tuning, expression, musicality, and balances (level differences among different instruments). It's quite like a numbing agent of the brain. If you could inject the part of your brain that processes hearing with novocaine, this would be similar to the effect of oversaturation. I would imagine that people of all walks of life have experienced this to some degree. I sometimes refer to it as "the wall," and when you hit the wall, there are only two cures. Time and fatties.

Hypersensitivity is the function of one's brain being so aware and sensitive to minute changes that you are beyond any kind of "real-world" standards of listening. It is the exact opposite of oversaturation. This temporary condition can make differences that are normally nearly impossible for the human ear to detect seem like enormously drastic changes. Although this condition is generally less debilitating than oversaturation, it can cause the wasting of inordinate amounts of time, as this phenomenon will cause one to endlessly make adjustments that seem to make a big difference but, in reality, make no difference whatsoever. Once again, there are only two cures. Time and fatties.

After twelve hours of intense listening, either one of these phenomena can occur. The best method of preventing these two temporary conditions is to take breaks. But breaks become less effective and are required more frequently as either of these disorders sets in, and at some point, only a good night's rest will rejuvenate one to the point of functionality. Unfortunately, rest and breaks do not appear time-efficient, and they are often abandoned for the far worse option of powering through.

Sometimes even a good night's rest can't prevent one from starting the day with either one of these ailments, as the cumulative effects of working long days on end take hold. And sometimes, *both* the hypersensitivity *and* oversaturation conditions can be present and occurring simultaneously. When this particular brain-fuck happens, *watch out,* because the phrase "dog chasing his own tail" is given a whole new level of meaning. Of course, on this project, while I have experienced all sorts of minor temporary semi-delusional states that occur over the course of a session (even without the fatties), oversaturation and hypersensitivity have not, to date, made the list.

What we needed today was focus and determination—a desire by everyone other than myself to make music and have the music captured as music as opposed to fodder for manufacturing something that resembles music. Cotton needed the gift of confidence. Really, the whole band needed that gift. Were I Knute Rockne, I'd likely have given the old "win one for the Gipper" speech. But I'm neither Knute Rockne nor the producer of this session. So I didn't.

Fortunately for everyone involved, Willy wasn't going to allow *any* of these disorders to enter our session this week. In fact, Willy seemed motivated to give this session the jump start it so desperately needed. I knew all this from our conversation this weekend, as he divulged to me his plan of attack.

"I think we need to record some takes of several songs and help build up some confidence in these guys," he said. "And we should experiment with not using a clik," he continued.

Thank God I wasn't drinking a cup of coffee when he said this, as it seems to me that's *exactly* what I said to him last week! Of course, I didn't mention any of that to Willy. I responded to him appropriately with agreement and praise, expressing my encouragement of such great concepts in recording.

When I arrived today, to my pleasant surprise, everyone was already at the studio. Willy, Lance, and the band were all waiting for *me*. This was a good sign. After greeting everyone on the patio, I quickly determined that the band was in fairly good spirits. I mean, Paulie Yore was still Paulie Yore, and you could tell that the "girls" still didn't like each other, but they *did* seem to be putting on an act. Although it seemed a bit contrived at times—"Oh, I'm sorry, after you, no, no, no, no, no, after you" (*puke!*)—it was better than the alternative of screaming and calling each other egotistical assholes while smoking and passing a fatty around. In my experience, that really brings down the vibe of a session.

Willy added another little twist to our session this morning, but fortunately we recovered quickly. He wanted to open up all the iso booths and record the band live—bleed and all. Bleed is the sound of instruments being picked up by the other instrument mics. I pointed out to Willy that by doing that, we would be hindered from doing super-microscopic editing—not that I was upset at that concept! By recording with bleed, you are allowing harmonic information onto the drum tracks; that is to say, chord changes or tonality. In other words, I could no longer edit based on drum patterns alone.

In the case of editing takes with bleed, I would have to take
into account musically where I was in the song when making an
edit. If I needed to replace a measure of a drum pattern in which
the bass player was playing a G, I'd have to take a measure in
which the bass player was playing that same G and with the same
rhythmic pattern—typically the identical measure from another
take. If I didn't, then the bleed of the bass and guitar in the drums
would rub with any retracked bass or guitar parts, and that can
be quite distasteful. Typically, this style of recording is reserved
for bands that can play a keeper take *together*, without having to
redo any of the parts—an unlikely occurrence in the case of this
band.

Recording without a clik can further reduce my editing options, as I have to use a measure that is close in tempo to the
measure being replaced—a hit-or-miss proposition at best with
someone like Dumb Ass on the throne.[37] But Willy didn't care.
He had decided that we weren't going to be doing such aggressive
editing. Not on two-inch tape we won't be! That would be nearly
impossible, and if not impossible, certainly time-prohibitive.

So we opened up all the doors, marked the mic placements
and distances from each amp, moved the amps into the main
room with the drums, and replaced the mics. We moved the
amps because if the bass amp and the guitar amps were too far
from the drummer, Cotton would sound as if he were lagging.
That's because sound travels so slowly.

The rule of thumb is that sound will travel one foot per mil-
lisecond (it's actually generally slightly faster than that, but the
speed of sound changes according to temperature and this ap-
proximation is close enough for the distances that we deal with).

Just five milliseconds can be the difference between the drummer sounding on top of the beat or in the pocket. Since the band wasn't going to be playing with headphones, the players' amps had to be a reasonable distance from the drummer.

Willy had the band start with a different song today. Wisely, he had chosen a song that would be close to the same basic planned drum setup as we had for the last. We spent about an hour making some changes to the drums and guitars to better match the song. Before I knew it, we started making takes. I could hardly contain myself as I sat in front of the speakers listening to the band actually performing (and I use that word loosely) for the first time during this session. I've certainly gone two weeks in a session with nothing to show for it, but at least in those instances I felt as though *some* forward progress was being made. It wasn't until some time later that we realized that those two weeks were lost. In this case, we were all too painfully aware of our lack of productivity.

Cotton played considerably better without the clik, and although I wouldn't give him an award for "overachievement in solid drumming," it seemed that we might come up with something usable out of the performances. Or perhaps I'm just being optimistic. Until we tried to put something together, we just wouldn't know.

After six takes of the first song, I convinced Willy (and it really didn't take much convincing) to move onto a second song, as opposed to trying to edit together a take. Normally, it's best to do your editing before moving on, because, if the band didn't nail a particular section of the song on any of the takes, then you can easily rectify the problem by focusing on that section. If you move on and you have to go back, then you spend an inordinate amount of time trying to reestablish a sound. As it is, it takes constant vigilance to keep the snare drum at the same pitch for each take.

Once we change over sounds, even with impeccable documentation, it's unlikely we could come close enough to make an insert of a section, although there are exceptions to this rule, hence my use of the word *unlikely*. Regardless, even if I *couldn't* edit something useable out of those six takes, it was better at this point to create the illusion of progress than to bring the session to a grinding halt again. Lifting the players' spirits and having them in the groove of playing was far more important than actually knowing we had takes at that particular moment. As far as the band was concerned, the track was in the bag and that was all that mattered. Illusion or reality, it has the same effect.

After checking to be sure that Lance had all the necessary notes (which I amended, as they were indeed missing crucial information), we moved on to the next song. The session ran as a good session should. We listened to the demo of the song. Willy went over the form changes from the original demo. We all discussed the planned sonic direction of the song. We changed out the snare several times, changed out some cymbals, switched to a different guitar/amp combo several times, and swapped out the bass several times, ending up right back where we started. As the band rehearsed with Willy, I would make adjustments. Then they would all come in and listen together to the sound of the recording.

Sometimes the processes of finding the right sound for a record can be a bit laborious. Sometimes it can be painless. Today the changeovers were middle-of-the-road. Willy had clear concepts in mind, and implementing those concepts was a matter of find-ing combinations of instruments that translated well. Where the process becomes laborious is when one's concept is not very clear or one's original concept didn't work as intended.

Finding the right source—that is, the instrument itself—is the lion's share of work when seeking an appropriate sound for a re-cord. It all comes down to the source. But the engineering side does come into play. Personally, I believe in making the record sound exactly as we (the producer and I) intend from the very start. I will distort drums to tape, compress them to tape, combine microphones to a single track, equalize, or do nothing at all. I will commit to tape whatever is required to make the drums sound like they should for the song. When it comes time to mix, I don't want the sounds to change at all. The mix should be done at the completion of the last overdub.

Sadly, even with this approach, on the occasions when my tracks are mixed by so-called famous mixers,[38] they try to change the sound of the record. It is truly heartbreaking to put as much effort as I do into recording a song, *exactly* the way it is intended to sound, only to have it homogenized by a mixer more interested in quantity than quality. But that's what the record companies want.

It's really an odd process, if you think about it. The record com-pany hires Willy Show, for example, to record the songs the way he is capable. Willy spends time and money getting everything to have a certain sound that is unique and consistent with the playing of the song and the performances. The record company then takes it from the producer's hands (*very* common), and has one of five mixers make it sound exactly like everything else on the radio. Then, as if that weren't enough, they have a mastering engineer[39] come in and stomp the last remaining bit of life out of the production and make it sound as two-dimensional and loud as possible. But I suppose that's a discussion for another time.

As we proceeded to make takes, it was important that the song at least *start* at the same tempo. This way there was a chance that we could edit sections between takes. So before every song, I would give the band the clik through the talkback speakers up until the third beat of the count-off. I always have a drum machine in the control room with me, and I would check Cotton's tempo with my own set of headphones as he played without the clik. Remarkably, he could actually hold a tempo fairly well. In fact, it's not uncommon for Cotton to finish a song at the tempo he started it. Granted he fluctuates during the course of the song, but overall I'm quite impressed with his ability to maintain a tempo.

When all is said and done, by the end of today, we managed to record two songs of six takes each onto four reels of two-inch tape. I have no clue as to whether we actually recorded something useable or not, and it doesn't even matter to me. At least we are getting takes down. Momentum is the name of the game right now.

The most promising development of the day is that Cotton may be gaining some confidence. The last take they played tonight was the best he's played this entire session. I'm not saying he's miraculously great—far from it—but I *have* been able to put away the barf bag.

For the moment, anyway.

– Mixerman

DAY 12

Girlfriend Day

POSTED: AUGUST 14, 12:29 A.M.

As I was driving to the studio, reflecting on yesterday's productivity, I had a very disturbing realization. Although we were making takes and progressing with the session, the band members seemed unfazed by such events. There was no excitement, no giddiness, no enthusiasm. It was like making takes with a bunch of robots. If the band is a bunch of robots, then Paulie Yore is certainly the King of all Robots with his monotone, "Yeah, I guess that's all right." Or if he got really excited he'd say "That's good enough, I guess." I wasn't holding much hope out for Yore, but I was hopeful that when we make a little more progress, the level of enthusiasm would elevate considerably. Perhaps even I was guilty of guarded enthusiasm yesterday. That would certainly be understandable after the two-week debacle we have endured thus far.

When I spoke to Willy this morning, he had made an interesting decision. He was going to hire some hotshot Radar editor from Nashville to come in and edit takes while we kept recording.

I didn't even know there *was* such a thing as a "hotshot Radar editor." Editing on the Radar is a piece of cake—do we really need a "hotshot?" I could just imagine Dude punching keys at lightning speed, as one uses designated macro keys on a Radar as opposed to using a mouse. Perhaps our hotshot Radar editor came of age when Commodore 64s were all the rage, giving him a distinct advantage over younger Radar editors who are likely hindered by the lack of a mouse.

Since when was Willy—the consummate Luddite's Luddite—willing to transfer the drums to digital format and edit them there? Granted, the Radar is probably the only digital multitrack machine in the history of such machines that I actually think sounds good (barring some serious hot-rodding). But that was quite a leap for Willy to make in such a short amount of time. Perhaps I had his ear and he trusted me now.

"I'm surprised at that," I said to Willy when he told me about the Radar editing.

"Yeah, well, we need to get a move on with this session, and you've already demonstrated that the Radar sounds great, so fuck it," he said as I could hear him sucking in heavily from what I assumed was the first fatty of the day.

Indeed, I thought to myself.

I certainly didn't complain about this new development. Shit, I couldn't have been more delighted to be relinquishing editing duties to someone else. If Willy had been a producer that enjoyed Alsihad, the session would have been paying for an Alsihah to be editing the tracks anyway. Besides, having one person editing while we continued recording would be a far more efficient way of working.

Then Willy further enlightened me on the subject of his great turnabout. He told me about a friend of his who is a somewhat famous producer in Nashville, who suggested that we quit fucking around editing two-inch tape and transfer the takes to Radar for editing, and Willy's friend recommended *his* guy for the editing gig. Being that Willy actually described Dude as "lightning fast," I've named him Fast Fingers McGuilicutty, sight unseen. Fast Fingers would be arriving tomorrow to start editing takes.

Further, I learned in our conversation that Willy had taken home a couple of the takes of each song from the running DAT (Digital Audio Tape). I keep a DAT recorder rolling at all times during the course of a session. When the band is making takes, Lance's job is to mark an ID at the beginning of each take and log the ID number and its corresponding take number. That way, if Willy or I want to take home a CD of some takes, all Lance has to do is look at his notes and transfer those takes to a CD. Running a DAT recorder at all times has the added advantage of allowing me to play back an idea or part that someone may have played accidentally but forgotten, and it can potentially provide interesting and fun interlude material for an album.

Willy had confided in me, in our phone conversation this morning, that the takes really weren't up to par and that the band was severely lacking energy. This was not a surprise to me. After all, the band *did* have an obvious lack of enthusiasm yesterday. It's not that either of us is incapable of listening to a take go down and recognizing that it's not totally happening, but we're dealing in relative terms here. Our ability to listen to a take has been tainted with the comparisons of what we had previously recorded. In comparison to our first recording with the band, yesterday's takes were a marked improvement. Improvement was a step in the right direction. In cases like these, where the playing is so hideously atrocious, knowing for certain whether takes are going to pass muster often requires a day away from the tracks and sometimes requires actually editing them.

Although the takes weren't happening, Willy felt that moving forward, as we have done, has been the right course of action. We could always go back and try to beat what we have recorded thus far. So long as there was improvement, Willy would allow the band to record takes and move on to the next song.

Even with the news of the takes not being up to par, I was encouraged and upbeat on my way into the session. Perhaps the energy level would improve today. As I was driving to the studio, I had made a decision that I was going to be as upbeat and as positive as I possibly could. Sure, I'm always positive at the studio. But today was different. Today, I was going to be the specimen of good vibes, positive thinking, and overly expressive enthusiasm. Perhaps my enthusiasm would be infectious, and the band would start to play with excitement.

Of course, no sooner had I arrived at the studio, convinced that I was somehow going to make a difference on the day's work, when I was instantly and completely deflated. There, at the table on the patio, sat two girls with Yore and Harmon. Girls in their own right certainly were not a bad thing, but these particular girls had two strikes against them. They were at a recording session in which there were no girls, and they looked suspiciously like girlfriends. A terrible, horrible feeling overcame me. These guys didn't *actually* bring their girlfriends to the session. Did they?

"Hi, how's it going?" I said coolly as I hobbled to the table at which the crew was sitting. I stood there with what I'm sure was an awkward little smile waiting anxiously for an introduction, which I didn't actually have the patience to wait for.

"My name is Mixerman," I said like a heathen, holding out my hand as if making an effort to show that I came in peace.

Heathen or not, sometimes my insight and ability to recognize a situation scares me. They *were* girlfriends!

What I wanted to do was cry, "No! No! No! No! No! No! No!"—over and over again as I slammed my forehead against the brick wall outside the studio. But I figured that would have been too revealing of my thoughts on this subject, so I smiled and welcomed our newfound intruders instead.

How could these guys be this stupid? One should *never* bring one's girlfriend to a session. It's like the first rule of recording. I think they teach this in kindergarten. Even my children know you don't bring your girlfriend to the studio. Guys don't act like themselves when their girlfriends are there. They get distracted, the girls get upset because the guys aren't paying attention to them, and then the guys get all pissed off because the girls don't understand that they're making a record. Then what typically happens is the girls split, the guys get pissed, and it's a fucking fiasco every time. My only hope was that the girlfriends were planning to leave and go shopping together. I clung onto that hope like it was Barry Bonds' seventy-third 2001 home run ball, as I proceeded to the control room and prepared for the day's session.

Willy walked into the control room, and I gave him what must have been a maniacally horrified look as he entered, because he actually asked if I was sick.

"They brought girlfriends!!" I blurted out in horror, with no thought to how that must have sounded or looked for that matter.

Willy chuckled. "I'm sure they'll be leaving soon," he replied.

But they didn't leave soon. They stayed the whole day, and for what had been the briefest of moments yesterday a decent, well-adjusted session would now be destroyed by the presence of alien intruders.

Don't get me wrong. I love women. *God* do I love women. I enjoy working with women in studio situations. What I don't like is girlfriends or boyfriends in the studio. In fact, boyfriends are worse! There's just no room for that shit. Band members and artists have to be unencumbered and free to be themselves wholly. Girlfriends and boyfriends only serve to aggravate, for they don't recognize the boundaries of concentration and focus that go into the creative process of recording.

It seems our visitors were intent on proving that my disdain for such things was warranted right from the start. The girls yucked it up on the couch in the back of the room while I was trying to get sounds. Anyone who has done any level of engineering at all knows it's *very* difficult to work while people are in the room talking. The only way to combat the noise is to turn up the volume of your monitors. However, the louder I turned up the volume, the louder the intruders would talk, until such a point that I was absolutely blasting the music, as the unwanted studio guests were yelling at the top of their lungs and looking at me as if I was doing something wrong!

"I'm sorry, but there really can't be any talking while I'm doing critical listening," I would say after muting the speakers. "You're more than welcome to go into the lounge if you like."

"Oh, sorry! We'll be quiet," they would respond, giggling, as if making my life miserable was somehow humorous.

Less than thirty seconds of silence would go by, and the whispers would start again. The whispers would soon turn into talking, and then yelling as the cycle would play itself out again, and I would calmly ask them to shut the fuck up in as pleasant a way as I could muster—perhaps too pleasant a way. Round and round we'd go in an endless cycle.

At one point, one of the girls realized that I could magically communicate with the boys by pushing a button and just talking, and the other decided it would be cute for *her* to talk to Yore.

In an elongated and exaggerated fashion, with a light Southern accent much like the blonde white-trash-factory-worker character that pretended to get pregnant in the movie *An Officer and a Gentleman*, she screamed, "Play louder, sexy!" She made sure that she yelled directly into the push button, as if by some miracle a solid piece of plastic with her thumb over it could somehow act as a microphone.

MOTHERFUCKER!

"Please!" I said, exasperated. "You really can't be playing with the talkback button. We're trying to make a record here," I continued, as I held out my hand in a gesture to demand return of the talkback remote control. Still, they wouldn't leave.

I had thought for hours about what I could say to get them out of the room. Many scenarios had played in my head in short little daydream sequences, as my brain attempted to come up with a reasonable solution to my problem.

"Get me a mic and set it up for the girls over there," I would say to Lance in one of my daydreams, as I pointed to the back of the control room.

"Why are you setting up a mic?" one of the girls would ask.

"So that I can record your singing," I would reply.

"But we're not singing," they would respond hook, line, and sinker.

"Oh! Right! Well then, how about you SHUT THE FUCK UP!" I would yell, to their horror and dismay. That would get them out of the room, anyway!

Had this little vignette actually happened, it surely would have gotten me in hot water with Harmon, who wouldn't understand at all why I was yelling at his girlfriend. I would have possibly gotten myself fired, a thought that is not so unappealing right about now. Worse yet, I might have to hang out for weeks with a guy whose girlfriend wants me fired. Even if *he* could somehow forgive me and understand why I snapped, his girlfriend would make sure that he hated me by such torturous techniques as endlessly talking about the incident.

Deciding that I perhaps wasn't the best candidate to ask the girls to leave at that particular moment, I decided it would be good if I let Willy act as the diplomat. I was at my wit's end where they were concerned, and one should try to get a disinterested party involved in such cases. Willy always seemed to fill this role perfectly.

Willy was great, because when I told him my problem, he poked his head in the door and held out a fatty and led the girls to the lounge as if the fatty were a flute, Willy was the Pied Piper, and the girlfriends were rats. So as the crew smoked a fatty, Willy came up with the new rule that no one was allowed in the control room while we were working. Everyone was agreeable, as most people are when they are smoking fatties.

Willy was quite tolerant of the fact that the girlfriends were there. At one point, when the girls were in the lounge and we were making a take, Willy said we would just have to deal with the "bitches" for now (his word, not mine). The way Willy figured it, the girlfriends might actually make the boys play more inspired. This hasn't been my experience in studio life, and it certainly wasn't evidenced by the band's uncanny ability to play a 120-beat-per-minute lullaby. But who am I to argue with success?

With the girlfriends now out of the control room, the remainder of the day went fairly smoothly. Much like yesterday, we recorded two songs today. Willy was working very hard with the band to try and bring up the inspiration in their playing. If I didn't know any better, I'd say the band and Cotton were starting to perform halfway decently by the end of the night. But I do know better. So much for being upbeat and positive!

I guess there's always tomorrow.

– Mixerman

DAY 13
What Up, Dawg?

POSTED: AUGUST 15, 12:09 A.M.

Whereas yesterday was a pain in the ass what with the presence of Paulie Yore's and Harmon Neenot's girlfriends, today was a pain in the ass times two. That's because Dumb Ass and the singer both decided to bring *their* girlfriends to the session too. Girlfriends were multiplying at an alarming rate. Tomorrow, could I expect the girlfriend ratio to double again? Perhaps Willy would bring his girlfriend and our soon-to-arrive comrade Fast Fingers could have his girlfriend flown in from Nashville. Lance surely had to have a girlfriend who had nothing better to do than to spend a day at the studio gabbing as she ate chocolate muffins. I have always had my suspicions about Magnolia—perhaps *she* could round up a girlfriend, and then we could have eight girlfriends tomorrow!

For the record, I really didn't give a shit that the girlfriends were eating chocolate muffins, as the runner was now buying ten of them or more per day so as to be sure that we never ran out. I considered requesting that the runner back off on the muffin count, but I was fearful we'd be back down to one muffin per day, as making requests at this studio was much akin to driving a large vehicle very fast and making sudden direction changes while on ice.

Four girlfriends is four girlfriends too many. I had to make a sign. I find signs to be an effective way to not only set rules but set them in an obnoxious way without actually offending anybody — mostly because rules usually come off humorous when posted as a sign. So I ripped a piece of paper from a pad, and I wrote on the paper.

NO GIRLS ALLOWED!!!!

No! No! No! No! I thought as I tore up that sign. That wasn't going to work. A sign like that would only serve to guarantee that the girls would enter the control room. I needed a girlfriend deterrent, not a girlfriend magnet. So I tried again.

NO TALKING IN THE CONTROL ROOM!!!!
TO BE STRICTLY ENFORCED!!!!

I liked that one. I was hopeful this would work, since, as it was, I was sure that I could hear the flock gabbing from down the hall through an airlock that is designed to prevent sound from entering or escaping the control room. I realize that my sign was neither super inventive nor very obnoxious for that matter. But the way I figured it, these girls weren't going to be coming into the control room if they weren't allowed to talk. Therefore, by placing the sign, I would be better able to enforce the rule, since the rule had been clearly and conspicuously posted.

Yeah, right.

As I was hanging my freshly written sign, out of the corner of my eye, I noticed a stranger coming down the hall. He was a short, lanky, meek-looking pasty-faced guy with a tiny goatee and spiked hair dyed pure blond. He was wearing a parka and carrying a bag that I assumed was made out of hemp. The stranger looked prepared for an Arctic dogsled competition, save the fact that he was also wearing knee-length shorts. It's ninety-five degrees outside, and this clown was wearing a fucking parka!

"What up, Dawg?" the stranger said to me. "Where da Bitch Slap session at, Yo?" he asked.

"Right here," I replied, preoccupied with the ideal placement of my sign and completely disinterested in pointing what I assumed was more posse to the lounge.

"I'm here to cut takes, Yo," the stranger announced. With that, it became apparent whom I was talking to.

It was none other than Fast Fingers McGuilicutty, in all his glory, standing before me, looking like a twenty-year-old idiot with a parka rated for forty below in the middle of summer in L.A. Out of nowhere it struck me that my Commodore 64 theory from yesterday was now shot to hell. Dude was too young to have ever used a Commodore 64. Perhaps he wasn't as fast as all the hype made him out to be.

"Ah-ight," I said, as I noticed that he was about the height of the girls, and lined my sign up to his eye level.

"Been having problems wit da bitches?" he asked.

What's with these guys and the "bitches" shit? I mean, yeah, I don't want girlfriends on the session, but it's not for some misplaced deep-down hatred of women.

"Word," I replied in a language that I thought he might understand.

My years of hip-hop sessions came in handy, as I could converse fluently with Fast Fingers, or perhaps I should say Fingaz. I knew the lingo and when to use it, and as far as he was concerned, I was one of the brothers. Strangely, neither of us was one of the brothers, but I figure that's just a technicality.

So I gave Fingaz the nickel tour. I showed him the room, and then the control room, and finally I showed him where the Radar was. As I stood there staring at the Radar, I realized that neither Willy nor I had considered where Fingaz was going to work. Editing in the control room was out. The iso booths wouldn't provide enough true isolation, and we'd likely want to reserve them for recording anyway. Willy's makeshift office was too far away from the control room, since we wouldn't want to have to keep moving the Radar. Really, the only place I could think to put Fingaz was in the bathroom, which was a reasonable distance from the control room. Fingaz didn't seem too thrilled with that prospect.

"What happens when someone has to go to the bathroom, Yo?" he asked incredulously.

"I guess you'll have to take a break," I said. I could hardly contain my laughter, and it got worse, because then I imagined someone taking a really smelly dump during Fingaz's forced mandatory break time, causing considerable contamination to the editing area. By the looks on Fingaz's face, he was imagining something quite similar.

This wasn't the first time that an editor has ended up in the shitter on one of my sessions, and I didn't find it any less humorous the last time it happened either. Being experienced in these sorts of things, I brought out some extra tapestries (which were also necessary for acoustical reasons, as large concrete bathrooms make for terrible acoustics), a plethora of scented candles, and some incense, in an attempt to try and transform the bathroom into what appeared to be a very vibey editing space. Okay, so it never quite made "vibey," as we couldn't really cover the commode, but it was certainly much improved, and the toilet would make a very convenient seat for anyone who wanted to come take a listen to what Fingaz was working on.

Willy loved what I had done to the bathroom after he figured out that I was, indeed, right that there was nowhere else to put Fingaz. Cotton pointed out that there *was* another bathroom down the hall, which I had forgotten about—mostly because I don't like that particular bathroom. I call it the "Trough," with its three urinals and three stalls. I hate using the Trough. I don't have a phobia or anything like that. I'm fine with the Trough at the mall or the movies or a restaurant. But I spend twelve hours a day at the studio, and I like having a private bathroom, much like the one I have at home.

With our makeshift editing suite complete, we set up the newest member of our crew in the bathroom. Fingaz had the Radar, a rack of three Dangerous Mixers,[40] and some powered speakers. We ran cables to and from the Radar between the bathroom and the machine room, and we transferred the takes for Fast Fingaz to get to work on. He immediately got to work. And work he did.

This guy really *was* lightning fast. He had the fastest fingers I've ever seen as he hit macro buttons left and right like he was a court reporter at a deposition. He'd cut, paste, scrub, mark, move, slide, chop. It almost seemed fake, like a bad movie where the guy is pretending to break into a supercomputer on the Internet by typing on a keyboard really fast. He was absolutely fantastic!

Now, with Fast Fingaz furiously editing away, we needed to start to make takes again. Occasionally girls would try to enter the room one at a time, and I would play Mind Tricks on them, forcing them to quickly close the door and go back to the lounge. But at one point, I was overrun by the four of them. My Mind Tricks were useless against such numbers, and somehow they figured this out.

Willy would let the girls hang for a while, and then he'd pull his Pied Piper routine again, luring them to the lounge down the hall with his fatties. Then Willy would return and we'd continue working.

As the day went on, it got progressively more difficult to find band members with whom to make takes. That's because they would usually be somewhere else with their girlfriends. The moment I'd find a player and inform him that he was needed, another band member would be missing. It was like the girls had cast a spell on the band, causing them to forget that this day was probably costing in the neighborhood of $4,000.

Whenever Lance was trying to find AWOL players, I would go and hang with Fingaz and get to know him a little better. I found it absolutely fascinating that this guy lived in Nashville. He would be the equivalent of an alien in Nashville with his appearance and the way he spoke. Things just didn't add up, and I so desperately needed them to. I figured I'd just up ask him.

"So where in Nashville do you live?" I asked, as if I knew more than one street there.

"Damn, maaan," Fingaz responded incredulously. "I don't live dare, yo. Jus' been cuttin' takes wit da man over dare."

"Word," I replied. "Well, where you from, Yo?" I asked.

"I live in da City, Dawg" he replied, which made a hell of a lot more sense than dude living in Nashville.

"You know dey don't let no Wegro live in Nashville," he continued.

I almost fell off the commode at that comment. Dude called himself a Wegro! I never heard of anything so ridiculous in my life! African-Americans haven't been referred to as Negros in thirty years, and for good reason! But Dude decides to call himself a Wegro? What a schmuck!

But then, at the thought of such absurdity on so many levels, I found myself laughing and unable to stop laughing. I was laughing so hard my gut started to hurt. (I'm *still* laughing.) This guy was a fucking classic! The fact that he couldn't understand what I found so funny about this statement just made my laughing fit worse. Finally, I had to get the hell out of there, because he was starting to get mad at me, and that was not helping me regain my composure at all.

When I went into the control room, Willy wanted to know what I was laughing about, and I told him. The two of us sat there for about ten minutes laughing so hard that our stomachs hurt. At one point, when we had almost gotten control of ourselves, we noticed Fingaz standing in the airlock with this confused scowl on his face as he was watching us laughing. This didn't help matters at all. Then Willy decided to fire up a fatty, and Dude came in to join the party.

"You bluntin'?" Fingaz asked.

"Not bluntin'," I said. "Smokin' fatties." I guess Fingaz found that acceptable, because he joined in.

We got one song recorded today because we could barely get the guys in the room at the same time. Fingaz got the first song edited and was halfway through another. Willy decided he'd listen to the edited takes tomorrow after the second editing job was complete

As much as Fingaz is an idiot with his whole Wegro terminology and the shtick that went with it, at least I could hang with the dude . . .

. . . which was more than I could say for the band.

– Mixerman

DAY 14

Up All Night

POSTED: AUGUST 16, 9:45 A.M.

It's 9:42 A.M. Friday morning. I've been up all night, and I've just gotten home. I'm going to bed, but currently there is the looming threat of having to go back to the studio this evening, although I wonder if that's actually possible. Yesterday's session was a doozy.

But then, aren't they all? Sleepytime for . . .

— Mixeyman

DAYS 14 & 15

Bring In the Posse Brigade

POSTED: AUGUST 17, 10:49 P.M.

Exhaustion has set in.

I did a seventy-two-hour session once (actually twice) with no sleep and no drugs, and I've finished entire records in that time. So yesterday's twenty-two hours could hardly be considered a marathon in the grand scheme of sessions. But it's still a long fucking day. When you compound a twenty-two-hour day with three weeks of twelve-hour days, the stress of a session that was doomed before it began, the relentless documentation of my daily events here, and a desire to actually see my family, the exhaustion can be overwhelming. I won't do anything this weekend except walk around like a zombie and try to be of *some* use to my family.

I arrived at the studio at 11 A.M. on Thursday, the fourteenth day of work on the Bitch Slap album. The day started fairly normally. Dumb Ass was sitting on the patio smoking a cigarette. Harmon and Yore were in the lounge playing video baseball, and the singer was probably in the bathroom fixing his hair, as he was prone to do on a regular basis.

Lance had arrived, like clockwork, a few moments after me, which seemed to be the trend these days, since he'd exhibited some innovation by training the runner to turn on all the mics and the tube gear. Willy arrived the moment I began enjoying my morning muffin and hugged everyone in sight. My new friend Fingaz rolled in on his first-class rental sled, which seems the appropriate terminology for his ride given his propensity for wearing a parka. Magnolia was arranging flowers in the kitchen, even though they make me sneeze, and I place them out on the patio on a daily basis. Everyone was present and accounted for. That is, everyone but the unwanted studio guests.

While I was very happy that there were no girlfriends, I was also a bit suspicious, and I have no idea why. To my knowledge, Willy hadn't banned them; in fact, at one point, he had expressed the thought that they might help matters, which they don't. So where were they? Did they actually work? I didn't dare ask for fear that one of them might take my inquiry as some sort of invitation, and the next thing you know, we would have girlfriends everywhere.

With the obligatory morning niceties behind us, it was time to work. Willy wanted to record one of the more creative songs. He searched through his cases of gear and instruments and pulled out this fantastic circus drum. It had what I can only describe as a "round" sound, as it had a front head on it with no hole. The lack of a hole causes the front head to resonate more, supplying a very distinctive sound much like John Bonham's kik drum heard on old Led Zeppelin records. We had to actually tie Cotton's stool to the drum in order to prevent the drum from migrating forward as he stepped on the beater, as this particular drum wasn't designed to be used on a drum set and had no floor anchors.

With the makeshift kik drum in place, we attempted to detune the toms to be exceptionally deep and resonant, but Dumb Ass totally fucked up the sound of them, since he has no clue how to tune a drum set. Seeing as I had only slightly more of a clue, I called the drum tech. That's not a problem, because fortunately we are right down the road from the rental drum tech and warehouse.

When the drum tech arrived some fifteen minutes later, he decided to put up some very large toms that he had in his truck, and he made them super deep. Of course, Dumb Ass, living up to my name for him, neglected to tell or—at the very least—remind anyone that he doesn't hit the fucking toms in this particular song, save the floor tom once in the bridge. And since that particular tom hit was eventually dropped at Willy's request, there were actually *no* tom hits in this song. Essentially, we went through all of that bother for nothing.

After a couple of hours of drum sounds and several glasses of water, I was in desperate need of a trip to the Trough—a place that I abhor even for such mundane routines as relieving my bladder. Normally, a walk to the Trough would be relatively uneventful, and I assure you, I will not make a habit of describing to you my bathroom visits. Today, however, along my journey to the Trough, I found myself passing an inordinate amount of strangers. It wasn't necessarily unusual for me to pass strangers in the hall, as there was usually another session going on in Studio II. But the people from Studio II didn't typically wander this far down the hall, as the complex was set up to prevent excessive fraternization between sessions.

Regardless, my need to take a leak had reached a high level of alert, so I hightailed it to the Trough. To my surprise, there were a considerable number of people *in* the Trough, as well. Normally with this many people in a communal bathroom, I would assume there was a string session going on in the next room. But these were definitely not string players. These guys appeared more like wannabe rockers from the Valley, laden with tattoos and piercing hardware. If this were a decade ago, they would have likely been viewed as a sordid and dangerous bunch of hoodlums. Now they're society's youth.

After completing my business in the Trough and feeling as though I somehow didn't belong (when in reality I was the *only* one who belonged), I headed back for the control room, which I have taken to dubbing the "Womb," as it is often my only true place of refuge on a session. When walking to the Womb from the Trough, one must pass directly in front of the lounge, and as I did, I caught an unsettling image through my peripheral vision. I stopped dead in my tracks, just beyond the entry to the lounge. I was just a few short steps from the safe haven of the Womb. I wanted to ignore it. I really did. But to ignore what I had seen — or, more accurately what I thought I'd seen — would be only to put off the inevitable. Slowly, I leaned back, half cocking my head to see more straightforwardly into the lounge and to the view of a throng of strangers mingling.

For the record, this was not some communal lounge for anyone who happened to be working at the complex. This was our own private lounge, or at least it was to this point of the session. I scanned the crowd in search of anyone that I actually knew, but to no avail. As I searched, the lounge people began to take notice of me, and I grew uncomfortable, as if I didn't belong there.

It didn't take me much more than a few seconds before I continued on to the Womb. I was fearful that one of the strangers might start asking me whether he or she could help me, as if I were somehow in the wrong place. The band was out in the room with their instruments, adjusting their amps, tuning their instruments, and testing guitars, and I could hear the evidence of this coming from the speakers. Willy seemed ready to move forward with our session as he sat perched in front of the console.

We jumped through the usual hoops of trying to find a guitar sound that best fit the production and the sound of the drums. Sometimes this can be like putting together a puzzle. Every instrument has to sound as if it belongs with the others. Everything starts with the drums. If the drums are more stylized, then it's likely that the bass and guitar need to be as well. But style isn't the only consideration. One must also consider the frequencies that instruments occupy and how that affects the other instruments.

The frequency range of human hearing extends from twenty hertz (cycles per second) to twenty kilohertz (20,000 cycles per second), although it is a rare person who can actually hear frequencies as high as twenty kilohertz, much as it's rare to find a person who is 115 years old. An instrument has a fundamental range within that spectrum. Without going into the physics here, and to put it as simply as possible, a bass covers the low part of the spectrum and a violin covers the high part of the spectrum. A metal tine struck with another tine would have almost no low end, and a bass drum played with a soft mallet would have almost no high end. Achieving separation between a bass and a tine is very easy, as they do not cross frequencies. Achieving clarity between a bass and a kik drum can require some attention, because they cover similar frequency ranges.

In this case, the kik drum was very round sounding and took up a lot of low-end space. So the bass had to have some mid-range attack to it in order to cut through. Half the battle is finding the specific instrument that works best in a particular situation. In this case, we knew that this was the kik drum sound we wanted, so we were looking for a bass that fit best. In other words, we were looking for a bass that had a very pronounced midrange. So we chose an instrument that had this precise characteristic—in this case a Höfner bass. This particular bass was over thirty years old and could have easily been used by Paul McCartney,[41] as that was the bass he typically used through his career, although we have no documentation proving Paul actually played this particular bass. Not that we needed any; this was a right-handed bass, and it has been well established that Paul McCartney plays left-handed.

Different guitars and basses made at different times throughout the course of rock history have distinct and unique sounds. The same can be said about guitar and bass amplifiers. That is why on high-budget sessions, such as this, there will often be as many as thirty guitars, many of which are quite old. Older instruments are usually referred to as "vintage." Much like vintage wine, they are called that because they are the cream of the crop and have aged well. Otherwise, they are just plain "old," which also has its place.

I've been on sessions where there were over a hundred guitars available to us. It's not uncommon to try five or six different guitars (sometimes more) through several amps to find a guitar sound that works best for a song. This is not entirely a hit-or-miss process, as discussions take place, citing particular target guitar sounds. Oftentimes, adjectives such as *warm, biting, bright, thick, crunchy, mellow,* etc., will be used in an attempt to describe a guitar sound. When that fails (and that fails often), then we reference CDs. It's also not uncommon to send the runner to the record store to buy specific CDs in order to demonstrate a guitar sound concept. Suffice it to say, when you are surrounded by guitars and amplifiers of many varieties, you have many options available to you.

After recording a few of the rehearsals and then listening back and making adjustments, we were ready to start making takes, but the band wanted a short break. So Willy and I took the opportunity to visit Fingaz and check out what he was working on.

Fingaz was almost finished with his third song, and he was more than happy to take a break from it and play us his editing job on the first one. Willy sat on the commode, and I sat on the sink, which wasn't very comfortable with a spigot in my back, not to mention the constant concern with catching fire from the surplus of burning candles surrounding me. Willy liked the first song's drum tracks, as the takes were a far cry better than our first attempts at editing Cotton. I think abandoning the clik track and headphones was beneficial to the overall feel of the drums. But the question was, Were they good enough? That question couldn't be definitively answered until we attempted to record the rest of the band over the edited drums.

While Fingaz certainly wasn't doing as severe an editing job as I had attempted on two-inch, there were still a lot of cuts, and the bass and guitar parts were rendered useless as the cuts were designed specifically for the drums. There was bleed from the other instruments on the drums, but the large majority of that bleed was on the room mics. I could always remake the room mics by blasting the edited drums through the PA system and recording the room mics again. Regardless, I didn't think the bleed was going to render the editing job useless. Still, this is the gamble that you take when you record with bleed.

As I said before, usually recording in one room, as we did, is reserved for bands that can play a song together without redoing guitar and bass parts. Still, I was fairly confident that we wouldn't have any problems, since Harmon and Yore were fairly consistent in what they played, and the replayed parts that they would have to lay down would likely work fine with the bleed that was present on the drum recording.

Willy and I listened to the rest of Fingaz's editing jobs. Willy suggested a few changes, and we left Fingaz to his work, as it was time for us to begin making takes with the band. Having briefly forgotten the presence of strangers outside or perhaps hoping deep down that they had left (I'm not sure which), I made my way outside of the Womb and into the cold cruel world of excessively tattooed and pierced Valley intruders. My hope of their mysteriously vanishing was dashed the instant I popped my head out the door, as the presence of strangers had not diminished, but rather increased. There were strangers everywhere!

Who were all these strangers?

As I made my way through the infestation of intruders, I was approached by one of the band's girlfriends whom I had supposedly grown close to. She hugged me, assuming that I actually liked her or that I wanted her around. I didn't. I couldn't even remember which band member she belonged to.

There were strangers in the lounge, the kitchen, the game room; they even spilled out to the patio area where the band was now hanging. As I passed through the kitchen to the patio and sifted myself through strangers trying not to touch any, as if they were cockroaches or something vastly more disgusting, I couldn't help but notice that our usual spread of muffins, bagels, veggie tray, and fruit basket looked more like the remnants of an Overeaters Anonymous party. There was nothing left save the unappetizing remains of ranch dressing dip, which had mostly been dripped across the glass table, randomly interspersed with muffin crumbs both large and small in size. If I hadn't realized it before, I did now. The intruders were there for our session, and they had absolutely no business being there other than to eat my food, drink my beverages, and take up my space that I use as refuge from the Womb. For one even needs refuge from Wombs occasionally. There was no doubt about it—I was in the midst of a Posse Brigade!

Regardless of the brigade, we needed to start recording. So I went to the patio to get the band, who were holding court with their posse while holding onto their instruments—Harmon with the Höfner bass in his lap; Yore with an electric guitar strapped to his shoulder; Dumb Ass with his drumsticks in his back pocket; even the singer was holding a microphone that we would most likely never actually use to record him.

"You guys ready?" I asked.

"Let's get to it," Harmon responded.

With those words, the band stood up in one swift uniform motion and, in formation, proceeded immediately in the direction of the room. Never before had I seen such a determined look painted on their faces as they made their way through the crowd to the large double doors of the complex. For the briefest of moments, I felt as though I were watching a real rock band, a successful band, somehow making its way through the corridors on the way to performing their last concert after a long career of making successful records and selling out large stadiums. Like they were of the caliber of U2. Like they were actually cool.

"C'mon, we're playing!" yelled Cotton at the top of his lungs almost directly in my ear as he gestured for everyone to follow.

WHAT????? NO! I thought in panic.

With that summoning, the Posse Brigade became a posse parade, as they followed the band into the room like they were being lured by Willy with a fatty. I couldn't believe my eyes. Everyone filed into the recording room. It was like the lights had blinked on and off at the intermission of a play to indicate that the show was about to resume. But this wasn't a show, so what the hell were these people doing? I stood there motionless in the middle of the hall, staring in disbelief with my mouth hanging open, as brigadiers displayed marked irritation toward me for neglecting to provide a fully unrestricted path to the recording room.

As the last person filed in, I was suddenly broken from my spell. I spun around and ran to the Womb, which could be entered from a separate entrance without going through the recording room at all. The moment I entered the Womb, I could hear the commotion of brigadiers coming through the speakers, their every move picked up by the numerous live microphones littering the room. Willy looked at me wide-eyed with his mouth open, and I looked back at Willy, as it was apparent that he was as taken aback by this event as I was. I had not seen Willy fazed by anything until now.

Since he was still experiencing the shock that I had just moments ago been snapped out of, I spoke first.

"Are they going to clap when they finish the song?" I said dryly.

At that comment Willy snapped to and immediately went to the recording room and motioned for the singer to come into the Womb with about as much grace as Dumb Ass had used to motion the Posse Brigade just moments earlier.

After an extensive debriefing, it became apparent that the band was taking Willy's own words to heart. They were searching for a way to get more energy out of their playing. Willy had told the band he wanted to capture them the way they played live, so they figured the best way to achieve said goal was to bring in an audience. Willy expressed concern over such possible negative events as crowd noise, applause, or screaming in the middle of the take, but the band assured him that everyone in the room had been prepped on the procedure, and that no one would make a peep. Willy decided to oblige, which he might as well have done, since everyone was already in the room and ready to listen. With that, the singer made his way back into the room.

Willy looked at me and said nothing as he sparked up a fatty that had been sitting on the console for some time. He didn't look particularly pleased at that moment.

We recorded the band, and they didn't play any better or worse with their manufactured audience of drones. In fact, the presence of that many bodies in the room changed the sound that we had worked so hard to attain. But I wasn't going to start readjusting things yet. Rather, I allowed the session to proceed devoid of adjustments, because, frankly, I've been down this road before. After three takes that were likely passable at this point, the band headed for the Womb, and so too did the Posse Brigade. Willy and I looked at each other with the sort of horror you would expect if a piano were about to land your head from ten stories above.

"Whoa!" he yelled out. "We can't have the audience in the control room. I'm sorry," he continued, which surprised the hell out of me, because Willy rarely seemed to make unpopular decisions.

Like disappointed drones, as if there was such a thing, the Posse Brigade filed back into the recording room.

As we were listening to the takes, I took my normal listening position on the back couch. The band liked to be in front of the speakers when listening to the takes, and Dumb Ass liked to sit in front of the console and drastically change my balances.

By the middle of the second take, which was sounding awful owing to Dumb Ass's clear lack of mixing skills, I was envisioning twenty strangers in the recording room with mics that I'd spent a considerable amount of time placing and positioning. Worse yet, I was envisioning them with *no* supervision.

I was overcome by instant panic. I believe I've told you this before, but even the tiniest change in a mic's position can drastically change the sound that is being recorded. If a mic is somehow moved, it can render a take useless because it can no longer be cut together with another take. I jumped up from my position in the back of the room, and saw that my worst fears had been proven true.

There, through the window, I could see a guy hanging onto the large boom stand that I was using to hold a mic over the left side of the drums.

MOTHERFUCKER!

Not only was he hanging on it with his arms twisted around it like it was a barbell, but he was swiveling it back and forth over the drums in fascination.

Another intruder was sitting on the guitar amp that we were using, leaning back on it like it was a chair and he was in junior high. For me to go into the room and start berating people would be pointless. The intruders were completely ignorant of what they were doing wrong. Willy was listening down to a take and was completely oblivious. So in an effort to stop the madness and as quickly as possible, I did the most irritating thing I could think of. I stopped the tape.

"I'm sorry to interrupt," I said, "but we have to get all those people out of the recording room." I finished as I pointed toward the room.

Everyone stood up to look out the window, and Willy gasped in horror.

"I know you guys want a live atmosphere and everything . . ." I said.

And with that Willy told the singer with a look of wild-eyed horror, "You've got to get them out of there!"

The band, realizing he was right, agreed and escorted the Posse Brigade from the room. I explained to Willy and the band that between the moving of microphones and the removal of a large amount of the best deadening material known to man— man himself—we would have to record over the takes that we had done thus far.

After repositioning the moved microphones, I returned to the Womb. Willy was on the phone. Let me tell you, it's nearly impossible to listen at a reasonable volume when someone is on the phone next to you, so I sat down to wait and told Dumb Ass over the talkback to do the same (which he didn't, so I just muted the console). Once I had settled down on the couch to wait, I realized that I was listening to Willy's end of a conversation with Jeramiah Weasel, the band's A&R rep. They were discussing the progress of the record, and Willy was deftly spinning an account of great accomplishment and wonderful performances. As the conversation progressed, I could tell that Willy was being pinned down for a time to come by, but Willy was an expert at thwarting such attempts and finally convinced Jeramiah that he'd call early next week to set up a time.

Shortly after Willy's phone conversation with Jeramiah, we began making takes again. But we could barely get a groove going as the band was beginning to take peculiarly frequent breaks. It wasn't so much the breaks in and of themselves that were peculiar, as much as it was the manner in which the breaks were being taken. Indeed, as one band member would proclaim the need for a bathroom break, the rest of the band would proclaim same. These guys didn't do anything well together, including playing music — why would they all want to go to the bathroom at the same time?

Of course, I already knew the answer to my own question, as the telltale sniffles of a session gone awry could be heard through the microphones each time they returned for another take. I knew then that the boys were partaking in, as Dennis Miller so brilliantly puts it, "Colombian Marching Powder." As if girlfriends and Posse Brigades weren't enough to slow down the progress of a session, I now found myself smack-dab in the middle of a gak-fest.

The gak-fest was like some sort of disease (as gak-fests tend to be) that everyone on this session caught except for me. After the band, it was Willy who started to leave the room. Then Fingaz was walking back and forth through the control room on a regular basis, since he couldn't get anywhere without walking through the Womb. Even Lance was starting to disappear for long periods of time and on several occasions claimed to be catching some sort of a cold out of cold season.

I tried to stay in the Womb as long as possible. I certainly didn't want to join the party, as I knew that the moment I were to do a gak, I would want to be anywhere *but* the studio working. But after sitting alone for some time, I decided I should see for myself what was going on.

The party was raging. There were volumes of liquor and beer being consumed. There was actually a tiki bar set up in the lounge where people were ordering drinks. The entire complex reeked of fatty smoke. Even though there weren't piles of blow on mirrors in plain view, the consumption of Marching Powder was about as clandestine an operation as an episode of *Survivor*, a television game show in which cameras record a contestant's every maneuver. The complex was overrun with a Posse Brigade in the partying mood. They could even be found at the pool table in Studio II's lounge, a faux pas of the highest order. At one point, as I gazed in amazement at the sheer scope of this party, I was offered a gak by the band girlfriend who'd hugged me earlier. But I turned her down since I didn't want to be up all night. As it turns out, I was up all night anyway.

We spent the rest of the night recording relatively little over a long period of time, as everyone who was actually supposed to be on this session was gaked up except for me. I was surprised that I wasn't being pressured to join in by the band, as that is usually the case on these sorts of sessions. By this lack of pressure, I could only assume that there was a limited supply. Unfortunately for me, that supply lasted the entire night and through the morning.

Even with the ten extra hours of recording time, we managed to accomplish less than usual. To say that it was difficult to get Willy or the band in the room at the same time would be an understatement, but to be honest, I didn't really try.

We did, however, manage to make a couple of takes throughout the course of the evening. The really pathetic part about that was the fact that Dumb Ass played considerably better gaked up then he did straight. Unfortunately, Willy couldn't really judge the takes very well in this condition, and he kept listening to the same take over and over between his partying. Perhaps what we needed to do was get Dumb Ass gaked up and Willy straight before we did drum takes. But the logistics of that were overwhelming to me.

I would have gone home if the session had actually broken down into a full-on party with no pretense of trying to make a record. I even asked Willy if we maybe should call the session for the night, but he felt that we needed to keep going because the label was going to want to hear some of the recording we've done so far.

So I stayed the whole night, the only sober person there. I didn't even dare take a hit of a fatty as much as I really wanted to. I was too afraid that I would break down and take a gak, since fatties late at night tend to have the effect of putting me to sleep. I had to avoid taking a gak at all costs, because I would have to face my children in the morning. I promised myself when my first son was born that I would never allow my children to see me in that particular state, and to date they never have.

By 5 A.M., most of the Posse Brigade was gone, but the band and Willy and the last remaining brigadier, who I am assuming was the supplier of the gak, were all still up and raring to go. Willy, somehow realizing that we had managed to get very little done through the course of the night, decided we should record some bass and guitars on the songs that were edited. Sadly, much like Dumb Ass, Harmon could actually play halfway decently gaked up. I just didn't want to test out his singing, because I was certain that no substance on earth could help that. Yore, who was normally a fine guitar player, went to complete shit on the substance. I spent the next four hours recording bass and guitars on two songs. The guitars were, for the most part, useless, out of time, and generally uninspiring.

In twenty-two hours, we recorded what could have been done in six. Willy wanted to come back again Friday evening but, as I'd suspected, that was canceled. I'm sure everyone felt like shit, and they probably still do, as those sorts of parties tend to supply hangovers that last for two days. Hell, it's taken me a full day to recover, and I wasn't even partying. As of this moment, I haven't heard from Willy about Monday.

Perhaps tomorrow.

Once again, I find myself in semi-poor spirits come the end of a week of recording on this particular project.

Although I think I'm becoming numb to the idiocy.

– Mixerman

DAY 16

The Looming of the Mooks

POSTED: AUGUST 20, 12:03 A.M. — WEEK 4

It seems that Willy is no longer interested in parties, audiences, or the like.

I can't really blame Willy for having participated in the festivities on Thursday night. After all, he *is* human, and I can't say that I wouldn't have done the same were I able to go straight home to bed and not to young wide-eyed children wondering why Daddy's acting so weird. I'm not sure what it is about Willy. He's one of the most likeable fellows I've ever met. I genuinely enjoy hanging with the dude. Unfortunately, if he continually lets the band run the session when they clearly have no clue how to run one, this album isn't going to ever be completed. I still can't figure out what Willy's angle is. Does he want this session to self-destruct? I wish I understood his motivations. But at the moment, I don't.

On Sunday, Willy set a mandate. There would be no more "bitches" (his words, not mine) or posse at these sessions. He told me this mandate over the phone, and in a *very* stern manner, as if I were somehow a part of the problem.

Uh, excuse me! Willy! Hello?! You're telling *me* this? I thought to myself.

I've been telling him for days that he should get rid of the girls. Why the hell was he telling *me* no more girlfriends? Perhaps he was worried that I would bring my wife or something. Who knows?

I really have no idea how or why Willy's decision to put an end to visitation came about. Perhaps a two-day hangover, along with the realization that there was absolutely no recorded music worth a damn on this project made him reevaluate his purpose in life. Perhaps the looming visit from Jeramiah Weasel was on his mind. Perhaps Willy figured that he'd better have something to play for him, although I doubt it. Jeramiah is small potatoes. After all, he's just a minion with a very large opinion. Regardless of the reason, Willy was making another good decision in a not-so-timely manner. But at least he made the decision.

Halle-fucking-lujah!

We began today by listening to the "powder" takes the boys had done on Thursday and Friday's marathon session. The guitar parts pretty much sucked, but Willy thought the bass parts were fairly good. Perhaps that had something to do with the fact that the only sober person in the studio was actually the one babysitting and directing Harmon that night. Plus let's not forget that, for some inexplicable reason, Harmon could actually *play* all gaked up. I actually considered purchasing some gak to have handy for the upcoming Harmon takes (and Dumb Ass for that matter), but I thought better of that plan, as it was fraught with all sorts of built-in disasters. That harebrained scheme was best left to the Ralph Kramdens of the world.

With the bass parts in decent condition on two of the songs, and the bleed having proven to be only problematic if the room mics were turned up too loud, Willy decided to move onto guitars. Yore wanted to use a VOX AC30 amp. That was Yore's amp of choice on everything. Anytime we were tracking, the first amp he would plug into was the AC30. Then Willy would convince him to use the Marshall or the Mesa Boogie or the Matchless that we had available. We had spent a good deal of time selecting an amp for this song during the tracking process. Willy liked the Mesa Boogie, and that's what we used when we tracked, but why then was Yore using the VOX again? It seemed a bit counterproductive, since we had already spent the time to select a sound that worked well with the song and drums.

Don't get me wrong, AC30s are great amplifiers. In fact, I love a good VOX, and I use them often in productions. But they could hardly produce the modern sound that Willy was looking for. AC30s are forty-year-old amplifiers—not that the age of the amplifier matters.

"Modern" can be very elusive as time marches forward, and if you're not up on the latest music, modern can very easily pass you by. AC30 amps have a sound that one might call classic, but a definitive classic sound scares the hell out of record companies, and when they listen to classic, they inevitably think something's wrong with the production. The real bitch is that sometimes classic is modern, but you just have to keep up with the times to know when that is, and then take advantage of that window of opportunity to be both classic and modern simultaneously. Regardless of all that, what the record companies *really* want is "now," because "now" is something that record companies understand.

Unfortunately for everyone involved, by the time a record comes out, "now" was "yesterday" and the record is in the shitter for not being modern enough, even if it somehow happens to be classic. Occasionally, a new modern sound is born from some innovative band, and every major label in existence then scrambles to sign anything and everything that sounds remotely similar to that band. Then producers, wanting to remain modern themselves, will try to make records with the similar bands, so that they can be a part of what's "hot." Of course, none of it really matters, because no matter what, any sound that happens to become "hot," "now," or whatever, can be directly attributed to the Beatles. The Beatles are as classic as they come, and the Beatles used VOX AC30 amplifiers on their recordings. So why the hell classic scares a record company is beyond me, since without the Beatles, we'd be fucked. There's going to be a quiz on this later, so try to keep up.

The bands that typically push "modern" in order to make forward progress are unsigned bands that make albums with a seasoned producer, who takes the band under his/her wing to try and make a record that pushes the envelope of "now." Since there is no label involved, "now" is no longer a constraint and "tomorrow" can be attempted at minimal risk. In these cases, the band will oftentimes be signed with its first record left as is.

The record company that happens to sign a band with a finished record is always sure to put out a press release stating that the band's record was actually the band's demo—even though the demo was likely made by the same guy the label just *hired* to make a record for them. Guys who make records don't *make* demos. They make records that are meant to be signed as records. But labels don't sign bands with records—they sign bands with demos and then decide whether they want them to make a record or use the demos. It's all very fucked up and defies logic.

The most humorous part of this process of making records (or sad, depending on your perspective) is when the record company Mooks want the record to have a certain sound. The Mooks can't make a record, so they hire a producer and then try to describe what they want the record to be to the producer. Usually Mooks choose very odd words for these descriptions, like *happy* or *green* or *icy*. Then when you think you've finally come to understand what the hell a Mook means, half the time it turns out the Mook wanted the complete opposite of what he asked for. The other half of the time the Mook just out and out changed his mind because the Marketing Mook told the A&R Mook they can't get the song on radio. Oops!

Then, of course, there are the conflicting Mook opinions, but I won't get into that right now. Basically, you can't listen to the Mooks at all because they'll fuck you up every time. Of course, then there's the catch-22 of this whole operation. Most producers are desirous to deliver an album that the Mooks are happy with, because they want to be hired again. So producers are typically interested in what the Mooks want, and oftentimes cover all the bases by recording what are essentially several different options of productions—leaving it for the mixer to sort out and decide which production works best for the song.

Don't get me wrong. Not all producers are kiss-asses, and not all record company people are Mooks. That would be like saying that all black men have long dicks.

I'm not a Mook bigot or anything like that. Some of my best friends are Mooks! If I worked for a record company, which isn't entirely implausible, I might even be a Mook myself. If I were, I'd be damn proud of it!

Regardless of my futile attempts at disclaimers, what I have described in this diary certainly isn't unusual in this business.

I can't really blame record companies and producers for capitalizing on what is basically a musical fashion trend. Logic dictates, if the fashion is hot, then that is the product the company should put out. Right? Unfortunately, this practice is done to such extremes that all music comes out sounding the same as everything else in its genre. This leaves little room for diversity in sound and music. Even if a producer *does* make a record that strays from the current trends, or is possibly unique in some way, the record companies are sure to put the productions through a sort of homogenization process. I call them mixing factories, in which one of five highly paid major label mixers stamps out mixes just like his last, with little regard toward the music or the production. No record is treated differently from the next. The homogenization process doesn't stop there though. The record must then be sent to a mastering engineer.

These days, the mastering engineer views his job as one of placing an identifiable sonic imprint on the record. More importantly, his job is to be sure that the record is "loud." So the mastering engineer proceeds to stamp out every last bit of dynamic range by using what is called a brick wall limiter. Imagine what would happen to you were you to be stopped at a high rate of speed by a brick wall. SPLAT! Well, it's no different when music hits a brick wall. The music becomes flattened, all depth is removed, and all changes in volume eradicated.

With the dynamic range reduced to the point that the soft parts are the exact same volume as the loud parts, the mastering engineer has accomplished what is referred to in this industry as "loud." Some mastering engineers, in an effort to make their records louder than the next, will make a record so loud it actually clips, which is a generally undesirable form of distortion (although there are certainly exceptions). Making records loud has become like a competition of sorts. But since little good comes of this competition, and since it has been greatly destructive to the overall quality of records, we call it a war. A loudness war; and we're in the middle of one now.

Interestingly, as these mastering engineers are making records loud, they are all the while complaining about how loud records are destructive to the quality of a recording. I don't blame them for complaining—it's true. Unfortunately, if they don't make their records loud, the record companies, the producers, and even the engineers will oftentimes bring their records to someone who will.

As I was listening to the guitar sound emanating from the speakers, I felt that it was a beautiful sound, and certainly believed it would have been appropriate for some song on the record—unfortunately, not this song. But we had been through this already, which is why we picked the Mesa Boogie after careful deliberation and much discussion. Meanwhile, Willy was pacing nervously, asking *me* if I thought that Yore's sound was modern, and asking *me* why Yore wasn't using the Mesa Boogie.

"I don't know," I replied.

Willy, in his typical fashion, allowed Yore to lay down his AC30 parts, rationalizing that perhaps he could mix it in with the Boogie, which meant that I was going to need about eight tracks for guitars. Hopefully, we wouldn't actually have eight guitar parts to be mixed together. I've been down that road before, and it's usually quite messy.

After Yore had laid down his first guitar part, using the AC30, the singer, who I think had just come from a manicure, as his fingernails were unusually shiny, wanted to lay down the double guitar part. Yore didn't want the singer to play the doubles, because he felt he could play the doubles faster, and he could. The singer didn't want Yore to play the doubles, because he felt the doubles would be better if they were played by someone else, and they would be. Willy decided to let *them* work it out as he went to get a fatty. This left me in the undesirable position of mediator, as I was asked point-blank what my opinion was.

I wasn't quite sure; one side of me wanted Yore to play it because I didn't want to spend two hours recording a double guitar with a hack guitar player. The other side of me felt it would probably be better for the record if the singer played the doubles, as I find those to sound a little less manufactured. Personally, I thought that it would be best with *no* double. It didn't need a double. But that would have been a futile course, as the argument would have been to lay it down in case we decided *later* that we needed a double. When in doubt, ask a question.

"Well, are you more interested in a perfect double, or the sound of a second guitar player playing the same part?" I asked.

Willy had walked in at that particular moment and gave the old "that's exactly what I've been thinking about" routine.

After three hours of debate—I'm not exaggerating, and it's not the first time in my career that a discussion such as this has stopped a session for that many hours—the band and Willy finally came to the conclusion that it would be better if the singer did the doubles. Of course, after all that, Yore wanted to do his other guitar parts first. So that's how we proceeded.

During the course of the three-hour debate, I visited Fingaz to see how he was doing. He was whipping through the editing jobs; in fact, he was almost done with the songs that we had recorded so far. This meant that, come this evening, Fingaz would be getting paid to just sit around. I'm sure he's getting a minimum of $500 a day, and he wasn't going to have to do shit for several days if we kept this course.

Not recording *all* of the basic tracks straight through is the most expensive way to make an album. That's because the session is paying for drum rentals, some outboard gear rentals, a large tracking facility (as opposed to a smaller and cheaper studio for doing overdubs), and, of course, Fingaz. When the snare drums sit in the room at $50 a pop, and entire kits at $250 a pop, and editors are sitting around at $500 a pop, and the studio costs $1,800 because it's a large tracking facility, it can hardly be considered working in a cost-effective manner.

Unfortunately, we were somewhat forced to work this way, as we are three weeks into the process and have relatively nothing to show for the time. The record company is going to want to hear *something*. Most importantly, we still don't know for sure that

Cotton's drums are going to pass muster. In my opinion thus far, they barely pass. They are wholly average, and even after Fingaz's super-skilled editing jobs, they're just okay. The real question is, Can the drums be disguised in such a way that they work?

Willy was obviously a man who wanted a record with some feel. If he wasn't, we'd have gone into Alsihad already. The editing jobs would take entire days, and everything—including the guitars, bass, and vocal, would be chopped up, tuned, and put together again like a chicken nugget—which, in many cases, is reconstituted. That is the way many, many of today's rock records are made.

If U2 were to put out *Boy* today, I contend that record would have been a sterile piece of shit. They really weren't great players back then. But U2 had a vibe, and they were innovative, and the fact that they weren't great players made the music all the more alive. Today, a young U2 band would have more than likely been destroyed by a producer and his Alsihad—that is, if they ever got signed at all.

We recorded Yore for a couple of hours, and had the distinct pleasure of his not really digging anything, and never having the decency of actually getting excited about his own record. When we finished with his parts, he insisted that he get to take a stab at his own double first. Willy agreed, but only if he did his doubles with a different guitar through the Mesa Boogie. Without saying a word, Yore complied. He recorded his double, and his guitars sounded *great*. The combination of the Mesa Boogie and the VOX supplied both classic *and* modern guitar sounds simultaneously. What more could you ask for? Unfortunately, the singer had arrived, and took over the playing of guitar doubles.

With the passing of the guitar from Yore to the singer, like the passing of the family business from father to son, everything went to shit. The guitar suddenly sounded wretched. Willy was asking me what happened to the sound, as if I'd changed something. So I spent the next twenty minutes trying to make the guitar sound close to as good as it did when Yore was playing it, and to no avail.

As with just about any instrument—and I do believe I've said this before, but I can't say it enough—the sound of a guitar lies squarely in the hands of the player. No amount of voodoo or engineering trickery can compensate for poor technique. So I tried to make the guitar sound as acceptable as possible, and we spent hours recording a part that had taken Paulie Yore only minutes to lay down. We did, however, complete the guitar parts on the song, which, when you think about it, is largely underwhelming.

Unless you happen to be on *this* session.

– Mixerman

DAY 17

Johnny Be Good

POSTED: AUGUST 21, 12:44 A.M.

Johnny is an enigma.

Johnny, the front man and singer for Bitch Slap, is probably one of the more self-obsessed people on the planet. Johnny fixes his hair approximately twenty times an hour. Personally, I can't tell any difference between the Johnny Ugly who starts to fix his hair and the Johnny Handsome who's finished fixing his hair, mostly because, to Johnny, a good hairdo doesn't appear to be a hairdo at all—quite the opposite, really.

I, having no experience whatsoever in the cutting of hair, could easily cut his hair for him without anyone being the wiser. A chunk out here, a chunk out there, here a chunk, there a chunk, everywhere a chunk, chunk, and BAM, we're done. I'm not sure whether he teases it, as I've never actually caught him red-handed with a comb or anything, but I have my suspicions. He doesn't seem to be a gel or hair spray kind of guy, although I think he might be surprised at all the extra time he would have if he just tried some.

Perhaps if I bought him some hair spray for Christmas he would be able to get it messed up to perfection and then spray it in place.

Johnny is the kind of guy you would expect all the girls would dig. He has a very symmetrical face with strong lines. He's definitely a handsome fellow. While he has an obvious obsession with shitty hair, that doesn't seem to be his only fetish.

Johnny Primper can't ignore his appearance, for even a moment. I haven't figured out how the hell he's going to sing, since between hair fixes he's constantly working on his teeth with this odd toothpick-like utensil with a string and a compact mirror that he keeps in what seems to be some kind of purse. Of course, Johnny claims his purse is some sort of European wallet.

Whatev.

I have this sneaky feeling that Johnny secretly wishes he were European, or at least what he *thinks* is European, because he hasn't changed his pants once in over three weeks on this session. I've gotten into conversations with him on this subject. He likes to go into these long drawn-out monologues about how washing jeans destroys them. He will talk endlessly in detail as to how they shrink, they fade, they soften (since when are soft jeans a bad thing?), and, most egregious of all, how the blue color will blend into the white threads throughout the jeans. It seems that rather than using the more modern cleaning methods of soap and water—or even dry cleaning solution, for that matter—he prefers the age-old tradition of air washing.

Air washing is the process of attaching the jeans to a clothesline from the waistband, allowing the full length of the leg to hang down, thus permitting the air to permeate the entire jean and, thereby, washing them. I suppose there must be some merit to the technique, because he hasn't started to stink or anything. I can assure you, however, that if Johnny Wellkept starts transforming into Johnny Stench, without hesitation, I'll tackle him down, remove his jeans, and wash them my damn self. I have to endure plenty on this session; I'm certainly not going to put up with my control room air being violated!

Johnny Fashion is also into his thrift store shirts and his vintage, 1980s-era Air Jordan sneakers that apparently Japanese sneaker collectors would pay thousands of dollars for. His shirts cost him $10 at thrift stores, but to hear him talk about it, they are like rare one-of-a-kind artifacts, and he can cite manufacturers, material, the year of production, and the estimated number of the shirts remaining in existence today. Personally, the way I figure it, if you're shopping in thrift stores for used $10 shirts, you might possibly consider selling your very expensive sneaker collection for the opportunity to, perhaps, buy a brand-new shirt at Saks. But that's just me, and this diary isn't about me.

I wouldn't say that Johnny is a particularly nice person. He puts up a good front. He sometimes can appear to be a nice person. He was cool when I was mixing for him a few years back. But these days Johnny Mr. Nice Guy can transform into Johnny Asshole in no time flat, especially when Paulie Yore is around. How these two formed a band together is beyond me. Johnny and Yore hate each other with a passion, and they haven't even made a record yet. At least John Lennon and Paul McCartney made a successful album or two together before *they* supposedly expressed their disdain for each other.

I don't think it's by accident that Johnny's the lead singer of the band. Not because he's an exceptional singer, because he's not.

But rather because, much like a three-year-old, he is egocentric and is of the belief that the world revolves around him. If one tries to have a normal conversation with him, it is only a matter of moments before the conversation is manipulated into a self-indulgent conversation about his experiences in life. Once that happens, one can't get a word in edgewise and might as well not even try. Usually, I just allow my mind to wander elsewhere as he chatters away. If somehow you are allowed a moment to speak of your own experiences, he cuts you off and goes right back to talking about himself. He finds very little humor in the words of others but finds himself to be absolutely hysterical. He's the kind of guy I loathe having to work with. If you think about it, he's probably the kind of guy *you* loathe to work with.

On my way to the studio today, Willy called me and asked me to start recording guitar parts for the next song and said that he'd be in later. This sounded like a good plan to me, until I got to the studio.

Upon entering the Womb, I heard the familiar sound of vocal scales that many vocalists use to warm up with, although not usually rock vocalists. It didn't sound quite like a yodeler with gout, so I was able to rule out a pending Harmon Neenot vocal session. With that welcome revelation, I was filled with an infusion of courage to investigate. So I followed the sound of the phantom voice. The howls were coming from Fingaz's makeshift editing suite, and as I arrived, I saw that it was, in fact, Johnny. He had seen me. Damn!

"Hey, man. I'm glad to see you!" Johnny said.

Just moments before he saw me, I knew exactly what was going on. Johnny wanted to sing. If only I had gotten out of there before he caught me, I could have started guitars, and he would have probably abandoned singing. But he *did* see me.

"Hey, Johnny, what's going on?" I asked in a cautiously friendly tone.

"I'm getting ready to lay down a vocal," Johnny responded, leaving little doubt as to his intentions.

Oh, joy!

Without even giving me an opportunity to respond, Johnny went back to singing his scales. I can't for the life of me understand why we don't set up our plans for the next day before we leave the studio each night. That would be a very good preventive measure for this sort of situation. Regardless, I certainly wasn't going to let Johnny just leave things at that.

"Willy called me this morning and wanted me to cut guitars with you guys on the next song," I interrupted. "Seeing as we're set up for guitars, it might be more efficient for us to continue," I concluded in what I felt was a very concise and logical explanation.

"Well, I'd rather record a vocal," he responded, in a very self-serving and emotional manner. It was obvious that his Mind Tricks were working on me, as I was frozen from pursuing this cause any further. Besides, if he was inspired to do a vocal, who am I to tell him to wait for the sake of procedure? It doesn't really make a difference whether we record guitars or vocals today. The only potential problem is that producers typically prefer to be around for vocals. The vocals are money. Nothing on the record is more important than the vocal. But Johnny Adamant wasn't leaving me much choice.

Surreptitiously, I instructed Lance to call Willy and leave a message telling him we were recording vocals as I set us up for such activities. I wanted to hear what Johnny sounded like on several varieties of microphones, so I had Lance set them up all in a row for comparison.

As Lance and I prepared to record a vocal, a stranger entered the Womb. I don't like it when strangers enter the Womb, but that's inevitable, I suppose. The stranger was a very short man in his mid-fifties, wearing a sky blue Izod shirt, a brown tweed jacket, and brown wool pants. He had his extra-long side hair combed over his bald head, and he wore perfectly round glasses. He spoke in what I can only describe as a booming and overly dramatic voice.

"I was told that I could find Johnny Handsome here," he said to me.

"Indeed," I said, in a language I felt he could understand, as I pointed toward the shitter.

The short man disappeared toward Johnny Coyote's howls, which abruptly ended as the two of them came back together in silence. The stranger chose to introduce himself, as I'm sure he figured it was highly unlikely that Johnny would think of such a thing. Apparently, the stranger was a vocal coach. His name was A. Scott Ascot (I'll call him Ascot for short).

Oh, this ought to be good, I thought to myself.

Ascot proceeded to coach Johnny with these very deep-breathing exercises, which is fine by me—what the hell do I care if Johnny hyperventilates before he sings? This guy really took breathing seriously. You could tell that breathing was truly exciting for him. I mean, breathing was like sex for this guy.

"Yes! Yes!" he'd yell as if he was mid-orgasm. Then he told *me* to join in. "You! You must breathe too!" he said to me. "Everyone must breathe. Breathe in . . . out . . . deeply . . . *deeply*!!!!"

Who, me? Why the fuck should I breathe? Johnny's been wearing the same damn pants for seventeen days—I'm not going to breathe deeply anywhere near the dude.

Ascot was a bit of a square fellow. He spoke very proper English, although he didn't have an English accent or anything like that. He was exactly as you'd imagine the nutty professor to be before Eddie Murphy did the movie and changed that image forever. I couldn't help but be amused by this little halfling of a man with his zest for life and his free expression. As I listened to him speak, I wondered to myself how a conversation between Ascot and Fingaz might go.

"Yes, yes, very nice to meet you, Fingers?" Ascot would say, overly enunciating Fingaz's name.

"Word," Fingaz would respond.

"I hear you're an editor," Ascot would continue.

"Word," Fingaz would reply. "I hea' you a pervert, Yo."

Suddenly I was snapped out of such thoughts by his hysterical yelling.

"Breathe! Breathe!"

I decided to exit stage left.

When I returned, Johnny and Ascot had completed their breathing exercises. I asked Johnny to sing a little bit of the first verse and chorus on each mic as I switched to whatever mic he was standing in front of at the time and recorded the examples. When Johnny sang on the first mic, Ascot announced from the back of the room, "Wonderful!"

Yeah, right. It sounded like shit. What the hell was *he* talking about? So I tried the next mic. "Eeeeeven better!" he yelled in a deep tone from behind me. It was worse. So I tried a C12. "That's the one!!!" he screamed at the top of his lungs, this time jumping up and down in his excitement.

"Do you mind?" I said turning to him.

He apologized, and as much as I really wanted to pick another mic other than the mic he'd screamed was "the one," it was without a doubt the best choice for this song. Once I swallowed my pride and selected the mic that my newfound dwarf comrade had deemed "the one," I had Lance move the other mics out of Johnny's way. Then I had Johnny sing the chorus for me, as I made some adjustments to the mic pre[42] and the compressor.

For the next two hours we cut vocals. Ascot took to commenting from the back of the room.

"No, no, he's not warm. He must be warmer!" Ascot said, telling me to erase it. Oh, great! Now I had Rush Limbaugh booming out orders on which takes to keep and which ones to burn. After a few takes, I had Johnny come in to the control room and listen. Normally, I would have discussed what I thought about the vocals that he sang, but I couldn't get a word in edgewise with Mr. Excitement in the back of the room providing misguided advice. We continued on, recording six more takes, each one getting progressively worse from the direction given by Ascot.

By the eighth take, Ascot declared from behind me, "He's almost there!"

On the ninth take Ascot inexplicably exclaimed, "He's past it! He's past it! His voice is shot for the day. He must rest!"

Did I miss something? Or did we go from "almost there" to "past it" in one take? What the hell was this guy talking about?

In between each and every take, Mr. Ascot would talk to Johnny about his breathing and opening his vowel sounds. Every take got progressively worse. By the time we were on the ninth take, Johnny was starting to sound like an opera singer.

I decided to play the last and most operatic of all the takes for Johnny Opera. He had a very stoic look on his face as he listened to his vocal that rivaled the Three Tenors' latest release. After I stopped tape, Johnny decided to get a second opinion, and it was about time, too. He turned and asked me what I thought. So I told him.

"I think you're in a rock band, and you should stop worrying about classic technique and start worrying about whether you're providing us with a compelling vocal performance," I said bluntly.

"So you're not compelled?" he asked.

I sat there for a moment, deadpan, hardly believing that he'd actually asked me that. My initial thought was "der," but as stupid a question as that was, it was considerably more intelligent than the large majority of Dumb Ass's questions. Even idiotic questions deserve a straightforward answer.

"Do I look compelled?" I asked dryly.

So we started over. Ascot, sensing his effectiveness waning, conveniently had another appointment, and he exited stage left as Johnny started to sing a vocal like he meant it.

Willy finally arrived and was happy that I had let Johnny Adamant sing, given that he was obviously "feeling it." After the vocal takes were done, Willy and Johnny set forth to comp (short for compile) the vocal, which is the process of selecting the best sections, lines, or even words from several vocal takes and transferring them onto a new track, thus making a compilation. This new track is often called the comp track or the comp vocal. Usually

I do the comps with the producer, but Johnny wanted to participate, and three's a crowd.

In my opinion, it's better for the singer to let someone else
comp the vocal and then listen fresh to the comp as a whole
performance. This prevents the singer or artist from becoming
oversaturated, and consequently unable to adequately judge the
comp as a whole. Aside from that, singers tend to get very preoccupied with pitch over performance, and good producers are
interested in performance over pitch. This case was no different,
as I listened to the back-and-forth discussions between Willy and
Johnny on pitch versus performance.

After about an hour, Willy and Johnny had come to an agreement on the comp, and I put it together for them by using their
comp sheet. A comp sheet is basically a lyric sheet with notations
as to which take is to be used for which lines. When the comp
was done, Willy and Johnny listened to it and felt that it was a
good vocal. Then Willy decided we should do harmonies.

At that point, Harmon was hovering in the room like a vul-
ture, and he had every intention of doing the harmonies. Harmon was trying to force his will upon everyone in the room by
setting himself up at the mic and preparing, as if he'd be surprised at the notion that Johnny wanted to sing the background
vocals. But Harmon is not skilled in Mind Tricks, and Johnny
Mindblock would have nothing of it. An hour-long discussion
ensued, which included the usual smoking of fatties and circular
conversations.

Eventually, after carefully weighing the ramifications of either
decision, Willy chose to have Harmon Neenot sing the harmonies. He exited stage left, knowing just how tedious the session

would soon become. I spent the next three hours, trying to coax a dying seal to sing in harmony.

I can assure you, that's no easy feat.

– Mixerman

DAY 18

Rollin' Fatties

POSTED: AUGUST 21, 11:44 P.M.

When I awoke, I realized that, once again, I had forgotten to establish today's precise plan of attack before leaving the studio last night. It's become obvious that Willy prefers to be the kind of general who gives me my marching orders on a need-to-know basis at the beginning of the day. Unfortunately, I must relay those commands to a bunch of nimrods who clearly prefer anarchy over any semblance of order.

I didn't even bother to call Willy this morning, as what he was planning to record was far less relevant than *who* actually had a bug up his ass to be recording. Once that band member stepped forward at the start of the day, then and only then would I know what we were recording—by default.

Today, it was Dumb Ass who was standing in the room performing lame and futile attempts at Mind Tricks. He, being of little brain, was not able to control me, but I figured I'd let him have his way. So I obliged him.

Dumb Ass was setting up what looked to be brand spanking new timbales in the room. I actually laughed out loud at the thought of Dumb Ass being so idiotic as to lay timbales on the only production that I could think of that might be ready for percussion parts. But he couldn't understand what I found so humorous, and with that, my laughter turned to horror.

"So . . . we're recording timbales?" I asked casually and cautiously.

"Duhuh, duhuh, you got it!" Dumb Ass stated with his usual and tiresome retard shtick.

As I walked away, once again baffled as to why a retard would *act* like a retard, I found Lance and asked him to set up a microphone, which was all well and good until Dumb Ass informed me that he wanted the timbales to be stereo. Ah, yes, stereo. So I had Lance set up two microphones for stereophonic recording.

It seems that everyone wants his instrument in stereo. Sometimes a stereo presentation of an instrument is a good thing. Usually, such presentation is not a good thing. Don't get me wrong—I tend to use the entire stereo image when mixing. I like very wide mixes with elements of the mix coming from the far sides of the stereo field. But unrealistic stereo presentations of a single instrument across the sound field are not, in my experience, an effective use of stereo. While there *are* two timbales, were you actually in the room with them, their sound would have a specific point of origin.

Still, it wasn't an unreasonable request. If Cotton wanted his timbales in stereo, I was happy to oblige. They could always be spread across a diminished field from center to right. They could even be broken down to a mono signal later, so long as I was diligent in my mic placement, for stereo miking does not always break down cleanly in mono due to phase cancellation.

Phase cancellation is a phenomenon that occurs when there are more than two microphones in close proximity to one another. Each microphone has a pickup pattern. When two microphones are close to each other, the pickup patterns of the microphones will have intersections. These intersections will cancel each other out, and there will actually be a cancellation of the sound wave and the sound as we perceive it. There are 360 degrees of phase. If two signals are 180 degrees out of phase from each other, they will cancel each other out completely. No sound will be heard.

Lesser degrees of phase will cause lesser amounts of cancellation, but they will still cause some cancellation. If there are severe phase coherency issues, the microphones will not combine properly in mono, and there will be a reduction in volume of the instrument. As an engineer, I must be careful that the stereo image breaks down well to mono, or there could be problems down the road. There are miking techniques that help to minimize this problem.

Some automobile manufacturers use phasing to cancel out the sound of the engine, making the cockpit completely devoid of engine sound. Occasionally on TV you might see two people with microphones get too close to each other. You'll notice that the sound starts to get weird and even disappear. This is a prime example of phase cancellation.

I'm not quite sure if Dumb Ass was trying to impress some Latin girl from his English-as-a-Second-Language class (it's well documented that his mother was a poor immigrant from Great Britain), or if he had just gotten a set of timbales for his birthday.

Tito Puente he was not, and the sound of a syncopated Latin tim-bale beat on top of a shuffle was just too much for me to bear. As far as I was concerned, it was high time that Lance get the record-ing experience his uncle so very much wanted for him.

"Lance!" I yelled out, as he was kibitzing with Fingaz in the shitter.

"You're in charge. Call me when he's done," I said.

I left poor Lance to get the experience of a lifetime as I took a lesson from Willy and exited stage left. Lance was now on his way to becoming a professional recordist. With my handing over the reins, he would have an "additional engineering" credit. In the not so distant future, Full Sail[43] students would be listening to his records and marveling at how great his timbale recordings were. Lance had completed the transition from assistant to engineer in an instant.

Of course, when I had returned, Lance was actually well on his way to getting a *full* engineering credit, because Dumb Ass had managed to record what I could only describe as a complete percussion clusterfuck. Aside from the timbales, which were ex-cessive in their own right, Dumb Ass also recorded an egg shaker, a tambourine, a woodblock (I swear I haven't seen a woodblock since high school), a cowbell, congas, and maracas—none of which actually went with the song or the production. Worse yet, Dumb Ass made sure to fill in every thirty-second note of the production with some form of percussion, and he did so with an incredible lack of skill or understanding of what excessively out-of-place and out-of-time percussion parts can do to a rock produc-tion. I chose to throw caution to the wind.

"I think Ricky Martin uses less percussion than that," I said.

Dumb Ass laughed uncomfortably and continued listening to his rhythmic disaster. After about thirty seconds passed by, it was as if my words had somehow percolated the tiny little area in his brain that the spoken word must successfully permeate in order to be processed and understood. He finally replied to my comment.

"I doubt it. Ricky Martin uses *a lot* of percussion."

I suppose I shouldn't expect that Dumb Ass might be able to detect the subtle differences between sarcasm and discussion.

When Dumb Ass was finished laying down his out-of-time percussion solo over the full course of the production, he asked me if I would make him a percussion-only mix.

"Will you be playing it for your mother?" I asked.

"Noooooooo," Dumb Ass replied, craning his neck out like a chicken. Had I an axe, I might have chopped his head off.

I wasn't in the mood for a journey to the Trough, so I had Lance make a percussion mix for Dumb Ass's future enjoyment as I went to take a leak in Fingaz's bathroom.

"What are you doin', Yo?!!!" Fingaz asked in a very distressed manner.

"I just finished eating some asparagus for lunch, and I thought I'd share," I replied. "I thought you were done editing."

"I'm checking, Dawg! You don't have to go number two, do ya?"

Fingaz made me laugh with that inquiry, and I began missing the toilet, which seemed to upset him even more. I think I got some urine on his parka, which lay dangerously close to the commode, but somehow he didn't notice, and I didn't dare tell him of the accident. He was, without a doubt, the most serious and uptight Wegro I've ever met.

I have no idea why I was in such a mood today. Sometimes I get like this when I feel the entire world has reached the epitome of insanity. Sometimes lack of sleep makes it worse. I think it's some sort of deep-rooted coping method that prevents me from going postal or something. When I get like this, my purpose in life is to fuck with everybody who crosses my path. No one is immune. Unfortunately, there was no one left. Yore and Johnny weren't around, and Willy still hadn't arrived.

When Willy finally did arrive, he was *very* interested in hearing the percussion parts that Dumb Ass was so excited about. Apparently, Dumb Ass had greeted him at the patio and informed Willy just how much his percussion parts were helping the song.

Yeah, right.

Willy was very keen on hearing them and, being mildly amused at the prospect of Willy's reaction, I obliged by pressing play on the tape machine. I made my way to the back of the room.

Willy sat motionless in front of the speakers. I was directly behind him at the couch, but when you've been working at a studio for longer than a day, you figure out that you can watch the expressions of people at the console from the reflection in the glass that separates the room from the Womb. I have a setting on the automatic programmed dimmer selector that allows me the maximum amount of reflection, and I often hit it just before I play someone something.

I could tell by the wide-eyed expression on Willy's face that he was appalled by the wretched percussion parts, although he had to bite his tongue because Dumb Ass was in the room. Slowly, Willy leaned into the console and started muting percussion parts and listening to each part individually with the track. I could see him trying to figure out what the hell was going on with these percussion parts. Finally, when the song ended, Willy stopped the tape and pronounced his feelings on the subject of Dumb Ass's percussion parts. He did so with supreme clarity and absolute conviction, holding back nothing.

"Uh . . ." he said.

I decided it might be best if I jumped in, as Willy was in the midst of a very awkward pause. "Perhaps it's a bit much," I chimed in.

"Yes, perhaps," Willy echoed as he snapped his head to look at me, seeming relieved that I had managed to bail him out.

"Well, I guess we could mute the woodblock," Dumb Ass replied deep in thought, "but that's a mix thing, right?" he continued.

"Indeed," I said with conviction, doing everything in my power to hold back my laughter at the incredulous look on Willy's face.

Willy explained to Dumb Ass that he needed to live with the percussion parts for a moment and pretended that he needed to run an errand for which he needed my expertise. Fortunately, Dumb Ass didn't question this, or worse yet, offer to tag along, so Willy's white lie didn't have to blossom into a tale that only Lucille Ball could rival. As we got into Willy's car, I knew exactly what the errand was that we were going to run. I'm not quite sure how I knew. I suppose sometimes you just get a sense for these sorts of things.

"Sushi time!" I exclaimed. And I was right!

Once Willy realized that I knew how bad the percussion parts were, he went through a variety of stages. First, he expressed relief that I wasn't the architect of such atrocities, then horror that Dumb Ass was. Then, after we had a couple of beers and some sushi, he couldn't stop laughing about it. Of course, my singing the song and dancing like a retard playing timbales wasn't helping matters.

I offered my consultation to Willy, expressing that I thought we should play the percussion for the rest of the band tomorrow, so they could be the ones to tell him it sucks ass. Then I suggested that we record guitars on the other song that Willy had already approved the drum edits on. He agreed, and that's what we did.

I felt fortunate, as Johnny-on-the-Spot wasn't at the studio when we returned. Apparently, he'd come and split when he heard we were gone. We were actually able to rip through guitars on another song with Yore. Willy decided to stick around tonight and run the guitar overdub session rather than exit stage left. He even ran the controls, as I lay in the back of the room on the couch occasionally shouting out orders like I was the producer and he was the engineer. As I did so, I did what any good producer would do.

I rolled a fatty.

– Mixerman

A Man, A Plan, A Canal, Panama

POSTED: AUGUST 23, 1:42 A.M.

I'll never forget the look on Paulie Yore's face as he stood in front of the console listening to the playback of yesterday's "Percussion Solo over a Production" debacle. I wasn't quite sure whether Yore was going to throw up, pass out, cry, or start laughing hysterically, but he could have easily made the transition to any one of those reactions. Yore decided to stop the tape around the time the maracas began their incessant chattering. He turned in a slow methodical fashion like a mannequin on a turnstile, and he gazed at me with absolute marvel in his eyes. Then he became animated again.

"Is this a joke?" he asked me as he held out his hands like one would to carry a folded blanket.

"I take it you don't like it," I replied sarcastically.

Dumb Ass couldn't have picked a more perfect moment to enter the room were his goal to get chewed out by someone who despised him.

"What the fuck were you thinking?" Yore asked as he turned his attention toward Dumb Ass.

"What'd I do?" Dumb Ass replied.

"These percussion parts suck!" Yore yelled in amazement. "Who the fuck puts a timbale on a shuffle?" he continued.

I was wondering that myself, but then the answer stood before me.

"I think he's planning on muting the woodblock," I said without thinking. I was sorry the moment I said it. Fortunately for me, there was no backlash for my poorly timed smart-ass remark, as they both chose to ignore me. Dumb Ass and Paulie Yore proceeded to get into it, and I exited stage left.

I was hanging out on the patio eating a chocolate muffin when Willy arrived. Not wanting Willy to walk in on the scene unprepared, I attempted to tell him mid-chew that Yore had heard the percussion parts. Willy smacked his forehead with the palm of his hand so hard that he left a red mark. He leaned back as if he were in excruciating pain that I had gathered was caused by the excessive force of his smack. Then I realized that Willy's expression of pain wasn't as a result of the smack, but rather from the ramifications of a missed detail.

"I totally forgot to warn Yore," he whined, still wincing.

I told Willy he'd better get a fatty and get in there quick, because Yore was tearing Dumb Ass a new asshole, and I didn't think Dumb Ass was going to take it anymore. With that, I now knew just what to say to Willy were we ever to participate in an inter-studio relay race. Willy bolted to the control room, and I, not wishing to miss anything, followed close behind.

When we got back to the control room, Yore was on his way out, and without a word, he split. Dumb Ass was bright red in the face and sitting on the couch in silence with his arms and legs crossed.

Willy, Dumb Ass, and I sat in the room in silence for approximately five minutes. Finally, I got up to get a glass of water, and on my way out of the room, I was handed a message slip by the runner. It was from Jeramiah Weasel, and the note was for Willy. It said:

To: Willy Show
From: Jeramiah Weasel

Please Call—Urgent.

I abandoned my water run and dispensed the slip to Willy, who glanced at it briefly, crumpled it up, and threw it toward the trash can. He missed. Dumb Ass split without saying a word. Since nobody was in the room, I took that opportunity to ask Willy about Jeramiah's pending visit.

"Will Jeramiah be coming over soon?" I asked.

"Not if I have anything to do with it," replied Willy curtly.

I decided to leave it at that, as Willy didn't seem to be in the mood to discuss it.

After Dumb Ass had calmed down and reentered the room, Willy had a heart-to-heart with him about the percussion. Willy selected his wording carefully, telling Dumb Ass that the timbales brought the song to a place that he wasn't envisioning. Willy put in the obligatory stroking by telling Dumb Ass that the percussion parts were very creative and interesting, but that the record label was looking for something a little more "straight-ahead." He told Cotton that rock radio might not play a song that had timbales on it, and that radio airplay was of great concern of the label. It was a great speech, and Dumb Ass seemed to be buying it.

"Well, what do you envision on this song?" asked Dumb Ass.

"At the moment, nothing," Willy replied bluntly.

Dumb Ass questioned Willy for a while longer, like a child asking why he couldn't have a dog, and then, seeming somewhat dejected, he split.

Great! There was nobody from the band at our session.

Fingaz moseyed on through the control room with the hood up on his parka, as if he had just entered the Hungarian Farmers' Club from a dogsled race in Barrow, Alaska. His parka smelled a little like pee to me (human, not dog), but I didn't say anything to him about it. Willy and I followed Fingaz to his shitter and listened to the edited takes. Willy approved one and gave Fingaz some changes on the other two.

By evening, Johnny had arrived, warmed up, and was ready to sing. Willy was controlling the tape deck, so I lay in my favorite spot—the couch in the back of the room. The back of the room is great, because it acts as a bass trap due to the wall. When you lie there listening to music, it's really bass-heavy and relaxing— hence the term "bass trap." Sometimes, if everything is going smoothly in a session, or if the producer wants to run the deck, I like to go to sleep back there. So that's what I did.

I was awakened from a dream state in which I was in a hot air balloon with Dumb Ass and his set of timbales. Dumb Ass was freaking out because he had a fear of heights. I was marveling at the fact that someone with a fear of heights would actually get *into* a hot air balloon, when Dumb Ass began repeating, "It's too fucking high. It's too fucking high," and then I woke up. It was actually Willy saying, "It's too fucking high," and that had some- how permeated my dream. After a moment, I finally understood what was going on. The song was in a key too high for Johnny to sing.

This sort of problem happens all the time, certainly more often than it should. Singers can get very stubborn about what key they sing a song in. There is definitely some validity to their stubbornness, as changing the key can drastically alter the feeling of a song. Unfortunately, if one can't sing the song in the key chosen, then where the recording process is concerned, that point becomes moot. As it turned out, Johnny McMyway didn't want to lower the key of the song, because he felt the song sounded better at the top of his range. That may be, but not today it didn't.

"I *told* him this song was too high," Willy vented out of earshot from Johnny, who was still in the tracking room. Willy now had his face in his hands with his elbows on the console, clearly dejected by this revelation.

That statement told me that this topic had been discussed before. Johnny wasn't willing to take Willy's suggestion to lower the key. Usually, if you get into the studio and the singer can't hit the notes, it's not because he can *never* hit those notes, but rather because he sometimes *can* hit the notes. That causes the singer to be overconfident and misjudge what his true range is. A singer's true range is what he can *always* sing. Even if you happen to get the singer on a day where he can just about make the notes, many times, the singer ends up sacrificing a good performance as a result of the brainpower being allocated toward the hitting of notes. When it is finally discovered that a song is too high for the singer, there are several options.

The key can be lowered using a function called vari-speed on the tape deck, which allows me to speed up or slow down the rate at which the deck plays the tape. If you slow down a tape with recorded music, the pitch goes down. The problem with this is, if you end up slowing the tape down too much, the quality of the voice can degrade upon playback at normal speed, causing the singer to sound like The Chipmunks. Another disadvantage to this method is that the tempo of the song is slowed down during the performance, and sometimes that can make the song just as difficult for the singer to sing. In that case, you are merely trading one problem for another, which rarely helps the cause. If slowing down the tape doesn't work, then retracking the harmonic instruments in the new key must be considered.

The harmonic instruments like guitar and bass and keyboards (if applicable) can be retracked, so long as the drums work in the new key. I'd say ninety-nine times out of a hundred the drums work fine, so long as there is no bleed from the other instruments. Let me repeat that last sentence: so long as there is no bleed from the other instruments.

If retracking isn't an option, the singer can try again another day, preferably on a day that he can hit the notes with relative ease. *Or* Willy could have him sing several takes of another song to really try to loosen up the vocal cords and then attempt the song that's too high again.

If our goal was to continue recording, it seemed our only viable option was to slow down the tape, and that's just what we did. But Johnny was getting frustrated and couldn't sing the song at the new tempo. So Willy went into the lounge and grabbed Yore's bottle of Maker's Mark whisky. I guess Willy figured he might get a take if Johnny got liquored up.

Since Johnny Rhythm didn't like singing to the song slowed down, we put the song back to its original tempo and pitch. Johnny pounded two full shots of Maker's Mark straight away and sang down a take. Between each of the first three takes, Johnny took another shot of whiskey, which made five shots in less than half an hour. I'm not sure that's what Willy had in mind, because not only was Johnny getting blasted, he still wasn't hitting the high notes, and he was beginning to slur his speech even in song. After the fourth take, Johnny pounded another shot and promptly pronounced that he needed to puke, so I quickly escorted him to Fingaz's bathroom, where he commenced a short prayer to the porcelain God. Fingaz crossed his arms over his chest and turned toward me.

"Oh, c'mon, Yo!" he exclaimed. "Dat shit gonna smell!!" he continued as he reached to cover his nose with his shirt. And it did smell.

Johnny Lush went to sleep it off on the couch, and Willy listened to the vocal takes. Before I went home, Willy decided that we would need to re-lay bass and guitars on this song, as the song was without question in too high a key. I pointed out to Willy that the whole band played in the same room, and with the drum bleed, changing the key of the song wasn't really an option. Willy made the only decision he could under the circumstances. We were to retrack the song in its entirety tomorrow.

I must be getting used to the idea of taking two steps back for every one step we take forward, because no matter how great today's setbacks may have been, I could take great solace in the fact that we had accomplished what I had hoped for more than anything else.

We had a plan.

– Mixerman

DAY 20

Marv Ellis

POSTED: AUGUST 23, 11:16 P.M.

Johnny Swerve was arrested for driving under the influence last night. Apparently, no one considered the fact that when Johnny woke up, he might drive home. But that's exactly what happened. Johnny had spent the night in a cell with a blood alcohol level of 0.1, which is two points over the limit in California. DUI is a serious offense anywhere, but in L.A., the penalties are phenomenally stiff. This could easily cost him between $5,000 and $10,000 when all is said and done. Willy was markedly distressed at this news, and you could tell he felt bad. I suspect Willy's going to be helping Johnny out with the costs of that bad play.

As far as recording goes, there was nothing unusual about today. Willy wanted to record with the instruments isolated again, so we moved the amps into the iso booths once again, and the band played with headphones. Lance and I readjusted the drums back to the setup that we used for "Song in Wrong Key." We referred to Lance's notes, which were beginning to look like a calculus lesson with his three-dimensional drawings and measurements of mic positions in relation to the drums. Dumb Ass continued to play without a clik. With preparations complete we retracked "Song in Wrong Key."

Fingaz, who had completed all of his work, was preparing for a weekend trip to Vegas by reading a self-help blackjack handbook. He was attempting to memorize when to hit, split, and double down, but he must not have had a very good memory, because I saw him split fives. What an idiot. I don't expect he'll be counting through five decks of cards anytime soon.

We spent until just before evening recording, and then Willy called a dinner break. The band eats atrociously, and neither Willy nor I can ever eat with them, as we don't like eating fast food on a daily basis. Conversely, the entire band wouldn't be caught dead eating raw fish, and I'm quite sure that I've never seen any of them actually eat a salad.

Willy perused the menu book and then dramatically slammed it shut with a *whack*. Willy looked at me, and by the grin on his face, along with the up-and-down motion of his eyebrows, I understood the meaning of this action.

It was sushi time!

I suppose the others had gone to KFC or something unappealing like that, while Willy and I took off for our sushi dinner, which was, without a doubt, the most enlightening sushi dinner I've ever had.

On the way to the sushi restaurant, Willy got a call in his car. Willy answered the call on speakerphone, holding his index finger sideways to his lips as he did so. On the other end was Marv Ellis, the president of the label, and the person who had agreed to pay Bitch Slap two million dollars to not make a record for over two years. Willy immediately asked Marv if he'd eaten, and before I knew it, we were on our way to meet Marv Ellis for sushi.

I've met plenty of record label presidents, although I'd never met Marv. I'd only known him by reputation. Record company presidents come up from all aspects of the business. I've seen Bean Counter Presidents, Promotion Department Presidents, A&R Department Presidents, MBA Presidents, Street Presidents, Gangster Presidents, and the newest fad, Producer Presidents. The side of the business that a president comes from often determines how he will run the label.

When a new president takes over a major label, speculation runs rampant about whether he's qualified to be the president of a corporation. The record industry doomsayers, who often run amok on the industry's Internet bulletin board called The Velvet Rope, usually hypothesize that a new president doesn't know how to run a business, or doesn't know music, or any one of a multitude of shortcomings that would make being a president a very temporary position. I suppose the speculation is usually correct, because other than a few standbys, most record company presidents are *exactly* that—temporary.

Personally, I couldn't care less about all of that. It's not like the president has any kind of power over what his employees do, because he doesn't. Many, many times, I have seen a president's signing get the cold shoulder by the A&R department or the marketing department, or worst of all, the radio department. The employees don't give a shit what the president wants. The employees in power positions do what *they* want. Sure, they provide plenty of lip service for the president, but when push comes to shove, one makes a name for himself in this business by discovering a hit act and then following it up with another. It's referred to as the Golden Touch, and if you are perceived to have the Touch, you will be the big winner in this business. In reality, the president is actually competing with many of his employees. The employees will undercut the president with their own agendas and then report back to him as if they gave it the old college try.

I'm sure that some presidents are able to thwart these sorts of attempts. I only know what I see, and I'm certainly not privy to the large majority of the inner workings of every major label. It's not my area of expertise. Perhaps it was different for Marv Ellis. If anyone commands respect, I'm sure Marv does. Perhaps he is immune to these sorts of political backstabbings that often occur within labels.

When we arrived at the sushi bar, Marv had not arrived yet, but there were three places reserved at the sushi bar, which was otherwise full. I have never seen spots reserved at a sushi bar. In a town of world-famous movie stars, record executives are generally considered small-time. I had to assume that Marv ate here on a daily basis to get such treatment. Either that or we lucked out. Judging by the pissed-off couple in the corner waiting for the bar, my guess would be against that of luck.

Willy and I didn't have to wait long, as Marv arrived only a minute behind us. He was an average-height guy, with an average build. He wore clothes that looked pretty casual but probably cost a fortune. A pair of jeans in this town can cost more than most Americans' suits, and I was pretty sure that this was the case here. We all sat down, and Marv told us not to bother ordering, because his chef would supply us with everything we needed. And the chef did, too. This place rocked!

The dinner was amazing, and Marv Ellis was very personable. He was sharing war stories with us about how he got to his position, as we plowed through many small vials of very expensive cold sake. Marv wanted to know *my* story, so I told him how I started out and the bullet points of my career. As the conversation progressed, the three of us got into philosophies of making records, and we spoke about the business and the future of the record industry.

Willy and Marv were obviously pretty buddy-buddy. It didn't take me long to realize that this was why Willy didn't give a shit about Jeramiah. This is the president's project, and Jeramiah is basically, as I stated earlier, just a minion with a very strong opinion.

As we were finishing our dinner, Marv Ellis finally asked what, frankly, I'd been waiting the whole night for him to ask. Were it me, this would have been my *first* question of the evening. But this guy went through a whole dinner before even mentioning it.

"So how's the project going, Willy?" Marv asked.

"It's going a little slower than I expected," Willy conceded. "I'm having problems because the drummer's not very good, and the band's resisting outside help. I've got a drummer lined up for next month," Willy continued, as I almost choked on my orange, which is what one typically eats for dessert at a sushi restaurant.

"Look, Willy. I don't care what you have to do. This band is my top priority. As far as I'm concerned, you have a blank check. If you need a year, then take a year. I don't give a fucking shit. Just bring me a record I can sell. Okay?"

The two hugged, and as Marv Ellis turned to shake my hand, he looked at Willy again.

"I have a feeling this guy is going to add a lot to this project. Make sure he stays on," Marv said to Willy as he hit me on the side of my upper arm and smiled. Then he got into his car that was waiting with the valet, and he drove off.

I stood there flabbergasted. Was this like some sort of joke? Was there a hidden camera?

I've heard of situations like this with virtually unlimited budgets. There's one very famous rock band from the early nineties that's been recording an album for the past few years with several different producers. But *that* is an established band. Bitch Slap is a bunch of miserable nobodies who were forced to write songs for two years.

I followed Willy like a zombie to his car, and he drove me back to the studio. He told me not to mention anything about the drummer—as if I needed to be told that! As he was filling me in on the importance of discretion, which I found nothing short of ironic given this online accounting of my days, the phone rang in Willy's car again, and he answered it on speaker. It was Marv, who spoke without introduction.

"Willy, do me a favor will ya? Let Jeramiah come by the sessions. He's driving me fucking crazy."

Willy agreed to let Jeramiah visit. When we arrived at the studio again, the band had split, and Willy called it a night.

I drove home carefully, wanting to avoid the possibility of a DUI myself. As I drove, my mind was racing with all the possibilities. Could I be on this project for a year? It's unfathomable to me, the possibility of working with this asshole band for a year. Then I would convince myself that it won't *actually* take a year. Marv was merely assuring Willy that he didn't have to worry about a budget—not for Willy to take a year to make an album. I was thinking about the opportunity (or curse) of recording a band with an unlimited budget. It's a well-known principle that you always spend up to your budget. So if there is no budget, what do you spend? Will we start recording guitar chords one string at a time? Will we record the same album three times?

Sure, the loot is good, but a year of twelve-hour days? I usually work a few months and take a month off. I would have no time off. I would be out of commission for mixing, which pays considerably more than tracking. Were I to somehow get myself out of this gig, I could actually work less and make more money. But that's always a gamble, because in this business, there are no guarantees. I could hit a dry spell and be kicking myself for not having kept the Bitch Slap gig. Of course, being out of commission by virtue of being stuck on a project for an entire year (assuming it went that long) is also incredibly risky. All of my current clients will have found new engineers to work with. It could become very difficult to get work after being on a project for that long.

Then my thoughts turned to the Dumb Ass situation. We've been recording him for weeks. Now I come to find out that Willy has another drummer scheduled to come in and lay down tracks on this album? How long has that plan been in effect? Has Willy known since day one, and so we've been doing nothing but biding time?

My head was swimming and still is swimming with all of these thoughts. I've got an offer to do another record right after the AES (Audio Engineering Society) convention in October. Do I turn that down? I'll have to make a decision on that by early next week.

Then there was that dinner. I mean, I consider myself a swell guy and everything, but there was something strange about that dinner. What about "the question?" This is the most important project on Marv's plate, and he saves asking how the project is going for last? The stream of questions and concerns running through my head are relentless and endless.

Not that any of this really matters right now. At this particular juncture, there's really only one thing that I can do that has even a chance of making any difference at all.

Crash.

– Mixerman

DAY 21
Film at 11

POSTED: AUGUST 27, 1:19 A.M. — WEEK 5

My first thought of the day, after realizing that I was going to have to go to another Bitch Slap session, was, *Why* am I going to another Bitch Slap session today? I was trying to explain to myself precisely for what purpose we would be recording today. It has now been established (to me anyway) that we will not be keeping any of Cotton's drums. Both Willy and I know that a new, yet to be named, drummer will be laying down these drum tracks. Did Willy think that we were going to record the music and then lay the drums to the preexisting music? I've done that before, and in my experience that methodology is, at best, a hit-or-miss proposition, so long as there's a clik. In *this* case there was no clik, and to lay down a decent drum performance over an existing track with no clik is exceptionally difficult to do well.

Perhaps our purpose in recording today was in order to further propagate the myth that Dumb Ass was actually being given a chance to prove himself before he was shit-canned. Perhaps it was to give Willy enough ammunition to convince the band that

Dumb Ass sucked ass. I looked at the situation from every angle and nothing made sense to me. Logically speaking, there was absolutely no reason for me to be at a Bitch Slap session today. But logic has nothing to do with a Bitch Slap session, so I certainly couldn't rely on that. Being a willing participant in the madness, I went to my session.

When I arrived at the studio, two huge plain white trucks and a generator were crowding the lot. This configuration of vehicles could only mean one thing.

"They must be filming in the other room," I said to myself out loud. Then I saw what appeared to be a temporary makeshift valet station, so I pulled up to it and handed my car keys over to a small Latino man in a red coat. He could have easily been a con man, preying on people in a hurry, but I gave him my keys just the same.

From the generator came a bundle of cables that were now holding ajar the main entrance to the building. I figured the heavy lines would be heading toward the other room in the facility, but they weren't. The cables ran down the hall toward the Bitch Slap session. All I could think to myself was, Please don't let this be for my session, please don't let this be for my session. Of *course* this wasn't for my session! I considered for a moment that this might be some sort of news-related event. Perhaps a recurring daydream of mine, in which Yore chokes the shit out of Dumb Ass, actually happened. But the trucks had no television affiliate markings, and there were no police or ambulances, so that couldn't be it.

I was passed by a burly fellow carrying camera tracks toward the Womb. Determined to put an end to the speculation, I attempted to stop the man.

"What are you guys filming?" I asked.

"Fuck if I know," the burly man responded. "I stopped keeping track years ago," he continued as he kept walking.

I accelerated my little mantra, as if I were the little engine that could. Please don't let this be for my session, please don't let this be for my session.

I followed the cable straight into the Womb, which was now infested with strangers setting up cameras, lights, cables, and tracks. The tracks and the cabling ran right through the control room through a double door air lock that just days ago provided safe haven and isolation from very loud drums and guitars.

MOTHERFUCKER!!!!!

I searched through the many strangers now infesting both the Womb and the room, in the hopes of finding Lance, but he was nowhere to be found. I picked up the phone and called the front desk.

"Find. Lance. Now!" I said, as if I were saying three distinct sentences.

"Okay," the voice quivered.

Then I decided I'd better go into the room and make sure my mics weren't being touched. As I entered, I realized that I was being followed by a tall, skinny dude with pants that were entirely too slim in the pant leg to be fashionable, carrying a camera on his shoulders.

"What do you think you're doing?" I asked, imagining that I must have looked like some dude who'd gotten busted by *60 Minutes*. The guy didn't respond; he just kept the camera focused on me. I kept on walking, and the skinny camera dude continued to follow me.

Okay, fine.

"Who's in charge?" I asked a guy who was setting up the tracks to weave through the Apartments we had set up in the room.

"Fuck if I know," the guy responded, and upon closer inspection I saw it was my new burly acquaintance whom I had met moments earlier in the hall. I felt like I was in a bad cartoon. Then Dumb Ass walked in, and I *really* felt like I was in a bad cartoon.

"You wouldn't happen to know what the fuck is going on here, would you?" I asked Dumb Ass, abandoning the usual exchange of niceties that occur before such statements.

"I think they're going to film the session," Dumb Ass replied, in his usual insightful manner. To which I raised my hands in disgust, as that was exactly the answer I *should* have expected from Dumb Ass. So I responded in song.

"*Yes!* But *what* are they filming, dear Henry, dear Henry, but *what* are they filming, dear Henry, but *what*?!" I sang to a melody that I remembered from decades ago in a skit on *Sesame Street*.

I was without a doubt becoming unglued where Dumb Ass was concerned. I was beginning to behave like Lieutenant Dreyfus who was literally driven mad by Inspector Clouseau in one of the *Pink Panther* sequels.

"My name's not Henry," replied Dumb Ass, who was now reaching new heights of stupidity.

As I turned to walk out of the room, I almost hit my face on the camera that the skinny dude was carrying. I stood there staring at him with my arms crossed and a look that could kill. Then I saw the formation of a tiny little smirk on his face.

I considered my options. I could threaten him bodily harm, but if he called my bluff, I'd be loath to actually do anything to him, as he would have actual proof that I attacked him. I considered the old Pied Piper trick of luring him outside and then, when his guard was down, running back in, closing the door and locking it. But that would only serve as a temporary fix, as people were constantly coming and going. As I pondered my options, through the control room window I saw Fingaz walking through to his shitter. In my mind I could smell the urine that I had sprayed on his parka just days before. I even think I could see the little stain from my position some forty feet away.

"If you don't turn off the camera and get away from me, I'm going to pee on your shoes, and if you don't believe that I will, just ask the guy with the pee-stained parka in there," I said pointing toward the control room and looking the skinny dude straight in the camera with an expression that would have easily won me a large pot in the World Series of Poker.

Wisely, he decided to put the camera down, and *finally*, I spotted Lance in the control room, so I went there.

"What the fuck is going on, and who's in charge?" I asked Lance, who was looking mildly uncomfortable as he looked past me in an odd sort of way.

A familiar voice came from behind me. "That would be me," the voice said.

No!

It was Jeramiah! I have met Jeramiah Weasel many times before, so I knew his voice. As I turned to face him, I couldn't help but think to myself that he was not a particularly handsome fellow. He stood there sipping his Starbucks Venti double soy mocha latte, with his supposedly stylish greasy hair, chicken pox scars, and a schnoz I could park a car in. Upon his nose he balanced a pair of lime-green, tinted sunglasses, which he wore regardless of the fact that he was inside. He wore blue jeans that were most likely purchased at Fred Segal, (one of the more expensive places to purchase blue jeans) and a Dixie Beer T-shirt, which I could only assume was some sort of collector's item.

"Hello, Jeramiah," I said, taken aback that he was in the Womb. Then I went to shake his hand, not the least bit embarrassed by what he had overheard me say, as it was a perfectly legitimate question.

I explained to Jeramiah that no one had informed me of the film shoot, that I couldn't find anyone in the film crew who knew what the hell was going on, and that there were some definite problems with the way things had been set up. I went into detail about the problems with tracks going through isolation doors, and bright lights making the tracking room so hot that the air-conditioning wouldn't be able to keep up, and the need to threaten camera men who wouldn't get out of my face. Jeramiah listened to every word without interrupting. Of course, much of it went in one ear and out the other.

"Well, you guys are just going to have to work around it," Jeramiah said, peering over his sunglasses with no empathy for my situation whatsoever.

"I see," I said, attempting to restrain myself. "Do you know how long they'll be here?" I asked as politely as one can after being snubbed so blatantly.

"As long as it takes," replied Jeramiah.

Great! Having Jeramiah on this session was going to be about as welcome as a case of the clap. I excused myself for my chocolate muffin of the day, but as I made my way down the hall, I ran into Willy, who was carrying two muffins, one in each hand. He was looking down at the cables and following them, much like I had when I first arrived. Willy spotted me and handed over one of the muffins without saying a word as he continued following the cables to the Womb. Jeramiah stood in the exact spot I'd left him, still sipping his latte and peering over his eyeglasses.

Willy looked at Jeramiah and then looked at the tracks that ran through the isolation doors, which once allowed us to monitor instruments through speakers, rather than through open doors. This made about as much sense as opening all the windows in the middle of winter and cranking up the furnace. Willy entered the Womb, stepping over the tracks, and sat down, still not saying a word as he pulled out a fatty. Once seated, Willy sparked up the fatty, dragged upon it, and swiveled his chair so as to look squarely at Jeramiah.

"Filming, are we?" Willy said.

The verbal thrashing and name-calling that transpired after this initial question was too personal and possibly too salty even for this diary. Willy, suffice it to say, was not ecstatic about the film crew being there and displayed considerably less elation at Jeramiah's presence. I've never seen a producer tear an A&R rep a new asshole as readily as Willy did Jeramiah. But given Willy's relationship with Marv Ellis, and given that Jeramiah "is the most miserable shit to ever walk the planet" (according to Willy) and was "nothing short of a figurehead" where Bitch Slap was concerned, it was certainly understandable.

Willy attempted to call Marv's office, but apparently Marv would be in Europe for the next two weeks and unavailable other than for absolute emergencies. I suppose Marv's secretary felt this situation didn't qualify.

Even with the reaming, Jeramiah was unfazed. He had no intention of removing the crew, and I'm not sure if Willy had any authority to actually remove the crew himself. So now it was merely a case of negotiation.

Fortunately, Willy did successfully convince Jeramiah that the cables and tracks couldn't go through our isolation doors, and that the lights could only be turned on when the crew were actually filming. The biggest point of contention in our negotiations was having the cameras in the control room. I didn't want cameras in the Womb for any reason. But Jeramiah was adamant.

Apparently, Jeramiah had hired a director and film crew to make a documentary of the Bitch Slap sessions. Jeramiah went on and on about the importance of "capturing what goes on in the trenches" for his documentary. To which I could only think to myself, Document what? Does he really think that anyone wants a documentary about a band that's been in the studio for twenty-one days and hasn't gotten shit done?

Ahem.

We didn't do any recording today, as the film crew was in need of its own setup day. They still hadn't cleared the iso doors by the time I left (which was early), but they promised they'd have them unobstructed by tomorrow. I'm not sure we ever came to an agreement regarding filming inside the Womb, and tomorrow we were to start recording each song with a film crew present at all times—the ramifications of which did not escape me. For every conversation, every slipped fart, every insult cast out of range of its intended mark would be captured on film.

That gig in October is starting to look better and better.

– Mixerman

DAY 22
Show Time

POSTED: AUGUST 28, 2:18 A.M.

Since there was no way around the fact that I was going to be on film, I decided I should at the very least dress for the occasion. I considered a variety of different looks, including the slovenly engineer complete with stained and holey concert T-shirt, stained jeans that were too big in the rear, much like plumbers enjoy wearing, and bright red canvas Keds sneakers. While I found the boldness of such an outfit inviting, I was concerned that people might misconstrue the intended satire of my garb.

Another concept was the well-dressed, suave, white-collar stylized engineer—complete with mint-condition Levi's Red Tag Jeans, my best Donna Karen sports jacket over a Wilke Rodriguez button-down shirt, finished with a polished black leather Hugo Boss belt and slip-on leather shoes from Italy that I fear might actually be from Ireland. Still, I liked the shoes. While this outfit was also appealing, I was afraid that Johnny might faint at the sight of my vintage jeans, or worse yet, try to steal them somehow. I also considered that my shoes might become a point of discussion causing great embarrassment, so I abandoned that ensemble. After debating for some time the exact look that would be best for appearing in a film, I settled on something familiar.

I decided to wear a god-awful Hawaiian button-down shirt for my film debut, as that is what Ed Cherney[44] wore for his cameo on the *Bette Midler Show*. I know, because I watched it. After all, I figured that was just the way engineers dressed for this sort of occasion. Who was I to argue with success? Of course, the Bette Midler Show didn't last long, but I really don't think that had anything whatsoever to do with Ed's shirt.

It seems I was the only person treating this filming as a farce, but I wasn't the only person to select my look carefully. Dumb Ass was looking *very* cliché, wearing shorts and no shirt. Harmon Neenot was the sharp-dressed man with a very nice pair of black dress pants, black leather shoes, and a black dress shirt unbuttoned and untucked over a bloodred T-shirt. Paulie Yore wore a Nirvana concert T-shirt and a pair of stonewashed jeans that I suspect he wore just to piss off Johnny, who has proven himself to be nothing more than a jeans snob.

Johnny was dressed in circa 1955 Levi's 501 jeans, which he claimed were not reissues, but the original jeans recently discovered in a large time capsule of a warehouse. His jeans were perfectly pressed without a crease down the leg, never washed, and never shrunk. If he even stood next to a glass of water, he'd get nervous. On his torso he wore what was a modern modification on the short-sleeved polo shirt. The shirt was made out of polyester and viscose (I checked, and, no, I have no clue what viscose is) and is designed to be worn two sizes too small. Johnny Buff suddenly looked as though he had large muscles with this shirt on, which I assumed was the intended result.

For all I know, Willy was wearing a silk robe, because he didn't even show up today. Perhaps he's boycotting the session. I couldn't say I blame him—I considered doing the same.

Seeing as the film crew was in full effect, the lights were blazing, and I was being followed by men with cameras recording my every deliberate move, I decided to play up to the part.

When I arrived at the studio, the band was already there. I had never seen them so pumped up to record. Dumb Ass wanted to start with a particular song and had actually selected the drums and everything. I was floored, as he was usually asking *me* to select his drums for him. Yore had brought in a guitar tech to change out his strings and intonate the guitars. Johnny was warming up, as if we were actually going to keep vocals that had excessive amounts of drum bleed on them. Harmon Neenot was warming up by playing classic Yes bass lines from the album *Fragile*. Chris Squire he was not.

When I walked into the room, Lance started laughing at my shirt, but fuck him, this was the shirt that engineers wore on film shoots! Although, I must admit, the humor in that was only apparent to those who saw that particular episode of the *Bette Midler Show*. Considering the show had been canceled, and considering I felt like an idiot in a Hawaiian shirt, I decided to consider another look for tomorrow.

Figuring that Willy would make an appearance sooner or later, and not wanting to appear on camera as if we sit around all day and get nothing accomplished, I decided to get the ball rolling. Dumb Ass was in the room and on the throne.

"*Kik*," I yelled into the talkback with authority and zeal. I was going to play the part of an engineer who could quickly fire through every instrument, further propagating the common myth that engineering is done in the control room.

"What?" Dumb Ass replied.

So I smiled for the camera.

"*Kik!*" I repeated through the talkback, while smiling for the camera.

"What about it?" Dumb Ass yelled out.

He was ruining my little scene.

"Play the *kik*," I said patiently.

"What for?" Dumb Ass replied.

I swear to God, this guy could fuck up a wet dream. My scene in which I get drum sounds in less than three minutes flat, like some Greek god–like engineer, came to a screeching halt. I was looking to perpetuate the image that this was a well-run session, and he was intent on keeping it real. And real is what the cameramen captured as I went around the same stupid-ass conversation I always have with Dumb Ass where getting drum sounds was concerned—all caught on digital film for the world to see one day. With that thought, I was beginning to regret my decision to wear a Hawaiian shirt, regardless of the precedent that had been set before me.

Once I finally assimilated Dumb Ass to the groundbreaking concept of checking drum sounds before making takes, I was able to proceed with that process and thereby temporarily leave behind the awkwardness and self-consciousness that had been plaguing me. After getting sounds for the whole band, I had them make a take.

For a band that typically sucked ass, they were displaying an actual ability to *play*. If I didn't know better, I'd say they were playing close to—dare I say it—great. Dumb Ass was finally laying into the drums with some authority, and he wasn't forgetting his cues. A few times I caught him twirling his sticks and even saw him throw a stick into the air once. Of course, he dropped it. Harmon was grooving like mad in his duds. Paulie Yore was doing windmills and goofing on Pete Townshend's two-legged hop move. He was laughing hysterically, as if Pete Townshend were somehow "cheese" (as Yore puts it). To date, I can't really recall ever having seen Yore laugh. For that matter, I can't recall ever meeting anyone who thought Pete Townshend was cheese.

As the band was making takes, I sat at the console and bopped my head around, as if I were thoroughly enjoying the playing. Occasionally, I'd get up and dance around a little, as Lance danced through my little area between the console and the counter, pretending to write down notes and enjoy himself. Even Fingaz was getting into the act, wearing his parka and dancing all hip-hop to rock tunes. At one point he disconnected the Radar controller and brought it into the control room. He began frantically hitting buttons, pretending to be editing and yelling like a mofo—"Aw shit! That's it, baby! Now we got dat bad boy down, Wiggah!"

Between takes, I would talk to the band, telling them things like, "You're on fire!" and giving them advice like, "Make it a bit more steamy in the bridge!" and "The last chorus is a bit flat— sharpen it up!" I even threw in the obligatory "It needs to be more green! Give me green!" The band looked at me strangely and said nothing. I was starting to regret my miserable little satire caught on film, and I now realize that this was a mistake. As much as I thought it would be funny for me to *play* the caricature of an engineer on a rock session, I had finally realized that I already *was* that caricature of an engineer on a rock session. And so my act was similar to feeding a pig pig. Not a good idea.

Since I could no longer enjoy myself with my new revelation that my life had been reduced to nothing short of trite, I decided to confess to Fingaz on camera that I might have gotten a little bit of pee on his parka. To add insult to injury, I explained to him that he was starting to smell a bit like urine and that it was becoming a bit of a problem. He just stared at me with a look that could kill, and I was doing everything in my power not to laugh.

"Aw man, why you be tellin' me this now?" he blurted.

Fingaz picked up his Radar controller and took it to the shitter. I followed him and begged for forgiveness, as I realized that my goofing around had gone overboard. After all, I'm only human—I make mistakes just like anyone and feel badly about them afterwards. I even offered a public apology to Fingaz on camera for the whole world to hear.

"I want everyone to know that I did not actually pee on Fingaz's parka. A parka with pee on it subjected to ninety-five-degree weather would start to stink like hell. I am here to tell you that his parka smells wonderful, and I will prove it to you now," I said to the camera in my staged apology. Then I took a deep breath from his parka and fell to the ground, as if I had passed out from the smell. For the first time since his arrival, I had discovered humor that even Fingaz could relate to, as he started laughing at my slapstick antics.

"You a freak, Yo," Fingaz said, laughing and pointing at me like I was a chimp taking a shit at the zoo.

There was no way around it. Cameras are no different from strangers in the studio. I can't actually feel comfortable about myself when there is someone present who has nothing to do with the session. Even if I could get past the actual person holding the camera, the thought that someone might one day watch this footage and judge my actions was just too weird for me. There is no question about it—I *hate* cameras in the Womb.

The director, whom I've dubbed Haired Director, was so uptight he could shit a diamond. He was not in the least bit pleased with my behavior. I believe he called Jeramiah Weasel on more than one occasion, but Jeramiah didn't bother to come by today, which I can't for the life of me figure out. This was his shindig, and he wasn't making an appearance? Haired Director was vibing me out, as if I were somehow ruining his production. One small part of me desperately wanted Haired Director to actually come right out and *tell* me that I was ruining his production so that I might have the opportunity to point out that he was in fact fucking up *our* production. Furthermore, if we make a record that has no chance of selling, he can be assured to have directed a documentary with no chance of selling. The film crew was the intruder here—not me. I'm trying to make a record. If it makes the band play better, then great, I'm all for it. But personally, I would be content to be out of it.

As far as recording was concerned (the unfortunate subplot of this debacle), we actually recorded three songs today. I didn't spend excessive amounts of time trying to dial in the exact sound. That's not to say I sloughed it off. Quite the contrary: I am very happy with the sounds we got today. Sometimes working on a guttural basis and not overthinking every decision is a very effective way of recording. It's actually my most preferred way of recording. Unfortunately, it's the least-used method of recording these days.

The way I figure it, the cameras are there to capture Dumb Ass's footage more than anything else. Since he was on his way out, this was their only opportunity to get shots of *him* playing, as opposed to the ghost[45] drummer they would likely bring in.

My feeling is this—if the band is going to play as well as they did today, then I'm all for the cameras. As far as the actual recordings are concerned, their presence has been positive. I suspect once the band gets used to the cameras, the playing will go downhill again, but for now, at least we were making progress. Not that it matters.

We're just biding our time.

– Mixerman

Audio Placebo

POSTED: AUGUST 29, 2:25 A.M.

Having learned my lesson on how *not* to act during a filming session, I decided to wear my normal studio clothes, which were basically jeans and a T-shirt. I typically bring a sweatshirt for when the air-conditioning becomes a bit overbearing. Of course, with all the film equipment in the control room, the sweatshirt was nothing short of superfluous. Between a large-frame console, enormous lights, massive amounts of outboard gear, and excessive bodies, the room never got below eighty-five degrees Fahrenheit.

I called Willy this morning to make sure that he would be coming today. He assured me that he would, but that he might be late. As usual, I filled him in on our progress. I told him of the band's newfound energy owing to the presence of cameras. He was obviously pleased with this news, but his pleasure was displayed only briefly, as he had important information to dispense. Willy began to warn me that Jeramiah would be coming today, and that I was not to change *anything* based on his recommendations.

Great! I thought to myself, another political hornet's nest. Just what I needed with cameras rolling.

Willy obviously had some inside information, because not only did Jeramiah show up, he was there before me. The second part of Willy's prediction came true just minutes after the session began. It seems Jeramiah was uncomfortable with my recording drums to just six tracks.

"That's two tracks too many," I replied, hoping he would drop it at that.

Then he began to tell me about how the "world-renowned" mixer Sir Arthur Conan Mixallot has become upset with him upon receiving so few drum tracks.

"Do the drums sound good to you?" I asked innocently.

"Well, yeah, I just think there should be more tracks," he replied, ignoring the logic that I had set forth in my question. I tried to just ignore his objections, but Jeramiah was a Mook's Mook, and he wasn't going to drop the subject. I tried to educate him, but he felt that Sir Arthur's opinion outranked mine. The expression of that sentiment did nothing toward his cause.

"Are you saying that Sir Arthur doesn't know what he's talking about? He *is* a highly respected engineer!" he replied, and so I abandoned that tack.

To discuss this subject further would only prove to be a complete waste of time. Jeramiah was being filmed, and he was not to be denied. Willy had warned me not to change anything. Even without such warning, I wouldn't likely change the way I had everything set up just to appease some A&R Mook's concerns that a mixer might be upset at having his hands tied later. After all, tying hands was my intention. Seeing as Jeramiah was pressing me so hard to change the drums, I had no choice but to give Jeramiah an audio placebo.

Jeramiah wanted twelve drum tracks, and I was printing six drum tracks. I didn't require an abacus to figure out that if I bussed[46] the identical set of drum mics to the next six tracks in line, I'd then have a full twelve tracks of drums. This exercise does nothing to change the sound of the drums. Two identical recorded signals summed together reproduce identically, save for a three-decibel jump in level. In other words, recording the identical six tracks of drums twice was nothing short of superfluous. All I was actually doing was making the drums louder. As far as Jeramiah was concerned, when I opened the other six tracks, the drums sounded much stronger, which they did, because they were louder.

Unfortunately, by appeasing Jeramiah, I'd allowed him to believe he could just push me around. So Jeramiah began to pick on other things that he felt weren't right. He felt that the snare drum really needed to "soar" more. I could tell that Jeramiah was a very persistent lad, and what he wanted, he was going to get. So I ripped a small piece of whiteboard tape that we use for labeling gear, and I wrote on it, "snare," and then I wrote, "soar," on another piece of tape. I carefully placed the "snare" label on an unused Pultec (the thirty-five-year-old analog EQ that I used on the drums), as that particular piece of equipment has very large knobs. The implementation of an audio placebo works best when done with large knobs, because the person being duped really feels that he's making a difference. Pultecs are also great for this because they have plenty of room for labeling, so I put the "soar" label directly above one of the large knobs.

"Turn this knob slowly—make *sure* you turn it slowly, because if you add too much soar, you could blow out my speakers," I told him as if I were telling a ghost story at a campfire.

"That's the soar knob?" he asked excitedly.

No, Jeramiah, it only becomes a sore knob if you play with it too much, I thought to myself. Unfortunately, had I answered in this manner my ruse would have been over before it began, as he surely would have concluded that I had set him up purely for that line.

"Yes, if you turn that knob, the snare will soar," I answered. "But for God's sake, be careful!" I exclaimed.

"How does it work?" he asked.

At this particular question, I was momentarily taken aback. How does the soar knob work? Was he looking for a detailed technical explanation that he wouldn't understand as to why the knob works? I considered saying that it worked through the power of suggestion, but that would also have given away the ruse. So I told him how it worked.

"It sends a harmonized signal through the flux capacitor chamber, which is then blended back in to the original signal using a time stretch mechanism," I explained, pulling from my genetically passed-on ability to spew phenomenal amounts of bullshit on the spot and actually sound credible.

"Whoa!" Jeramiah exclaimed, in awe of my expertise in such things.

And so Jeramiah ever so carefully toyed with his soar knob. I'd be surprised if he actually turned the knob more than a millimeter at a time. With each millimeter, I could see the expression on his face change at the obvious results. He kept adding the tiniest

215

amount of soar at a time, until such time that he realized he had added too much, and he backed it down a notch. When he had settled on just the right amount of "soar," he smiled, as if he could hear a difference. And I nodded enthusiastically.

"You know what?" I said, acting shocked and simultaneously impressed, "I thought it had enough soar, but it's better now. You really have good ears!"

Lance, being privy to the entire episode of audio placebo, concluded that he deserved to be in on the fun. "I think you should add 'thump' to the kik drum," he interjected. So I made a "thump" label.

This sort of fun went on for the better part of an hour. As Jeramiah continued to turn knobs, he was obviously convinced that he was actually making a difference. There was an abundance of handwritten labels scattered over the knobs of unconnected gear. I was running out of knobs as the control room began to look like an elementary classroom with words taped up everywhere. Words such as "sheen," "warmth," "crack," "heat," "brass"—don't ask me, Jeramiah wanted the guitar to sound more "brass." Who am I to disagree?

Finally, Willy arrived, and he immediately began scanning the gear rack. The band was playing a take, and Jeramiah was standing in front of the console with this smug little grin on his face, as if he'd actually made a difference. Willy began to further inspect all of the labels, and I grew concerned that he might blow the gag.

"Jeramiah made some improvements to my sounds," I said. "Do you like how the snare soars now?" I said, as I pointed to the "soar" label on the Pultec.

Willy looked at me and smiled.

"I think it's soaring a bit too much," he replied as he reached to tone it down a notch.

Jeramiah questioned the validity of such an adjustment and expressed a slight concern with making such a move in the middle of a take. But Willy insisted it would be fine and that he'd only moved the knob a little.

"But the tiniest adjustment on that knob makes a *big* difference!" Jeramiah professed.

I kid you not.

Willy was obviously very pleased with the results. He listened as he smoked a fatty, at one point slightly confused at my double tracking of the drums. He looked at me in his confusion, and I shook my head as I rolled my eyes in the direction of Jeramiah. Willy caught my meaning and said nothing of it. He felt the drum playing had improved enormously, which it had. So much so that Willy was now prepared to abandon the ghost drummer concept. I warned him that we'd better keep the cameras here, and that we'd better get down the songs as quickly as possible before Dumb Ass turns to shit again. He concurred.

We recorded another three songs today. Fingaz was editing the first three very lightly, mostly by taking sections of the songs and cutting them together. We now have six songs in the bag and in which the drums are pretty good, certainly acceptable. We would likely fire through another three tomorrow (knock on wood). There is a total of seventeen songs to record, which in my opinion is seven too many, given the process of recording this band so far.

Even with the progress that we were making, I still have to make a decision on my October session. I was only booked on this session for two months' time, and that is the full extent of my commitment. If the record goes over the allotted time budget and I'm booked, then it is bad planning on their part. I should not be expected to leave my schedule open-ended in order to accommodate lack of efficiency. Leaving is not a problem. I won't get a rep as a quitter, as I will have accomplished what I was contracted for. Typically, I prefer to see a project through. It's better for the continuity of the project and it's often better for me. I prefer to stay on a project as long as possible, because I might very well get the opportunity to mix it, seeing as I have the track record for that. If I leave now, I'm guaranteed *not* to mix it.

As much as this diary has been a great outlet, I cannot make a decision to continue with the most dysfunctional gig in my career purely for the opportunity to document it. To further complicate matters, I am highly suspicious that this journal may be getting into the wrong hands. While many have predicted the likely end of my career with such brash disregard for the sanctity of a private session, the pundits have failed to take one fact into account.

There's no such thing as bad press.

– Mixerman

DAY 24

On Strike

POSTED: AUGUST 30, 2:34 A.M.

Today's session was canceled, so I spent the day with my family. It was great to spend the day with them, as I wasn't so wiped out that I was just trying to do my best to put the old game face on. My son, at the age of six, has an insanely intelligent grasp on humor. Today, as he was doing everything in his power to suppress a smirk, he said to me, "Daddy, when I grow up I'm going to become an expert on not being funny."

I'm not sure whether that line translates in print, but live, it was nothing short of hilarious. I call my son "The King of Funny." My son calls me "The King of Daddy"—and it's true.

Having a day like I had yesterday makes me want to quit the business of making major label records. Why should I spend twelve hours a day working with a bunch of shitheads, making a record that has no chance of ever being heard by anyone, when I could spend eight hours a day with gracious, appreciative people making a record that has no chance of being heard by anyone? Oh yes, the money. But honestly, the money isn't worth it. In

California, it's not as if you get to keep any of it. So what's the point?

The best albums that I have mixed in the past two years have been made by unsigned artists who paid for their own record to be made, very small indie label artists and major label international artists with small budgets. I take on these records because they inspire me musically, and *that* is why I got into this business. I do records like these for a fraction of what I charge a major label, although in the greater scheme of things, it's still not cheap. But I'm happier doing these types of records. I'm sure a large part of the reason is that I choose the project, rather than the project choosing me. Plus, the people are generally nicer to work with.

Making music is sort of like dating. If you see a girl that you think is drop-dead gorgeous, but then you go and talk to her and she is obvious trash, her appearance changes for the worse. Music is similar in that you can love the music, but once the people who make the music turn out to be shitty or uninspiring, the music quickly follows suit.

Apparently, Willy was refusing to record until the film crew was gone (or so he says). He was trying to reach Marv Ellis in Europe. I guess we're on strike.

I wonder if I'm getting paid.

– Mixerman

DAY 25
The Offering

POSTED: AUGUST 31, 3:14 A.M.

Willy called this morning and put the green light on the session. It seems that some middle ground had been reached between Willy and Jeramiah. For the time being, the cameras were only to be permitted in the room. The Womb was now considered a camera-free zone, which made it feel considerably more Womb-like. I was grateful for that compromise as cameras in the control room were exceedingly obtrusive. In the tracking room, however, they were somehow providing the necessary inspiration for Dumb Ass to play like a man.

Today, and for reasons that are not entirely clear, I took a different route to the Womb. It is not uncommon throughout the course of my day to walk through the tracking room on my way to and from the Womb. But it *is* an unusual path for the beginning of the day.

You see, there are two ways to get into the Womb. I can enter from the hall, which extends the length of the complex, turns to the right, and runs past the lounge. Or I can enter through the room, weave my way through the Apartments, and cut through one of the iso booths. That is the path that I chose today.

Walking through the room allows me to make sure the Apartments are tidy for the guys, that the mics haven't obviously been bumped, and that the mic lines haven't excessively tangled. There are other potential hazards, but you get the gist. My walk-through would be much akin to a pilot's walk-around before actually flying the plane, save for the fact that I typically can't actually kill the entire band by performing a poor inspection. I suppose I just wanted to make sure that everything was the same as I had left it, since the film crew still had access to the room.

Willy and Jeramiah were in the Womb. They were in front of the console, an area that can be plainly seen through the glass from just about any vantage point in the room. It would have been nearly impossible for me not to notice them, as they were quite obviously engaged in an animated and heated debate, about what, I still don't know. An argument between Jeramiah and Willy in and of itself was not an unusual event given the contentious nature of their relationship. What I found peculiar was how blatantly and abruptly the argument had ended upon Jeramiah's notice of me.

When I entered the Womb, Jeramiah seemed cold toward me, and Willy was obviously quite irritated. Willy proceeded to spark up a fatty, which he seems to keep an endless supply of, as I rarely see him actually roll them. He offered me a hit, but I was already paranoid enough as it was, and I declined—although, in actuality, Willy's fatties don't make me paranoid. What makes me paranoid are heated conversations ending at the sight of me.

Jeramiah hung around uncomfortably, as if he didn't know what to do with himself. He tried to strike up conversations with me that were awkward at best, and I certainly didn't attempt to make them any less awkward. All of my audio placebo labels had been taken down, and I couldn't help but wonder if this is what Jeramiah was arguing with Willy about. I found out later that Willy had curtly asked Lance to pull them down with no explanation. But why?

The only member of the band who was in the studio was Dumb Ass, and he was in the room playing his drums. Since everyone in the Womb felt this compelling and annoying need to talk without having a single thing to actually say, I chose to break up the awkwardness with a quick listen to Dumb Ass playing the drums. The drum heads were shot.

I wandered into the room and offered to call the drum tech, but Dumb Ass didn't seem too thrilled with that concept, as he silently stared toward me, cautiously shaking his head.

"What do you mean, no? Dude, your drum heads are shot; we need to get the drum tech in here."

"Naw, naw, I don't need that. I tech my own drums," he replied, sounding like a kid who didn't want to admit that his mom picked out his clothes for him.

I was astounded by this statement. You do? I was thinking to myself. Then I almost ran into a cameraman standing next to me. With that near miss, I was provided with the insight which explained his resistance. How could I forget? We were being filmed. If only George Orwell could see us now. We were like in some sort of 1984 biosphere. Just what we needed.

There could be no doubt the cameras provided unbridled inspiration for the band, but they also pushed the bullshit meter off the charts. God forbid Dumb Ass actually admits on camera that he uses a tech to either replace or tune his drum heads. Every great drummer I've ever worked with, save one, has a drum tech. That's not to say the greats can't tune their own drums—quite the contrary, they can. But the greats *do* typically use drum techs. Was it too much to admit that the not-so-great drummers use drum techs?

Since the bullshit meter was clicking like a Geiger counter in Chernobyl, I pointed out to Dumb Ass that we needed to change all the heads and that he was needed for going over arrangement details.

"Well, okay. You can hire a guy to put my heads on, and I'll fine-tune them after he gets them on there," Dumb Ass replied, like a caricature of Cliff Claven from the television show *Cheers*, who I can only assume was his childhood hero.

"Indeed," I countered, in my best Art Bell[47] impersonation. I immediately regretted having said that, as that comment would, without a doubt, make the fucking film—a fact that had me reeling inside as I would never want anyone to actually think I say the word *indeed* with any semblance of sincerity.

This would have probably bothered me for longer had I not caught Willy and Jeramiah squabbling again in the Womb—a squabble that also ended abruptly as I made my way back toward them.

Ignoring the fact that this kept happening, I informed Willy and Lance that we couldn't record until we replaced the drum heads. Lance left to call the tech, and I went to the couch to lie down for a while. The way I figured it, if Willy and Jeramiah wanted to argue, they could go somewhere else. But they stayed, and Jeramiah sat down on the outboard counter, where he could have a discussion with me as I lay on the couch.

"I was wondering, what are your plans as far as this session is concerned?" Jeramiah asked.

What an odd question. What are my plans? Uh, gee, I don't know. You'd think I was about to date his daughter or something. In which case the answer would be, I intend to fuck her, Weasel. Come to think of it, change the "her" to "it" and I had an answer that would have been a brutally appropriate reply to his question.

As much as I would have loved to respond to him in that manner, I knew I had to be cautious with how I answered this question. I certainly wouldn't want to give the impression that there was no way in hell I wanted to be working on this session anymore. This is L.A., and that would be too honest for anyone in L.A. to handle.

"I've kind of agreed to work on a session in October," I replied.

"With who?" he asked. *Whom!* I thought to myself, as if that was any of his fucking business.

"I wouldn't want to jinx it."

"So you're not committed?"

I preferred to be the one asking the questions.

"Why do you ask?" I said coyly.

Then Jeramiah proceeded to tell me that they liked the job I was doing and that he wanted me to stay on. I told him that I was pretty much committed to this gig in October, but Jeramiah wasn't satisfied, and he actually asked me if I had a deposit.

"No," I foolishly replied to Jeramiah's nosy inquiry.

I had played this conversation so well to that point, why the hell I answered "no" to that question is beyond me. I should have said, "Of course," and I laid there wanting to punch myself repeatedly for such a stupid response. I was even half tempted to say, "Did I say no? I meant yes." But he wouldn't have bought it.

Jeramiah spent the next ten minutes lecturing me on the risks of this business, pointing out that it would be in my best interest to stay on a guaranteed gig, as opposed to a gig that could possibly fall through. Then he went into how this record was of the highest priority at the label, and that it was going to be a huge-selling album and would be a high-profile gig for me. Then he moved into telling me that I should be more responsible with my scheduling, and that I should expect these sorts of sessions to go over in time, etc. . . .etc. . . . blah, blah, fucking blah.

My kingdom for a clothespin! The room was starting to reek from all the bullshit that was being thrown about. Does this guy think I was born yesterday? Finally he wrapped up his monologue.

". . . and I think it would be in your best interest to see this project to its completion," he concluded.

I lay there on the couch contemplating that phrase. "To its completion." What a concept. And then I started thinking about how rare it is these days to have the opportunity to record and mix an album in its entirety. Sure it happens, and I've done it myself. Too often, however, the mixes are sent out for the purposes of stamping a mixer's name on the product. This project surely was not going to be an exception to that trend.

Mixers are hired to supply one of the following: their time, their mixes, or their name. When an engineer is first starting out, he is usually charging for his time and that includes his time for mixing. If an engineer starts to attempt to specialize in mixing, as I did for so many years, then he is hired for his mixes. In that case, the mixer is paid for his mixes and is charging for a certain quality of work, attention to detail, approach, and fresh perspective.

A very select few mixers become name mixers, and they are hired specifically for the purpose of having their names placed on an album. Labels want the name mixer because he is associated with "big hits." The thinking is if the Program Director (PD) of a radio station sees that Sir Arthur Conan Mixallot mixed the album, the PD could be more likely to listen to the song or possibly even to select the song. The competition to get on radio is so fierce that labels will do anything they must do in order to gain an edge.

There is no real evidence that Program Directors actually care who mixed a song. The fact of the matter is, if the song and production are great, then the PD will spin it and see what the reaction is. If the reaction is strong, it gets more spins. Unfortunately, if the mix is weak, then the production is weakened, and the song likely won't get played. That's why the mix is so important.

As a consequence, name mixers are typically guys who have put out a significant amount of successful work. Unfortunately, what happens is that the name mixer becomes like a factory, partly because he is so in demand all he does is mix day in and day out. Because of this, rather than approaching each record as a separate work of art, the name mixer tends to stamp a particular "sound" on the record by using such things as sample replacements.[48] Worse yet, the processing chains (EQs, compressors, effects, etc.) tend to remain constant so as to maintain a certain consistency. This means that every instrument goes through a certain channel on the module at a certain level with a certain processing chain, and each instrument for each project gets the identical treatment. Unfortunately, this consistency usually provides good—but not necessarily great—results. That's because there is no one way to mix that works for every production, yet this is often the approach of the name mixer. I suppose good work (as opposed to great) along with the name often causes the Mooks to believe that the mix is somehow great.

Now, judging whether a mix is great or not is subjective, and one can only truly judge whether the mix was brought to its maximum potential if one is intimate with the raw tracks. Even then it's just an opinion, which is what makes this business so difficult. All decisions must be based on opinion. Yet an A&R representative keeps or loses his job based on facts—sales numbers are facts.

I have recorded several albums in the past two years that have been mixed by the biggest names in the business, and I have always been sadly disappointed with how homogenized everything sounded in the end. It's as if a name mixer goes out of his way to stamp every bit of uniqueness out of a production. There is nothing more aggravating than recording an album to have a certain sound that works with the songs and the production, only to have someone come in to make it sound like everything else on the radio. Jeramiah's phrase "to its completion" intrigued me, as it suggested that I might actually be able to negotiate for the mix. This concept was nothing short of appealing to me.

What I had to determine was whether I really wanted to record this project to its completion. Mixes can only rise to the maximum potential of the production. At the moment, that potential was not as high as I would have hoped, although since the cameras had arrived, the drum tracks have been remarkably usable. I could only assume the quality would improve tremendously with a drummer-for-hire. The way I see it, it's feasible for an excellent album to come out of this, mostly because the songs are good.

After some time of processing these thoughts, out of nowhere, I came to a decision. I marvel at the brain's ability to do this. It's much like how a woman's egg will immediately refuse penetration from any other sperm once the first sperm makes contact. My brain had hardened and made a rash decision, allowing for no negotiation. There was no way I was going to record this album to completion. To me, it just wasn't worth it. There was no reason for me to stay on this project. The project in October was a good one, and I should take that.

"I'm pretty much committed to the session in October," I repeated.

I might have been better off telling him I'd think about it, but there was no point in stringing him along, since I was so sure of my decision to move on.

Willy, who had been silently leaning in his chair with his legs up on the console, leaned his head back and to the side as he spoke.

"Perhaps the label would be willing to up your pay," he said, looking at me sideways, as he was likely too comfortable to actually turn around completely to look at me.

I lay there silently on the couch, with my hands behind my head, fingers linked. First I glanced at Willy and then intently watched Jeramiah, who looked incredibly uncomfortable and was obviously taking some time to think about this.

"Yes," Jeramiah said slowly, while looking at Willy. "Perhaps we would. What would make it worth your while to turn down your October gig?"

I stared at Jeramiah, who was staring nervously back at me. I lay there, not knowing for certain why Jeramiah was making such an offer. I also knew the price I wanted, but I really didn't know whether I should say it. It wasn't so much that I was worried he'd say no. I was worried he'd say yes.

As I processed all of this, I was interrupted by what I can only describe as one of the loudest crashes I've ever heard in my life. It came from the tracking room.

Jeramiah whipped around, and both Willy and I stood up. We all stood there in absolute amazement with our mouths wide open. One of the large slabs of glass that separates the control room from the tracking room had been completely shattered. There are actually two separate panes of solid inch-and-a-half-thick glass with about a foot of space between them. That's because the best isolation occurs when there is space between two hard surfaces. That isolation was now compromised.

We all ran into the tracking room to investigate what had happened. Dumb Ass was lying on the floor, writhing in pain and holding his wrist. He was covered in glass, and we helped him up carefully dusting him off. On the floor was a massive light that moments earlier had been precariously perched in the air on a huge lighting stand.

Lance took Dumb Ass to the emergency room, where it was later determined that he'd broken his wrist in two places. Exactly what happened still hasn't been entirely sorted out. At the time of incident, the cameramen were on a break. Their timing was impeccable, as cameras are sure to be in my face during my lame attempts at sarcasm, yet are nowhere to be found during what had to be one of the more spectacular falls in studio history. Since Dumb Ass had gone to the ER, we only had the eyewitness account of the drum tech, which was incomplete at best, as he hadn't seen the entire sequence of events.

What we've pieced together is that Dumb Ass was lighting candles in the guitar area and got his foot caught in one of the lighting cables, causing him to trip and fall backwards rather violently into the stand that held one of the big lights. The light was a bit top heavy, and Dumb Ass was no Jack LaLanne, which proved to be a bad combination. Dumb Ass somehow managed to land on his wrist with the full weight of his body, causing great trauma. He's lucky that's all that happened with all the glass that was everywhere. I've never seen an inch-and-a-half piece of glass shatter like this. It was un-fucking-real!

If I weren't convinced before, I am now. This session is cursed. It's time to bring in the sage weed for burning in an attempt to shoo out the evil spirits, because this session is an endless string of bad scenes. At every turn, there is a new setback, disaster, or inconvenience. Actually, my kingdom for an inconvenience! While the idea of having a ghost drummer has been nothing short of appealing, Dumb Ass has finally been playing well enough to keep the gig. So what does the poor schmuck do? He goes and breaks his wrist.

I told Jeramiah I'd think about my plans where Bitch Slap's recording was concerned over the weekend. Given all the commotion, he accepted this without attempting to close me. Now I must spend the weekend considering exactly what my soul is worth, albeit with a limited-use clause.

I suppose that makes it worth considering.

– Mixerman

DAY 26

It's All in the Mix

POSTED: SEPTEMBER 4, 3:14 A.M. — WEEK 6

There have been events over the course of this diary that I have found to be suspicious. While I have no lack of confidence where my personal likeability is concerned, I felt Marv Ellis's enjoyment of me and his overt vote of approval for my role in this recording process to be slightly overstated. In fact, I couldn't help but get the feeling that our entire dinner was staged. And what of Willy discussing the importance of discretion, post our dinner with Marv? Was that some sort of warning? I found that discussion to be nothing short of odd.

Then there was the sudden and inexplicable removal of the audio placebo labels: soar, thump, and the like. In and of itself this wouldn't have been nearly as suspicious had I not witnessed those heated arguments between Willy and Jeramiah. What of Jeramiah's sudden coldness toward me? Surely he was aware that I'd played him for the fool. But how did he find out?

As if that wasn't enough to pique my paranoia, there was the "name your price" game. I've been negotiating with record companies for over a decade. To date, I have never seen the recordist get to name his price. Why was it so important to Jeramiah that I stay on the session? I'm just the recordist. There are many, many qualified engineers with whom Jeramiah has worked over the years who could easily come in and take over. It's not like there's some sort of flow going here. Quite the opposite, really.

Still, after a three-day extended leave of absence from the Bitch Slap madness; after countless hours of strategizing, hypothesizing, and the like; after the relentless pursuit of playing out possible scenarios in my head, I have come to the conclusion that I should abandon my suspicions as nothing more than paranoia. For even if I were correct, no matter how I play the game in my head, it is, without a doubt, best if I ignore completely the possibility that this diary is somehow being read by the record company and continue on as if there were an elephant in the middle of the room that everyone was conveniently choosing to ignore. So that is how I shall proceed with these journal entries from this point forward.

Recording drums today was out of the question since Willy's prescheduled ghost replacement drummer wouldn't arrive in town until next Sunday. It's just as well, because the panel of glass that Dumb Ass shattered with his extraordinary grace was still missing. The sonic isolation that we once enjoyed was now compromised. Willy was considering keeping the takes that Dumb Ass had done. Apparently, he wanted to finish the productions in their entirety before actually making that decision. I suppose upon the completion of Fingaz's editing of the Dumb Ass "camera" takes, it was quite conceivable that we would have the drum tracks for half an album. Willy's plan was to try and lay down the overdubs on as many of those songs as possible.

First up was Harmon Neenot, the bass player, well established as one of the most god-awful singers on the planet, perhaps even in the universe—as I couldn't imagine an alien sounding quite so wretched. Harmon could have easily been one of the lead singers of Milli Vanilli, as he would have likely been on even par with Rob and Fab, the two non-singers of the group.

Milli Vanilli is famous for one of the biggest scandals in the history of the music business. They were like the Quiz Show of the '80s. Scandalous! The vocals on Milli Vanilli's hit album (approximately ten million units sold) were not sung, as advertised, by the two handsome front men of the group, but rather by ghost singers. Apparently, Rob and Fab wanted desperately to sing their music live as opposed to lip-synching, but, alas, weren't up to the task, and people quickly realized that these two couldn't possibly have sung the vocals as presented on the album. Upon the discovery that Rob and Fab couldn't even carry a tune, let alone sing a hit song, Milli Vanilli had their Grammy and their RIAA (Recording Industry Association of America) record sales awards revoked. There was even clamoring from advocacy groups that consumers should get their money back, although I really don't know what came of that.

Apparently, the listening public finds it distasteful to buy a CD that is a misrepresentation of the truth. Personally, I don't see the difference between hiring a ghost singer who can actually sing in tune and using software to redraw the waveforms of notes, thereby putting a lousy singer in tune. Both cases are egregious misrepresentations of the truth. I suppose it's also tolerable for the drums, bass, and guitars to be played by someone else, as long as it's not the singer who is replaced. For some reason, as long as the singer is actually the true source, and technology is responsible for the manifestation of misrepresentation, this is somehow acceptable to us. Perhaps, deep down, we are comfortable with these distortions because we are all still incredibly grateful to the photographer who edited out that awful blemish from our school picture. I know I am.

I went in a little early today, as it was necessary for me to make some slaves of the edited drums. As I was driving, I was encouraged by the fact that I wouldn't have to deal with Dumb Ass anymore. It was the best drive to the studio I've had in some time. The way I felt, you'd have thought I was going up to Big Bear Mountain for a much-needed mini-vacation. I was elated. Of course, that elation was shot to hell the moment I pulled into the parking lot, as there, on the patio before me, was Dumb Ass in all his glory, picking his nose and eating his boogers with the hand that had the cast on it. I made a mental note not to sign his cast today.

As Dumb Ass followed me into the control room like he was my most loyal dog or pig, as if I were the sort of person that would own either, I felt as though I had hopped right into a pool of quicksand. I was sinking, and quickly. For what I had failed to take into account was that if Dumb Ass wasn't playing the drums, then he'd never be in the drum room. And if he was never in the drum room, then he'd often be in the Womb. The presence of Dumb Ass in the control room was similar to being in a womb with a ripped placenta—very uninviting and distressing to the occupants.

Dumb Ass was exercising his true talent in life—making the lives of those around him miserable. He wouldn't leave me alone as he yapped endlessly. I had a job to do, and I was trying desperately not to pay him any attention. But he was as irritating as a fly that had nothing better to do than buzz endlessly around my head.

In reviewing Lance's notes, which were nothing short of a thesis on the concept that too much information can be equally as debilitating as not enough, I was attempting to decipher exactly which songs had slaves, which songs didn't, and which songs Fingaz had finished editing. Dumb Ass was still firing questions at me relentlessly, and although I'd tell him that I really needed to concentrate on what I was doing, this would only buy me about a minute before regularly scheduled interruptions resumed.

At one point, Dumb Ass brought a tambourine and started playing it with his left hand as I was listening to a take.

"Hey! I can still play percussion on the album!" he proclaimed.

He could have just as easily been clenching the tambourine with his teeth and shaking his head, because that's about how fluidly he played. Finally, I just told him that he was being excused from the Womb, and he started laughing like a retard, as if I was kidding.

"Do I look like I'm kidding?" I asked him as I pointed to the door and he slunk away. Good dog.

Both Willy and Jeramiah arrived around the same time today. From the moment Jeramiah got out of his car, I could tell that he was dying to get me alone. He was surely determined to pin me down on my schedule. But after an entire weekend of pondering what staying on this gig was worth to me, I decided I wasn't going to name a price at all. Jeramiah would have to make me an offer that I could refuse.

I pulled every trick in the book to thwart his maneuvers to speak with me. Mind Tricks were proving useless, but I knew he wouldn't want to discuss my fee with any of the band members present. I even hung around Dumb Ass in order to prevent the inevitable discussion. To be sure, my desire to avoid a conversation with Jeramiah was fierce, considering I was willing to subject myself to the constant idiocies of Dumb Ass.

Once Harmon Neenot had arrived, we prepared for recording bass parts over the drums. Personally, I'd rather have a weak drummer on a record than a weak bass player, as it's really the bass that anchors the song. There are those that might argue this sentiment, but they aren't here, now are they? A great bass player can even make up for less-than-stellar drumming.

Unfortunately, Harmon wasn't making up for shit. I think he's been playing with Dumb Ass for too long, as Harmon has the identical, sickening rocking-back-and-forth motion in his playing. I've never heard this phenomenon in a bass player before, and I hope to God I never hear it again.

About midway into the recording process, my carpal tunnel was killing me from the number of punches I had to make. Finally I just switched to my left hand, which isn't so much of a problem, except that I couldn't face Harmon. For logistics alone, it became necessary to turn the remote around. This is nothing short of a circus act when you consider that the remote for a two-inch machine is cumbersome at best, weighing approximately fifty pounds, connected to large umbilical cord of wires that tend to get in the way. To make matters worse, the umbilical cord was just about at its limit, making maneuverability extremely poor, at best. If you've ever watched the *Peanuts* cartoon where Snoopy has a wrestling match with a lawn chair, you have an accurate depiction of what I was going through trying to turn around the machine controller.

The film crew managed to somehow convince Willy to film in the control room, since there was really nothing going on anywhere else, save Dumb Ass practicing his imitation of a quadriplegic percussion player (personally, I would have thought that to be more than worthwhile footage). I watched him through the one pane of glass, the other of which would not be replaced until a custom piece of glass arrived. The replacement glass had been rush-ordered, and was due to arrive sometime on Friday.

Although it was Willy who had granted permission for the film crew to enter the Womb, either he didn't want to be filmed, or he had no desire to spend the afternoon recording half a measure of bass at a time, so he exited stage left with Jeramiah. Lucky him! This left me to record Harmon with a camera in my grill.

Harmon was so flustered by the camera that I had to try to convince him that he would ultimately have approval of the final cut. I wanted to point out that it wasn't in the record company's best interest to let the world see that this band couldn't play for shit, but I decided against that tactic. Rather, I explained to him that this was the process we go through, even with the best players.

As much as I loathed going into the telling of white lies, so long as I was able to expedite the recording of bass parts, I could live with myself. Besides, appeasing Harmon was always of great importance as he was without a doubt the most vocal, and certainly the most abrasive, member in the band.

Harmon's whiny voice is so piercing and so brutally annoying that sometimes I consider purchasing a chalkboard on which I could scrape my nails in order to drown out the sound of his voice. It's that bad. Because of his unusually irritating voice, he has the unique capability of winning arguments with little to no resistance. The repelling nature of his voice was the antithesis of a Siren. In fact, I would like very much to see a battle between a Siren and Harmon Neenot, as I'm sure that he would emerge victorious, causing the Siren to run for cover.

Along with his annoying voice, Harmon has some atrocious manners. He farts constantly, which, unfortunately, is his least egregious offense on good etiquette. I absolutely refuse to ever shake his hand as he constantly picks his butt, and as if that wasn't bad enough, he will invariably smell his picking finger. If his hand isn't somewhere near his ass, then one can usually find it planted firmly in the waistband of his pants, much like the character Al Bundy from the *Married With Children* TV show. He is so much a caricature of disgusting habits that one can't help but focus on the humor of such blatant displays of grossness. Still, Harmon's idiosyncrasies (okay, I'm being kind here, savor the sensitive moment) are relatively harmless, as long as you don't touch him and as long as you're not a woman. It's the women who should avoid him like the plague, as proven by how he treats his girlfriend.

Harmon derives great pleasure from putting down his girlfriend. He calls her trailer trash to her face, which to me is the epitome of the pot calling the kettle black. In his defense, however, I must say she *is* trailer trash. I wouldn't admit that to him, though, as I could only imagine that might further encourage such statements. When she'd call him on his cell phone, he'd yell at her, calling her a bitch and telling her that he was busy. He would then proceed to tell her that she should know better than to call him when he's busy. How does someone know that you're busy when they're calling you on the phone? And why would you answer the cell phone if you're busy? But I didn't dare ask him that for fear that I might have to listen to a ten-minute explanation of how she's just a fucking whore who needs to be kept in her place. Just the thought of having to listen to him talk for that length of time is too much for me to bear.

Strangely, despite Harmon's bad manners and poor behavior toward women, which I could easily chalk up to the results of poor upbringing; despite vocal cords that could rip through steel, which I couldn't really hold him accountable for as that is the work of nature; yes, despite his many shortcomings Harmon was the member of the band I could tolerate the most. As much as it pains me to say this, all things being relative, he is without a doubt my favorite member of the band.

What I find most interesting is how someone as uncouth and as vile as Harmon could actually be such a great songwriter. In my opinion, he's hands-down the best songwriter in the band. Of course, he doesn't tend to write the sensitive songs. How could he, with his personality and a voice that would make any young femme run for cover? These sorts of songs are reserved for lead singer Johnny Hard-On. Harmon's songs tended to be the everyman, mantra-style songs. They're usually incredibly infectious, and one can't help but sing along.

I was checking our bass work on the third song by the time Jeramiah and Willy had returned. I gave up my chair to Willy and allowed him to listen to what we had done. Then I made the tactical error of sitting on the couch in the back of the room, thus giving Jeramiah the opportunity to speak to me. Still, I couldn't avoid him forever, and at least I had gotten some work done.

I can't stand discussing business bullshit before I've gotten work done. It throws off the whole day to be thinking about what someone said to you, or how someone has lied to you, when that has little to do with actually making a record.

"So have you made a decision?" he whispered to me.

The music was playing, and it was unlikely that anyone could hear us. Feeling somewhat lazy, I chose to remain on the couch.

"I've decided to let you make *me* an offer," I replied quietly.

Jeramiah sat there without saying a word for quite some time. I was going to allow him to take whatever amount of time he needed. The ball was now in his court. Willy had moved on to the next song before Jeramiah finally decided to speak again.

"How about if you get first shot at mixing the album," he quietly said, looking me straight in the eye.

I was floored. Getting first shot at mixing the album could quite possibly make the misery of recording Bitch Slap worth my while. At least I would know that the quality of my recordings will likely be retained in the mixes, as opposed to getting back mixes that sound nothing like the record was intended to sound. Even the producer is often disappointed when mixes return, as his hands are tied when a big-name mixer is hired.

At this level of spending, it is rare for anyone other than the biggest "names" in mixing to have the "opportunity" to mix this kind of project. I say opportunity, but really, to a name mixer, it's no opportunity at all. It's just another paycheck, and for good reason: The paychecks are quite large, anywhere from $50,000 to $100,000 for one or two weeks' worth of work. Anyone fortunate enough to command that kind of money is typically profit-sharing, as well, with the usual cut being 1 percent of the MSRP (Manufacturer's Suggested Retail Price), paid by the artist and forced by the record company. At $17 a CD, that can add up to a nice chunk of change if the album is a hit.

The record companies will have anyone who will listen believe that a mixer commanding that kind of money (and I'm not by any stretch of the imagination complaining) has an uncanny ability or knowledge of how to mix a hit. But the reality is that these mixers actually have many more flops than they do hits. But because of the level of spending, they get considerably better opportunities for hits, thus giving them more hits, and thus charging the record companies more money.

Were I to get paid based on the high hopes of record companies, I'd be retired by now. That's because the Mooks are so accustomed to blowing smoke up people's asses, they start to believe their own hype. Oh, how many times have I gotten a record that was supposed to be an opportunity for me? *Hah!* Even a "sure thing" is suspect at best. No! One is only given the opportunity in this business to work on great music, or meet great people — not to mix a hit. Being given the opportunity to mix a hit would require a crystal ball, and I can assure you that the record companies have not a single crystal ball among them.

A label's desire for me to mix or to not mix a record has little to do with the quality of my work. I have a track record of mixing well-respected albums. I still do a considerable amount of mixing. It's just that these days I also do a lot of tracking as well. Really, the only reason I took this gig was because it would give me an opportunity to work with Willy Show. The more big-name producers that one can have as one's clients, the better.

I suppose from the perspective of the label, having me mix the album isn't really taking a chance. It's not like they never use alternate mixers — they do occasionally. It's not like they *must* use my mixes if they don't like them for some reason. They only have to pay for them. But having the first shot at the mixes gives me a leg up, as any subsequent mixes are being compared to mine rather than the other way around. Although this might not seem, on the surface, as any kind of advantage, given human nature, it is.

Jeramiah had made a reasonable offer. But if I was going to record and mix this album, then I was going to want to profit-share. So I decided to up the ante a little.

"I want my full mix rate, plus a point and I'll want it in writing," I said, staring him down like I held five aces to his pair of twos. And Jeramiah nodded unenthusiastically in agreement.

"My manager will call you in the morning to hammer out the details," I said, shaking his hand and going back to the console to see how our bass overdubs held up to the scrutiny of Willy Show.

Willy was fine with the bass parts, and wanted to lay down some guitar, so we summoned Yore from the lounge and recorded the guitar parts on one of the songs. Suddenly, mysteriously, I was beginning to enjoy life as a recordist again. And while I'm not deluding myself that this project has even the most microscopic, minuscule, infinitesimal chance of ever even being released, let alone being successful, there was still a chance. At this particular moment, I am enthusiastic, as now I have a vested interest in this project.

Funny how that works.

– Mixerman

The Hidden Benefits of Eating Sushi

POSTED: SEPTEMBER 5, 2:59 A.M.

Fingaz, who was mysteriously absent yesterday, went to Vegas for the second weekend in a row and was now moping around as if he were Paulie Yore. Unfortunately, the poor lad got suckered by the lure of winning a little, only to lose a lot.

The last time I went to Vegas, I mixed an album there, and I spent two weeks living at the MGM Grand. Let me tell you, fourteen days in a Vegas mega hotel is twelve days too many. Apparently for Fingaz, two trips to Vegas is one trip too many, because he lost his ass. I couldn't get an exact figure out of him, but I have this sneaky suspicion that Fast Fingaz was going to be Not-So-Fast Fingaz from this point forward.

"I be workin' too fast, Yo! I'm almost done and I lost my loot to da man!" he said to me. Perhaps it was this particular statement that gave me such a sneaky suspicion.

Feeling a bit devilish, I pointed out to Fingaz a bit of little-known trivia.

"You know, not too long ago they didn't even allow Wegros in the casino. You know, back when Vegas was run by the mafia."

"Word," he replied with conviction. "Dey oppressed my peoples," he informed me.

"Word," I replied back, and Fingaz left for his shitter, as I sat there simply amazed at some of the conversations that I have on this session.

Johnny had come to the studio directly from his attorney's office. Apparently, his lawyer was incensed by the fact that Johnny was caught driving intoxicated and was fighting his DUI arrest. Perhaps he was declaring the case unconstitutional. I'm not a lawyer, so I really wouldn't know much about these things. Regardless of Johnny's legal woes, he wanted to play guitar. Yore was already preparing to do same. I've been down this road before.

This time, I just lay on the couch as Johnny and Paulie Yore argued for the better part of an hour. Far be it for me to interfere in a turf war of this magnitude. Every now and then they'd try to suck me into the discussion, but in the course of being a dad, I've learned to grunt in ways that indicate no position whatsoever, and so they would be momentarily confused and then go back to their bickering. I was just grateful that Harmon wasn't around, as I wouldn't have gotten a wink of sleep with that cheese grater of a voice in the Womb.

The idiocy between Johnny and Paulie Yore would have likely continued for hours had Willy not shown up. Willy, being sensitive to vibrations of discourse, immediately noticed tension in the air. Either that or he heard the yelling from down the hall as the argument was beginning to spin out of control. Willy, a skilled diplomat and having a firm understanding of how to mediate such disputes, sat both Johnny and Yore down to work out their differences in a manner he could call his own. He sparked up a fatty.

It wasn't long before I was again being asked my opinion, and since Willy was now present and the fatty had made its way to me, I decided to tell them what I thought.

"I think Yore should come on Mondays and Wednesdays, and Johnny should come on Tuesdays and Thursdays, and the two of them should alternate Fridays," I said as I sat up, slightly groggy from my nap. At first I wasn't sure whether the three of them thought my idea was brilliant or idiotic, as they sat there staring at me silently with their jaws slightly ajar. Then I decided to hedge my bet.

"Or . . . not," I said as I toked on the fatty.

Without comment, the three of them went back to their discussion. They were making about as much headway with Willy's presence as they were without it, save the fact that they now had the munchies and wanted to eat lunch. Me too! We ordered lunch, and Willy made an executive decision.

"Why don't we allow Johnny to lay down his guitar parts today?" Willy said to Yore as he put his hand on his shoulder lovingly. Okay, not really lovingly, but there was a certain tenderness to his approach that I hadn't witnessed before.

Johnny is exactly the person whom I would have picked, were I the producer and had something else to do for the day. Without embarrassment, or the least bit of concern for appearances, Willy exited stage left, leaving me to the mess of recording guitars with the guitar player of lesser proficiency. Yore exited stage right, clearly displeased with Willy's executive decision.

I began recording Johnny Knuckles as he struggled through guitar parts that a second-year guitar student could have played with ease. Somehow, the simple parts were nothing short of challenging for Johnny. Perhaps his poor performances could be attributed to the cameras that were once again in the Womb. Johnny seemed to be concentrating more on how cool he looked on camera than on how well he played. It's not often that I get the chance to see windmills in the control room during guitar overdubs. Of course, it was just another inappropriate goof on Pete Townshend. If *only* Johnny were as cool as Pete.

Johnny's instrument was a beautiful vintage fire red Gibson 335, an instrument that he didn't deserve to play if you're the type that believes fine instruments belong in the hands of fine players. I am that type. We had the guitar plugged into a 100-watt Marshall head through a 4 x 12 Marshall cab.

I always have Lance by my side during the recording of Johnny Tone-Deaf's guitar parts. That's because Johnny can't tune his own guitar. Being a keyboard player, I'm not super fast at tuning guitars myself. Lance, who I have discovered through the course of the session to be a pretty smokin' bass player, was also a fairly decent guitar player. Consequently, Lance was quite capable of tuning guitars, and quickly. This was Lance's job. Johnny didn't seem to give a shit that the cameras were capturing this so long as his hair was properly mussed up, and so long as he looked cool when he was playing.

After about two hours of painstakingly recording rudimentary barré chords, we finally had the first set of guitar doubles completed. Willy had been back at the complex for about half an hour, and upon my invitation, he came in to listen. Johnny was considering warming up for singing, but Willy felt that Johnny's voice was a bit "husky" tonight and for this particular song, so he sent him home for rest. Dumb Ass was in the room for the second day in a row practicing his left-handed percussion act—an act that hadn't improved in the least. Thankfully, Willy told Dumb Ass to go home too. Most intriguing of all, he dismissed the film crew for the evening.

I couldn't for the life of me figure out what kind of work we had to do, let alone work that required the removal of the film crew. I couldn't make more slaves because Fingaz was moving like molasses since his fleecing in Vegas. He had nothing for us to listen to. I didn't really have any tasks to do. Lance was completely caught up with his documentation, as we have both been keeping on top of our work. So what were we going to do? Then Willy gave me that look I know so well. My favorite Willy Show look. The look that indicated he was feelin' it. It was the look of a man that understands not only *how* to run a session, but when to run *from* a session. Yes, Willy had given me *the* Look. It was sushi time!

I jumped for joy!

"Before we go . . ." Willy said, neglecting to end his sentence. I watched him intently as he walked into the room. The way he said it, I didn't get the impression he had forgotten something there. He had obviously left his statement open-ended for a reason. Willy walked methodically to the rack of basses in Harmon's Apartment, thoughtfully picked out a bass, and carried it back to the Womb. Willy walked right up to Lance and handed it to him.

"Learn the bass parts for this song, and when we get back, we're going to re-lay them," Willy stated matter-of-factly.

I had to cover my mouth as I half laughed, half coughed, half spit. It wasn't as if I found this funny, although right now I do. No, it was the sheer boldness of such a move. I was merely having an involuntary reflexive physical reaction to the shock of such a surprising development. Lance appeared more dumbfounded than even I was, as I seriously considered walking up to him and closing his jaw out of courtesy. Lance was obviously gravely concerned about the ramifications of being caught red-handed doing such a thing. Who could blame him?

"What if Harmon comes by tonight?" Lance asked with a quiver in his voice.

"He won't," replied Willy, as he headed out of the Womb, signaling for me to follow.

Willy may have been willing to take such chances, but I wasn't. I instructed the runner at the front desk that he was to call Lance immediately in the Womb if anyone from the band arrived at the studio. Further, I instructed the runner that he was not to leave the desk position for any reason whatsoever. Willy found my precautions humorous. I found them to be nothing more than, well, precautious.

Willy and I made the drive to Nozawa, my favorite sushi restaurant in L.A. If you sit at the sushi bar there, you're not allowed to actually choose what you eat, and I always sit at the sushi bar at Nozawa. It's a very small place nestled in a tiny strip mall on

Ventura Boulevard in the Valley. If you sit at the bar, the sushi chef, who is also the owner, will not even allow you to make a request, as he will have you removed if you try. I know one person who was removed for simply requesting a California roll.

He's the sushi version of Jerry Seinfeld's Soup Nazi: I could easily imagine him saying *"No sushi for you!"* There are signs all over the wall that say, "Trust me," in both Japanese and English. But this little restaurant is worth the chef's idiosyncrasies because the fish is so phenomenally fresh and of such high quality that it literally melts in your mouth. To date, I have not been asked to leave the establishment, but that's because I'm very prudent: I make no sudden movements; I thank him and bow my head to him on a regular basis; I speak only when I am spoken to; and I *never* look him in the eye. He always smiles at me when I'm leaving, because I think he derives enjoyment that I am so fearful of him.

As Willy and I were sucking down the most fantastic halibut sashimi in ponzu sauce with scallions, I broached the subject of assistants replacing bass parts.

"Don't you think Harmon might figure out that someone else is playing the parts?" I asked.

"If he does, he does," Willy responded, as he took a bite of raw halibut. I couldn't help but think that our surroundings were inspiring this sort of Zen-like response. I had heard all that I needed to know at that point, and so I abandoned the subject. I was considering asking him more questions about the project, but somehow I doubted that even *he* knew the answers to my questions, and so I would allow it to unfold for me as pleasant little surprises, much as it has to this point.

As we drove back to the studio parking lot, I was relieved that there were no Bitch Slap vehicles in the yard. We went to see how Lance was doing, and not only had he learned the parts, he had already laid them down. Holy shit! What a difference it made! The song had come alive. I could now actually groove to the music. I was having a physical reaction that I have not had on this session to this point. Willy was also moving to the music.

"Did you change anything?" I asked Lance.

"No," Lance replied. "I think the bass parts are great—he just can't play them very well."

The ramifications of this were mind-boggling. Half the band will have been replaced with session players. One of the session players was unauthorized by the band. I suppose if the final product is going to improve from such misrepresentations of the truth, then what's the harm?

After all, I can keep a secret.

– Mixerman

DAY 28

Shortypants

POSTED: SEPTEMBER 6, 4:53 A.M.

Willy asked me to come in early to record Lance today. We laid down the new bass parts on the other two songs, which still had Harmon's performances on them. Lance had taken home a CD that he had burned for himself last night, so we were able to start making takes the moment I arrived. Once again, I set up our runner lookout to be certain that we would have ample warning should someone from the band arrive.

Now that Lance was the bass player in the group, unbeknownst to any of the others, he thought it would be great to have *me* assisting *him*. He had me looking up his notes on Harmon's bass settings. It was bad enough that Lance's playing was so far superior to Harmon's, but we at least needed to use the same bass and amp settings. I obliged the little shit, but I assured him that this would be the last time. I also took the opportunity to point out just how handy the notes had become.

Lance laid down the parts in one take each, with only a few punch-in fixes here and there. As long as I've been in this business, it is still remarkable to me to hear the difference between a player who can play the notes and a player who can play the music. Lance was playing music. Still, even though Lance played the identical part, I feared that Harmon would notice. It's hard *not* to notice the difference.

Lance had recorded the bass parts on different tracks, so now I had two basses, and I needed to dispose of the evidence. I don't ever erase anything without the producer signing off on such a decision, and as it turns out, that was a *very* good policy, since Willy didn't want me to erase the old bass parts.

"If we get caught, I don't want you to have to rerecord those bass parts again," Willy said.

Oh, right! If *we* get caught! Now I'm some sort of accomplice in this unilateral decision of Willy's? To make matters worse, if *we* get caught, then *who* would have to endure the hours of painstaking drudgery of recording bass with Mr. Butt Pick himself? *Me!* And at precisely that moment I had an "aha." Did I really want to spend hours rerecording these bass parts? I now understood exactly what Willy was driving at, and so I backed up the bass parts to Radar with the code name "Operation Stinky Fingers." I would tell Fingaz when he arrived.

Even though Lance had played exactly the same notes as Harmon, the new performances were so musically superior that it brought the track to life. There was no doubt in my mind that Harmon would notice a difference. The big question was, Would Harmon buy the explanation as to *why* it sounds different? Well, in order to have such an explanation one must first invent it. So that's just what I did.

I decided to give the monitor mix[49] a little boost with some compression. I put a Crane Song STC-8 on the stereo bus,[50] which is similar to supplying an instant injection of turbo charge to a mix. Stereo compression from a high-quality unit like the STC-8 tightens up the low end of the monitor mix, and congeals or "glues" the instruments. There is a very short list of compressors that I'll use on the stereo bus, even if it's just for monitoring. The reason being the stereo bus is basically the summing of the *entire* sound. There is nothing more important than the stereo bus, and I choose my tools for this application *very* carefully.

The way I figured it, if I compress the monitor mix, the whole track would sound so "finished" that Harmon might think the compressor is responsible for bringing his performances alive. So that's what I planned to tell him.

As I prepared the monitor mix of the second Dumb Ass "camera" take, I sensed the presence of a stranger. When I turned around I had noticed that the sanctity of the Womb had indeed been violated.

The stranger was a very short man wearing his pants entirely too high above the waist, along with a cowboy hat and a pair of Porsche teardrop sunglasses that were far too large to be fashionable, unless somehow I had been transported to 1985 and no one informed me. The stranger also donned what I would assume were snakeskin cowboy boots, although, not being an expert in leather, it's quite possible they were fake. All that was missing was the string tie.

The short man was lighting up a cigarette, which I assumed was a Marlboro and which is a big no-no in the Womb. I had no idea how long he may have been there, as I didn't notice the door open. I stopped the tape and turned to address him as he was violating my airspace with his cigarette and I was certainly going to let him know about it. But before I could get a word in, he spoke to me.

"I'm Shortypants, Bitch Slap's manager, Where's Willy?" the man said curtly.

Seeing as we were introducing ourselves, I followed suit.

"Mixerman, Bitch Slap's engineer. Howdy!" I replied in a way I felt he might understand.

He didn't seem very interested in either my identity or my role on this session. In fact, he seemed quite preoccupied as he looked around the room as if in search of a lost set of keys. My curiosity got the better of me.

"Did you lose something, partner?" I asked.

"Where's Alsihad?" he said gruffly.

"We're not using Alsihad," I replied.

"*What?*" he yelled. "Why the hell not? Do you know what year this is? No wonder this shit is taking so long," he continued yelling as he walked out of the room in a huff.

I decided to remain in the Womb, as it was calm there. Lance came running in to inform me that Willy wanted a good mix of the bass, drums, and guitars on last night's work. After about ten minutes, Willy and Shortypants entered the room, and Shortypants was again smoking in the control room. Upon closer inspection of Shortypants' cigarette, I realized it wasn't a Marlboro after all, but a Lucky Strike. Regardless of the brand, just five minutes of smoke in the room can close my sinuses up like Fort Knox, which makes it impossible to hear properly. But I certainly wasn't going to tell *this* pistol to put it out. Not yet, anyway.

Willy played him the track that I had just rough mixed, and Shortypants was happy with how it sounded.

"Good! Good! What else do you have for me to hear?" he asked gruffly.

I almost had to spit out my coffee, which I had just taken a sip of, as there really was nothing else for him to hear, but I certainly wasn't going to say that out loud.

Yore walked into the room, and then Willy handled Shortypants's request beautifully.

"We've got several songs in various states of completion, but nothing I'm comfortable with playing for you today. Besides, Yore's here and we should really get to work. Studio time costs a lot of money."

"You're damn straight it does!" Shortypants yelled like the sergeant from the television show *Gomer Pyle*. "And who the hell is paying for these cameras? It won't be Bitch Slap, I can tell you that!" he added.

I guess he felt the need to continue on, because that's exactly what he did.

"I still don't understand why the fuck you're bothering with all this archaic technology, Willy! Kids today, they don't give a shit about this analog crap. Get Alsihad in here and finish the fucking record already."

I just couldn't get over how someone who was smoking Lucky Strikes and wearing Porsche sunglasses and snakeskin cowboy boots was telling *us* that we were somehow behind the times.

"Now that Cotton has broken his wrist and we're hiring a session drummer, we really won't need Alsihad," Willy said as he attempted to guide Shortypants out the door.

But Shortypants wasn't about to leave. He wanted to know all about the session drummer and the timeline. He wanted to come by and listen to more of the record. Shortypants made all sorts

of complaints until Fingaz walked in from his shitter and interrupted the lashing.

"What up wit dat Operation Stinky Fingaz proj, Yo?

Shortypants had a look on his face similar to how a cat would
look had an unfamiliar dog entered the room.

"Who's this?" Shortypants asked in wide-eyed amazement.

Willy introduced the two of them. I went to a spot in the room
where I wouldn't be noticed, signaling Fingaz to shut the hell up
with a dirty look and the universal "cut" sign made by running my
finger across my neck. Shortypants was interested in the "Operation Stinky Fingers" project, but fortunately Fingaz came up with
a well-thought-out clever little story to explain his gaffe.

"Aw, dat was a joke, Dawg," he replied as he exited back to his
shitter.

Finally, and with a most confused look on his face, Shortypants
left the room with Willy.

Yore wanted to hear what we had done on the song last night
as well, so I decided to print the instrumental monitor mix to
DAT, while Yore was listening back to the track. This way, I could
play it in the future without having to perform a mix on every
playback.

For the first time, Yore was somewhat impressed.

"Wow!" he said. "It's really come alive. What'd you do to the
track? The bass sounds killer now!"

I couldn't help but laugh aloud. I tried not to, but there was
just no way that I could be asked that question so directly and not
chuckle.

"That would be the stereo compressor that I'm using on the
mix," I said.

"Well, keep that on there all the time then," he said.

"I'm planning to," I replied, and so we laid down guitar parts on the other two camera takes, as perhaps Johnny took my advice to come on alternating days with Yore.

But that would be just too good to be true.

– Mixerman

DAY 29
Technical Difficulties
(As Opposed to Just Plain Difficulties)

POSTED: SEPTEMBER 7, 3:21 A.M.

Today we didn't do shit, not that this is much different from any other days, but at least on those days, I've got some good stories to tell. An entire portion of the board was spitting and distorting badly. The glass had arrived, so rather than wait around half the day, we decided to let the studio have a maintenance day to put in the glass and fix the console.

Willy is considering working Saturday, although I seriously doubt that's actually going to happen.

Monday the new drummer arrives for more takes.

– Mixerman

DAY 30

Blistered

POSTED: SEPTEMBER 10, 2:54 A.M. — WEEK 7

Shortypants must have thrown a hissy fit of epic proportions with the label, because the film crew was gone by the time I arrived today. From conversations throughout the course of the day, I gathered that the label was planning to pay for only half of the filming costs. That means the band would have to recoup the other half through its royalties. In other words, the band wouldn't make a dime until half the money that was spent on the filming was paid back to the record company. This is a very common contractual agreement for music videos, but as far as Shortypants was concerned, to have the band recoup the cost of some sort of documentary wasn't going to fly. Apparently, the label was willing to negotiate on the recouping issue where the documentary was concerned, but Shortypants didn't want the replacement drummer on film anyway, as that would probably look bad. I can't say that I disagree.

It was nice to walk into a studio that was private again. Having the cameras gone was like having an oppressive dictator removed. No longer would I have to be careful about anything that I might say or do, for fear of how I might appear were I to be edited out of context. Best of all, I could pass gas again with absolute confidence.

Our new drummer was already hammering away at the drums. I didn't dare go anywhere near the tracking room while he was playing, as he hit those drums so fucking hard. Holy shit! I waited until he stopped before I made my way in to introduce myself.

"Mixerman," I said to the new drummer, as I held out my hand to signal that I came in peace.

"Blister's the name," responded the drummer as he accepted my peace offering.

Blister was wearing a black sleeveless T-shirt that had "Go fuck your mother" emblazoned on the front of it, beige hiking shorts, and yellowish-brown work boots. If I hadn't seen him drumming, I might have thought he was coming in to do some caulking work on the freshly inlaid glass. Around his neck hung a string with two bright orange earplugs, slightly soiled with ear wax on each end. He was completely bald and was sporting the mandatory tattoos on his body. Some of them were likely covered by his most pleasantly inviting T-shirt. Oddly, his personality was nothing like his dress code.

"How do you do?" he continued, after introducing himself to me.

"I'm fine, thank you," I responded.

"Very pleasant day outside, wouldn't you say?" he added.

"Indubitably," I replied as Fingaz, who happened to be walking by, did a double take. "Word," I said to Fingaz, who nodded his head as if he now understood the meaning of "indubitably."

Blister's drum kit had been delivered and set up early that morning by his cartage company. It was nothing short of overwhelming. He had two kik drums, two snares, seven toms, and nine cymbals, which was one kik drum, one snare, four toms, and five cymbals too many for this particular project. This kit was entirely inappropriate for the style of rock music we were recording. Rather than hurt his feelings by asking him to trim down his set, I decided it'd be best if he came to that conclusion on his own. I escorted him to the Womb and played him some music.

In listening to the takes we had done so far with Dumb Ass, Blister wisely came to the conclusion that his kit was slightly excessive for the style of rock music that we were recording.

Indeed!

Thankfully, he removed the extra kik drum and the extra toms, and went with the much simpler setup of one kik, one snare, three toms, and four cymbals. There will be a test on this later.

Once we got the drum set together, getting drum sounds was a breeze. Typically with a player as good as Blister, all I really need to accomplish is getting the mics positioned in the right places. I've said this before in this diary, but I'll say it again. Mics cannot effectively be placed by sight. Regardless of how many times I say it, this is a mistake that I witness frequently. I've even had producers ask me to move mics from positions that looked wrong to them, but the best mic position cannot be predicted—it must be found.

I sent Lance out to move mics around as Blister played. Anytime Lance found a magical spot, I'd yell, "Stop!" in the talkback. Even though I had the room mics positioned for Dumb Ass, this was a different player who beat the hell out of his drums. My current positions were not "givens" for the new drummer.

The room is the majority of the sound, so I started with those mics and then we started to add mics that would act as support to the room mics. Blister was so good at balancing the mix of his own kit that I really only needed four mics total, the two mics directly over the drums called "overheads" and the two room mics. But I still put a kik and snare mic to tape, as these always come in handy, particularly for songs that rely less on the room sound.

We had drum sounds in about ten minutes flat. I guess everyone else figured it would take longer than that, because the rest of the crew didn't show up until 4 P.M.

Harmon was the first to arrive at quarter of four, and he immediately wanted to hear the rough mix of the takes that Yore was so amped up about. I wouldn't say I was nervous, but rather concerned that Harmon would notice that his bass parts had been replaced. Lance, on the other hand, was visibly shaking and sweating bullets as he loaded the DAT to play for Harmon.

Harmon totally grooved on the song and without even turning down the music, yelled out, "What the hell did you do to the bass?"

I decided to treat that as a rhetorical question, since I wasn't about to try to communicate over the blasting music. Besides, it wasn't a question I actually wished to answer. After he had completely listened to the first rough mix, Harmon turned down the volume to speak to me.

"You're a fucking magician!" Harmon exclaimed in full whine, as he stood up and began picking his ass. "My bass parts have come alive, man, what the hell'd you do?"

I fed him a bunch of bullshit about compression and gave him made-up philosophies on the benefits of recording bass without compression and then adding it later. I further confused the issue by telling him that I was now putting a compressor on the stereo bus, and that this was making the third harmonic distort slightly on the bass, allowing for the first harmonic to react with the odd-even harmonic contingency. He listened very intently as I pontificated.

"Well, whatever the fuck you did, keep it up, Bro!" he said, punching me in the arm with the side of his fist.

Harmon listened to the other two instrumental roughs as Johnny and Paulie Yore arrived. Dumb Ass didn't come to the studio today, which made things unusually pleasant. Willy walked in last. He immediately looked over at me, as if to get some sort of sign that the bass replacements had not been discovered. I smiled and gave him a thumbs-up, the international sign for "everything's cool." Judging by the look on his face, my gesture seemed to be enough to put his mind at ease.

"Damn!" Harmon replied again, as he turned around and saw Willy. "That's kicking some ass now!"

"I think so too," said Willy as he sparked up a fatty, standing there like he was Humphrey Bogart lighting a cigarette.

Blister was introduced to everyone in the room. Willy gave him and everyone else in the room a hug and kibitzed for awhile. Once niceties had been sufficiently exchanged, we cued up the rehearsal demo of the song we were planning to start with. Blister listened to the song once and then asked for it to be played for him again. He made out a chart for himself while the rest of the band made their way into the room.

It didn't take but a few minutes to select the proper guitar and bass for the tracking of the song. Everything seemed to be working like clockwork.

Then we hit a snag.

Apparently Blister didn't want to play without his earplugs in. He had grown quite accustomed to playing this way, since he was on tour for the better part of the year. Even with his headphones turned all the way up, there wasn't enough volume to permeate the 25dB reduction caused by earplugs.

My first course of action was to change his headphones. Some headphones appear louder than others, so I gave him another brand of headphones. This particular brand tends to have a bit more mid-range than others, and they don't have cloth covering the element that presses against the ear. The cloth tends to act as a filter of sorts to high frequencies. So do earplugs. Unfortunately, the headphones were slipping off, but with a few adjustments, we got them to stay comfortably.

Even with the change in headphones, Blister couldn't turn them up loud enough, so I had Lance set up a completely different amplifier for Blister's headphones. He used a 500-watt Hafler amp, which would certainly be more than enough power to blast through the earplugs. The band used little mixers to supply them with a headphone mix. Being that Blister was now on his own amplifier, I had to make a cue mix[51] for him on the console, which I did as Lance continued to set him up.

Unfortunately, the headphones were so loud that the sound was bleeding into all the mics. Even when everyone was playing full blast, it was a problem. As if that weren't enough, at one point in the arrangement of this particular song, the drums stop with a crash cymbal and the guitar plays a riff by itself as the cymbals are dying out. Unless we were planning to eventually stop the drums abruptly with a mute, which is a very unnatural sound and quite probably inappropriate for this particular production, the bleed was going to be a problem as the clik track was pounding away through the break for all to hear. As if that wasn't enough of a problem, the headphones were still sliding off Blister's head.

I suggested that we either go back to the original headphones that were softer and didn't slide off *or* that Blister remove the plugs that were making it necessary to turn the phones up so loud. Logic didn't seem to be Blister's strong point, as he didn't like either of those suggestions. Suddenly, Blister had an idea of how to solve both problems, and in one fell swoop. He suggested that we gaffer tape the headphones to his own head, and while this was a plan that I would have expected Dumb Ass to come up with, the fact that Blister had no hair on his head certainly made it feasible. So I summoned Lance to get the gaffer tape, which is very sticky black tape used to anchor cables in order to prevent people from tripping and knocking things over with disastrous results.

Ahem.

We proceeded to tape the headphones tight around Blister's head, attaching the tape like a headband placed just above the eyebrows. Blister played about ten seconds of the song with the band and yelled at the top of his lungs, "YEAH! THIS IS GREAT! LET'S MAKE ONE!"

"Okay!" I yelled to him through the talkback that went to everyone's cans,[52] which I suppose was too loud for everyone else, as they all ripped their headphones off and gave me looks of disgust. I actually took a journey to the room to tell the band in person to turn down my talkback mix fader so that phenomenon wouldn't happen again. Once back in my position in the Womb, I asked them to play the break in the song in which the headphone bleed had been problematic. Fortunately, the bleed had been substantially reduced to the point that I could barely hear the clik track in the drum mics during the break. So we started making takes.

The band was playing great. Even Harmon played better with Blister, although I doubt Lance's newly acquired job as bass replacer was in any kind of jeopardy. Johnny was actually singing his ass off, for once, and Yore, who usually played well, was playing a bit more youthfully and recklessly than usual. In fact, the take was feeling so good by two minutes into the song, I thought they might actually get their first song in one take. This was nothing short of staggering, given the way this session had gone to date and coupled with the fact that Blister had never actually played the song down. Unfortunately, their chances of getting a "first take" went right out the window at around the two-minute mark, as the drums suddenly stopped and were inexplicably replaced by the sound of screaming.

The rest of the band immediately stopped playing, as we all just stood there watching Blister screaming as he flailed about violently, ripping at his gaffer tape headband and the earpieces of the headphones. I'm sure everyone was frozen, since nobody knew exactly what the hell Blister was doing. At first I thought maybe he had made a mistake, and he was just being funny in an overly dramatic sort of way. But that didn't really seem his style, as to this point he had been quite reserved. Finally, when I saw the tears coming down his face, I realized that he was in pure agony.

He ripped and yanked at his headphones as he jumped up and down like a monkey in the jungle. I ran out to help him, but before I got there, he had finally managed to rip off the headphones, which now lay in a mangled mess on the floor. He was still howling in pain as I looked at his ears, which were beet red.

I quickly grabbed the cold bottle of water that he had next to his kit, and without really thinking, poured water on one of his ears. As appreciative as I thought he should have been for my trying to help a guy out, he sure did give me a dirty look. Lance had run to get some ice and finally arrived with two measly little cubes. I took the ice cubes from Lance, and I immediately held them against Blister's ears, which also got me a dirty look. Seeing as my help wasn't appreciated, I just handed Blister the ice and let him do it himself.

When I finally picked up the headphones, I realized exactly what had happened. The elements had gotten so hot that they'd begun to burn Blister's ears. The element is basically a piece of metal that has holes in it to allow the sound of the music to escape. The imprints of those holes were now emblazoned on each of Blister's ears. Fortunately, his burns weren't severe enough to warrant a visit to the emergency room. We let him ice them for the better part of an hour before we began making takes again.

The rest of the night was fairly uneventful. Blister decided it would be best if he played with headphones that had cloth over the element and without the use of earplugs, or excessively powerful amplifiers. I concurred. After making some slight form changes to the song, Willy felt as though we had a take that he liked. So I made him a rough, printed it to CD, and we all split for the night.

Despite the mishap with the excessively hot headphones, all in all it was a pretty good day. As good as Blister is, though, I question whether he's the right drummer for this album. While his playing is miles ahead of Dumb Ass's "bucking bronco" technique, something's not quite right. Certainly there are positives that Blister brings to the other players, but overall, I'm not sure he fits the vibe. But then, that's not my call—that's Willy's.

That's why he gets the big bucks.

– Mixerman

The Inevitable Meltdown

POSTED: SEPTEMBER 11, 3:22 A.M.

When I woke up this morning, I was in great spirits. And why wouldn't I be? We were recording with an excellent drummer, the band played well with him, and Dumb Ass wasn't there. The absence of Dumb Ass alone was enough to give me renewal of spirit.

It's not so much that Dumb Ass is evil or mean. Quite the contrary, he's harmless. But as harmless as Dumb Ass is with his retard routines, he has no understanding or feel for silent cues. Ignoring Dumb Ass is useless, because he never gets the hint. So you have to spell it out for him.

"Please, I have to complete this task right now and it requires concentration," I would say to him regularly. But he still wouldn't get it.

Regardless, I'm always extremely nice to the guy face to face. It'd be a lot easier if I could just act like the band and tell him to shut the fuck up, but that doesn't really help matters, and technically, he *is* the client. In general, I've found it be a good policy to avoid telling the client to shut the fuck up.

Seeing as this was a Bitch Slap session, there was no way in hell I could expect to have two good days in a row, and I certainly wasn't going to get my hopes up. So rather than allowing the usual tack of thinking positively at the beginning of the day only to have my pleasant thoughts shattered to pieces, I prepared myself for the worst. I tried convincing myself that Dumb Ass would be at the session, and I mentally prepared myself for such an event by repeating over and over that Dumb Ass was definitely going to be there today. The way I figured it, I would have a positive uplifting experience if I were somehow wrong, but I would be unfazed if I were right. Of course, my plan failed miserably, for when I arrived today and saw Dumb Ass on the patio, I was devastated. I swear to you, had someone at that particular moment told me my cat died, the news would have likely cheered me up.

No sooner did I get out of the car than I was flooded with an endless barrage of questions. He was like a one-man mob of reporters that I couldn't get past. He wanted to know all about yesterday's session, and what I thought of the replacement drummer, and yadda, yadda, yadda. So I told him that he should listen to the take for himself. When I finally got into the Womb, which was anything *but* that with the presence of Dumb Ass, I had Lance cue up the Blister take. Dumb Ass remained motionless as I played the recording.

"Well, I think it sucks," Dumb Ass announced dramatically after the take was finished.

"Really? What don't you like about it?" I asked.

"The feel's all wrong! That's not how I play."

I couldn't help but think to myself, That's the point! Of course, Dumb Ass was oblivious to the fact that he was being replaced for his substandard drumming. As far as he was concerned, he would be playing drums on this album had he not broken his wrist.

It didn't help that Fingaz was adding fuel to the fire.

"Dat shit sucks, Yo!" he said as he entered the room, being savvy enough to know what was going on.

"See, even he thinks so!" said Dumb Ass.

"He didn't even hear it!" I yelled in amazement.

"Oh, I heard that shit stinkin' up the place from down the hall, Yo." responded Fingaz as he pinched his nose and nodded his head up and down in an exaggerated fashion.

It was quite obvious to me what was going on here. Fingaz didn't want to be out of a job, so he was pulling a sabotage ploy. Even though I had to agree that Blister was not necessarily the perfect drummer for the project, he certainly wasn't "stinking up the place." What did Fingaz think he was going to accomplish by trading one great drummer for another? He'd still be out of a job by the time he finally finished editing the last of the camera takes. Of course, Fingaz was working at such a leisurely pace by now, I wasn't sure he'd ever be finished.

In short order, the rest of the band, including Blister and Willy, had arrived. The blisters on Blister's ears were looking much improved, but you could still see the imprint of the speaker element on his ears. I couldn't help but laugh aloud as I wondered if the imprint would be permanent. Blister didn't take kindly to my finding humor in his plight, so I got another dirty look, which only made the situation funnier to me.

Willy wanted to immediately move on to the next song. So we repeated yesterday's process of listening to the demo a couple of times, allowing Blister to chart out the song, discuss arrangements, and adjust sounds.

The band played down its first take of the song, which, from my experience, was a decent take and worth saving. From Dumb Ass's experience, which is somewhere between zilch and none, it was the worst take in the history of takes. He would have interrupted the band in the middle had I not physically stopped him. As the band was playing the last chord of the take, Dumb Ass was already on his way to the tracking room, where he could be heard discussing the idea that a drummer should somehow never strive to play in perfect time.

Willy sat at the console with his face in his hands, as if he just couldn't watch. Blister was looking up at Dumb Ass with absolute amazement. Johnny just lay down on the couch in his Living Room, and Yore decided it was time to have a drink. I was listening intently as Dumb Ass proceeded to show Blister a better beat for the song. He even went so far as to ask me to roll tape for him.

"Should you really be playing a hi-hat beat with a broken wrist?" I asked over the talkback.

"Just roll it!" he yelled in a most hostile manner. So I obliged.

Blister was taking it all in stride, and when Dumb Ass finished his most god-awful presentation of how to play drums, which in reality should have been a seminar on how *not* to play drums, Blister took his position on the drum throne again.

"I'll try to incorporate that into my performance somehow," Blister said to Dumb Ass cordially. That was good enough for Dumb Ass, who appeared somewhat pleased with himself as he reentered the Womb.

275

So the band made another take, and when they finished, Dumb Ass grabbed the talkback remote from my hand. I had considered holding tightly and not releasing it, but then I couldn't think of anything I'd regret more than getting into some sort of juvenile tug-of-war contest over a talkback remote. As far as I was concerned, if he wanted to make an ass of himself, that was his prerogative.

"That's getting closer!" yelled Dumb Ass right into the button that he was pushing, which is not a microphone, and if it were, he'd have been covering it with his thumb. "You're still playing too good," he continued.

Paulie Yore, fresh from polishing off a tall glass of Maker's Mark, had reached the end of his rope.

"What the fuck are you talking about?" Yore exclaimed, his voice coming through the speakers. "We're not going to play the song shitty just so it matches your bullshit drum takes!"

Thus began a fight of epic proportions, with the meanness of this session reaching new heights. Even Willy's fatties were no match for this particular exchange of blows. The atmosphere was so heavy, so disconcerting, and so vile, I could hardly stand to be in the room. Unfortunately, I needed to prepare for the worst, as I thought for sure the shouting match was going to escalate to a physical confrontation.

Physical confrontations are not good under normal circumstances. They are even worse when surrounded by hundreds of thousands of dollars worth of microphones and guitars. Both Willy and I were trying desperately to separate the group before such an event occurred. Blister obviously wanted no part of this particular vibe, so he exited stage left without a word to anybody.

In most cases, some of the abuse being dished out could cause a person involved to ultimately have regrets. In this case, I don't think any of them would have regrets later. The room was thick with disdain, the likes of which I've rarely seen before. This was two years of battle scars and pent-up frustrations coming to a head. Nothing was held back or left to the imagination. This was the Mother of all Fights and was meant to be so. The insults and the criticisms were designed to wound swiftly and deeply, and with no regard for one's fellow man. Going into specifics of what was said would be of little use for the purposes of this diary, and expressing that kind of detail would likely make the arguments seem silly. But I assure you they were far from silly and nothing short of distressing and draining.

Dumb Ass had finally had enough and went into the control room. Yore split, and Johnny wasn't far behind, although I doubt they went anywhere together. The battle was not a pile-on but rather a free-for-all, and Yore and Johnny certainly didn't have a shortage of disdain in regard to each other. Harmon generally didn't enter the fray, although when he did, he acted as an accelerant to the flames, as that was his role in this band. They all had their roles—Dumb Ass the Scapegoat, Paulie Yore the Victim, Johnny the Instigator, and Harmon Neenot the Accelerant. It's no wonder they can't take each other any more—they are a truly volatile and explosive combination of personalities.

Dumb Ass was the last to leave. He had given notice to Willy that he wouldn't be coming back. Willy didn't seem in the mood to convince him otherwise, which I'm grateful for. Besides, there was no point in that. At the very least, Yore, Johnny, and Harmon can coexist with each other. It was Dumb Ass who was as inept in his role as scapegoat as he was as drummer. For a great scapegoat is held in high regard for preventing such disintegrations, not causing them.

And so Dumb Ass has quit the band, which may or may not be a bad thing. It depends on what the record company wants to do about it. Willy told me that he'd call me tomorrow after the dust settled. I suppose there's always the possibility this whole argument will blow over, and Dumb Ass will be back again tomorrow. It's hard to guess.

I have to say, today's meltdown was never a matter of "if" but purely a matter of "when." It was the inevitable meltdown of a band that got into this for all the wrong reasons and was signed by a label for all the wrong reasons. Nothing is immune from being wrong on this session, including me. Even this journal is wrong, but you know how the saying goes —

When in Rome . . .

– Mixerman

DAY 32

Day of Reckoning

POSTED: SEPTEMBER 12, 3:12 A.M.

It's impossible for me to speak accurately on all the inner work-ings, jockeying, cajoling, manipulating, influencing, parleying, and negotiating that go on the day after a session blows up to the proportion that Bitch Slap's has—generally because I'm not privy to most of it. I can assure you that were I able to document such events, this entry would be far superior in both its entertainment and informative value to anything that I've written to date.

I'm sure there was every combination of phone calls that one could imagine among the characters in this saga. Willy to Marv, Marv to Jeramiah, Jeramiah to Shortypants, Shortypants to Marv—you get the picture. I'm also confident that the subject of those conversations had most of all to do with the acceptance of Dumb Ass's resignation, or the refusal of such, and all the ramifi-cations of either decision.

I've been right smack in the middle of these sorts of discus-sions. I can pretty much tell you everyone's position just from what I know of each person and from similar experiences.

First we have Marv, the president's president, who was willing to spend any amount of money it would take to make Bitch Slap a hit. That's all that Marv cares about. The band that he paid two million dollars for *must* be a hit. As far as Marv is concerned, he wants Willy to make him a hit record: If that meant hiring a drummer or finding a replacement for Dumb Ass, then so be it, just so long as he delivers a hit (as if there is such a thing before the fact).

Next, we have good ol' Jeramiah Weasel. Without a doubt, he would want to start auditions immediately. Most likely, he would want to audition drummers from once successful and now defunct bands, so as to have a "name" player in the group.

Shortypants I don't know from Adam. If I had to guess, I'd say that Shortypants wants to convince Dumb Ass to come back. Shortypants likely worries about the ramifications of losing a band member and what that might do to Bitch Slap's chances of ever even getting a record out.

Willy's easy. He, without a doubt, wants to hire a studio drummer, lay down the tracks, lay down the overdubs, and get the hell out of here.

Fingaz, who, much like me, has no say-so whatsoever in this decision, was probably hoping that Dumb Ass would have some sort of miraculous recovery and play drums again so that he could keep working.

Me? I always have an opinion. The bottom line is this: Dumb Ass's wrist is broken in two places and will not heal quickly. Once it heals, it will take Dumb Ass time to get into his top form, which is, on his best day, shit. Dumb Ass is hardly a super-important member of the band. He doesn't write any of the songs, he's not marketable, he's not particularly good looking, and he doesn't even keep a steady beat. So why the fuck keep him around just for the sake of keeping him around? He quit, so I say let him go.

I spoke to Willy early this morning. He wanted to record guitars on the tracks we already have, but ultimately, that was going to have to wait until tomorrow. Willy would be in meetings all day, discussing the dilemma at hand. I attempted to extract some information from him, but at the time, I think there was little to extract. Today was Bitch Slap's day of reckoning.

For me, it was just a day of rest, and a much-appreciated one at that.

– Mixerman

DAY 33

We Be Cruisin'

POSTED: SEPTEMBER 13, 4:32 A.M.

As smart as I think I might be sometimes, it's days like this that make me realize I don't know shit. As much as I pride myself on reading the subtle cues of others, such as recognizing when someone is mildly uncomfortable or if someone is being less than forthright with me, and as sensitive as I am to vibrations going on around me, I *still* can't predict the twists and turns of a session. Quite honestly, I rarely even try. Today was just further evidence as to why I shouldn't try.

Willy called early this morning, waking me from a deep sleep.

"We're on. Noon start," he said abruptly after I picked up the phone.

I suspect Willy called me early so as to prevent me from being able to go into a million questions that he obviously didn't want to answer. His plan had succeeded, for I was barely able to get anything more than a grunt, and Willy was quick to hang up after receiving such acknowledgment.

I left my house at 11 A.M. and arrived at the studio forty-five minutes later. I was greeted by Lance with a cup of coffee and a chocolate muffin. I pinched myself, which I realize is sort of a cliché reaction, but I was doing it more for the outward effect of it than actually trying to determine if I was somehow dreaming.

"What do you know?" I asked instantly, not even bothering to comment on the fact that Lance had arrived before me, and I was fifteen minutes early!

"Nothing," Lance replied as he shrugged his shoulders and spilled a bit of coffee. I thought of asking Lance what time it was, but I feared he might have actually gone for that one and spilled coffee on my new shoes — the ones I bought yesterday.

Anytime I get a day off from a long session, I usually go shopping, because it might be months before I get the opportunity again. I love my new shoes, but more than that, I love my new socks, of which I bought thirty-two pair.

I replace all of my socks on occasion, and I like to have a full month's supply on hand, as I can fit the whole lot in the washer in one load. Sometimes I buy a new supply of socks just so I don't have to wash the dirty ones. Occasionally that gets my wife to wash them for me, since she doesn't want me buying new socks when I have a laundry basket full of perfectly good socks were they not dirty. With these strategies in place, I find that I only have to wash my own socks about three times a year. I suppose I could just use a fluff-and-fold service, but for some reason, that gives me the creeps. It's all very convoluted, and besides, I digress.

Since I hadn't the foggiest idea what the plan was for today, I decided to sit on the patio with my coffee and muffin and kibitz with my main man Lance. This was highly atypical for me. I usually prefer to go straight for the Womb, as there's a good reason why I call the control room that. It's where I'm most comfortable. But being that I am this odd combination of recluse and socialite, I was feeling comfortable with the concept of having some fresh air with my breakfast.

I marvel at what breaks in routine bring to me. Sometimes I wonder what I must miss in life, because it seems that anytime I break up my routine, I make a discovery so valuable that I can't quite fathom going through life without it. Like the time that I picked up the newspaper while I was traveling out of town and read the obituaries, which I *never* read, and in it found the obituary of a lost acquaintance. Had I not read it, I can assure you that I wouldn't have ever found out that he was dead. Although that's probably a bad example, since I didn't really like the guy. Or like the time that I inexplicably decided to walk outside to smoke a cigarette (years ago, back when I smoked) only to watch a guy hit my car as he was parking and then drive off. I got the motherfucker's license plate number and had him busted. There's a point to all of this aside from the one on the top of my head.

You see, if I had done what I normally do, which is go directly to the Womb, I would never have gotten the opportunity to see a full-on, brand-spanking-new stretch limousine pull up with Dumb Ass's head sticking out of the sun roof as he toasted the neighborhood with champagne. I also wouldn't have seen Dumb Ass, Harmon Neenot, Paulie Yore, Johnny A-Go-Go, Marv Ellis, Marv's superfine girlfriend, and *Fingaz* stream out of the limo like an endless parade of clowns from a Volkswagen Beetle. Nor would I have seen the clowns impeccably dressed and acting all chummy like the Mother of all Fights had never even happened.

Dumb Ass gave me salutations as he walked by. The rest of the crew stayed out in the lot by the limo except Harmon, who came up to me, greeted me, and proceeded to tell me, out of nowhere, that the band was going on a cruise.

"A cruise?" I asked in an astonished manner. "With Cotton?" I continued.

"Yeah, well, some counselor is coming with us, and we're going to work out our problems," he responded, as if he actually believed that was possible "We have to set our boundaries," he finished.

I stood there half smiling, unable to move. I was almost going to laugh, but I willed myself from that. Yore waved to me from across the lot, and I waved enthusiastically back. Then I turned my attention back to Harmon, who was now picking his butt, even as well dressed as he was.

"I assume you're going right now," I said, and Harmon nodded. "Fingaz is going with you?"

"Yeah, well I guess he's done with his work until we get back, so we figured we'd bring him along . . . for comic relief," Harmon answered.

But what of *my* comic relief?

I couldn't believe it. Motherfucker! Fingaz gets to go on a cruise? Anyone who doubts that life just isn't fair needs to read this diary—at least up to here—for it now contains undeniable proof of this fact.

"When are you coming back?" I asked inquisitively and still, quite frankly, in absolute disbelief.

"I think like Tuesday or something like that. That's not even the best part, Bro!"

I couldn't wait to hear the best part.

"We get to keep the limo and the driver for awhile. Shortypants negotiated for all of it."

I just sat there on my stool with a stupid grin on my face. Without my realizing it, Marv had made his way to me, and he shook my hand with both of his.

"Hey, glad to see you again, Mixerman! I'm going to get these guys away from the studio for a few days. You and Willy do what you need to do. We need *hits*! Give me *hits*!" Marv said to me with great zeal, as he raised his arm in triumph and then lowered it to punch me on the arm in just the perfect spot so as to cause enormous pain.

"Okay," I said stunned. Marv was already walking back toward the limo as my arm throbbed.

Dumb Ass walked out of the studio carrying a prescription bottle, and he waved to me as he ran to the limo and got in with the rest of the crew. "*Hits!*" yelled Marv toward me, as he was the last to climb into the limo. Then the limo drove away.

The sequence of events that had just occurred before me was, without a doubt, one of the greatest lessons that I could walk away with in a lifetime of lessons that simply pale by comparison. For I now understood exactly how one should deal with a band full of losers who can't play well together and can't get along. I now understood how you convince an expendable player who throws a hissy fit and quits because he's not getting his way to stay. You supply the entire lot with a stretch limousine and brand-new clothes and you send them on a cruise for five days and four nights, along with the president of the company and his super-hot girlfriend.

Then there was the other lesson. If you're the Radar editor on the album, you get to go too!

The whole limo bit is the oldest trick in the Biz. It's easy to get artists to do what you want if you let them live large. Living large is just as bad as drugs, because the artists will agree to just about anything as they are in an altered state of mind. They couldn't fathom the loss of such perks as a driver, getting into exclusive restaurants and not having to pay the bill, having someone else buy them expensive handmade clothes, receiving expensive gifts, etc. It's considerably cheaper for a label to make artists feel and look like millionaires than it is to actually *make* them millionaires. Record companies do it all the time, especially when they want something from the artist. But what do they want? That's the question.

Willy finally drove in, as I sat there still dazed from the events that had just transpired before me. He walked up to me and asked how my day off was. I told him it was fine, and I showed him my new shoes and socks. Then I told him that I had just seen the band and heard about their little voyage. Willy told me that Shortypants had negotiated for it, and that he wanted the band to stay together rather than holding auditions in the middle of the project. The label insisted on the counseling sessions, and Marv volunteered to go along with them. Gee, I wonder why.

"Will Marv be attending the counseling sessions?" I inquired, not really expecting an answer.

Willy proceeded to tell me that Blister wouldn't be joining us anymore. Apparently, Blister had made it abundantly clear that he wanted no part of these, and I quote, "idiots." This made me ponder how it was that a drummer who thought it was a good idea to wear earplugs and then blast as loudly as possible headphones gaffer-taped to his head understood so readily that working with idiots was not a positive career move—a lesson that I am apparently still learning. But then things made slightly more sense, as Willy explained that this wasn't the only reason that Blister was gone. Dumb Ass had successfully negotiated power of veto over any drummer used to replace him. Oh, great! Now Dumb Ass is choosing the drummer!

"How did that happen?" I asked shocked and dismayed.

"It was part of the negotiations," Willy responded.

I decided to leave that one alone temporarily and move on to the more imminent question on my mind.

"So what are we doing then?" I asked naively.

"We're going to smoke fatties and make a record," Willy said, signaling me to follow him.

I followed Willy to the room where he pulled out his 1967 Gibson SG Custom as he asked Lance to put up the first of the camera takes. Willy plugged the guitar into a variety of amplifiers and switched guitars a few times—once to a Fender Telecaster Custom from the early '70s and once to a 1957 Gibson Les Paul Gold Top. He tried several amplifiers, as well, until he found the sound he was looking for. All I had to do was open up the channel in order to get a superior tone, because Willy was simply an amazing guitar player.

Once Willy had gone through his arsenal of possible guitar sounds, he proceeded to replace the guitar doubles, recording over Johnny Rotten's guitar parts, thus sending them to Bias

Beach[53] for a permanent vacation. I found this mildly humorous, as I'd spent hours with Johnny recording those parts. Now, in about twenty minutes' time, Johnny Bye-Bye's guitar parts had all been replaced on the first song, and they sounded and felt a million times better than before.

Then Willy, Lance, and I got into a Science Experiment. A Science Experiment is a hit-or-miss attempt to find some unique sound to serve a role in the arrangement. Once started, the Experiments tend to grow and take on a life of their own—hence, the term.

Willy wanted an "eerie spaceship" kind of sound, so we brought in his pedal board and started playing with delays and effects on his guitar. He was using an EBow, which is a handheld device that emits a magnetic field. When the EBow is held close to the strings, it forces them to vibrate and "sing" in a very legato sort of way. We recorded the guitar to another pedal that Willy uses to sample (record) and loop[54] anything that he plays. Once sampled, he can reverse the loop and manipulate it in other ways.

We tried running the sound through a Leslie (which is basically a spinning speaker that distorts, used for Hammond B3 organs), and we fired through a succession of amplifiers trying to find the perfect sound. We tried a Vibro-King and a Tremolux, among others. At this point, I can't even remember what we ended up using. The moment we got the sound we liked, we recorded it, and that was that.

Science Experiments are my favorite part of a session. I enjoy them thoroughly, and I wouldn't think twice about spending two hours or more trying to create some magical sound through guitars, amplifiers, effects, and miking techniques. In fact, that's about how long we did spend, and the sound was killer. Of course, it only comes in one part of the song for about ten seconds, but I think it was well worth the time. More importantly, so does Willy.

The overdub session is the time to do Science Experiments. There's no bigger drag than doing a Science Experiment during a mix. Mixes should be done as quickly as possible. Sure, there are times that a Science Experiment will come up in a mix that no one thought about, and that's fine. But too often, people know that they want to put some wacky sound somewhere in the song, but then save the creation of that sound for the mix. That's a big mistake, because mixing is a flow-oriented job. Once you lose the flow, it's very difficult to get it back. Science Experiments are flow stoppers and are not enjoyable when one is under the stress of completing a wholly separate task.

When we had finally finished our Experiment, Willy and I went on a break to eat some sushi.

When we got back to the studio, Willy had Lance play bass parts on some freshly edited "camera takes" There were three of these, and they were the ones that Fingaz had been editing for what seemed to be an eternity after losing his ass in Vegas. I couldn't figure out what the hell Willy was playing at. Certainly Harmon's bass parts on the raw takes were shaky at best. How was Willy going to fool Harmon into thinking that the new perfectly played Lance bass parts were his? I pointed out my concerns.

"You realize that you're replacing parts that are scratch[55] tracks," I stated.

"Yep," said Willy as he was rolling us a post-dinner fatty.

"Well, there's no way that we're going to fool him with this," I continued.

Willy smiled and sat back in his chair as he kicked up his legs on the console and sucked on the fatty.

"That was part of the negotiations, too," Willy replied with a smile.

"Word."

– Mixerman

DAY 34

Wanted: Singer with Pleasant Personality & Professionally Cut Hair

POSTED: SEPTEMBER 14, 5:16 A.M.

I think the concept of sending the band on a cruise with a shrink to work out their problems is as ridiculous as it is brilliant. I'm not entirely sure how long Bitch Slap will be bon voyage, but clearly, each day they were out of the studio would be a day that Willy, Lance, and I could make great strides toward the completion of records. Particularly in light of the fact that we no longer had to hide from Bitch Slap the fact that they were being replaced.

These days, it's somewhat unusual to replace band players with session players. It's not entirely uncommon with drummers, but most producers will just settle for the band. It's also not uncommon for producers to lay down their own guitar parts or even keyboard parts. For the most part, though, rock music has become so edited and so manufactured that people don't even realize how lousy it is anymore. The bar has been lowered to such an extent that a band like Bitch Slap, which has average to below-average players, could have been edited on Alsihad and fit right into the mainstream. But Willy doesn't make albums like that and, fortunately, neither do I (to date).

It was kind of strange not having the band around. I felt as though my children had all gone off to camp, and the house, or in this case the Womb, was empty. I found myself longing for some of our old family rituals, such as cell phone detail.

In most studios—and this one is no exception—there is a large counter that separates the back of the room from the listening position behind the console. Horizontal space is at a premium in the studio, and the counter is a magnet for all sorts of personal paraphernalia, particularly cell phones. People store their wallets, sunglasses, pagers, phones, change, and messages on the counter. The problem is, for some inexplicable reason, everyone leaves his or her phones turned on while making a take.

Cell phones that ring or that automatically check for messages can make an electrical impulse that will not only be heard in the speakers, but will be recorded to tape. Not to mention the fact that listening to takes as cell phones are ringing left and right can be nothing short of distracting. Training people to either shut their cell phones off or to put the phones in the lounge is useless and hasn't worked to date on any session that I've ever been on. Even signs don't work. People never remember. So before every take, Lance and I have to be sure the room is clear of cell phones, and we have the extraction of phones down to a science.

Here's how the operation works: As soon as the band leaves the room, Lance runs to the door and opens it as I throw him all the cell phones that are on the counter, one at a time in quick succession. We also keep count, so that we know if we're missing one, that way we can make sure that nobody has accidentally brought it into the tracking room, which is worse than a phone being left in the control room. When a phone makes it into the tracking room, it is guaranteed to ring on a good take. I'm almost positive I read this on my brother's Murphy's Law poster that he had framed and hung in our bedroom when we were kids.

Lance would catch the phones one at a time, gently slide them down the hallway, and then close the door. What I find most intriguing is that not one person has ever once mentioned anything about the fact that his phone was on the floor outside the control room. The band would pick up their phones like droids and reenter the room as if nothing was out of the ordinary, and their equipment was right where they'd left it. Of course, they then leave the phone on the counter again.

Today, I started by recording bass parts with Lance, who was now partially rewriting the parts to their betterment. I wasn't quite sure whether that had been discussed in Willy's bargaining with the band, but I didn't give a shit either. Consequently, I didn't bother saying anything about it. Willy made phone calls in the lounge as he waited for us to complete the task, and when we had, Willy wanted to lay down some simple percussion.

I love doing overdubs when all the mics are up in the room for tracking, because I have a plethora of mics to choose from quickly and painlessly. There are probably as many models of microphones as there are models of cars. While they are all similar in function, they are also unique. Selecting a microphone for an instrument or an overdub is sometimes arbitrary, but usually quite deliberate. Most good engineers don't usually like to hold up a session in order to find the perfect mic for a tambourine.

While the source is always the most important part of the re-cording chain, the microphone will color the source—sometimes positively, sometimes negatively. The real bitch is that sometimes negatively coloring a source is a positive for a given production. This was such a time, as I wanted the tambourine to sound "thick and chunky" as opposed to "light and jangly." Seeing as I didn't have any Pultecs with a placebo "chunky" knob at my disposal, and seeing as every tambourine in the building sounded jangly, I was forced to use my choice of microphone to achieve the sound I was looking for.

I tried several mics, and ended up on a Coles 4038, which is a ribbon microphone. A ribbon microphone has a diaphragm made of ribbon, as opposed to a capsule made out of whatever capsules are made out of. I wouldn't know because I engineer from a pure-ly musical background, not a technical one. The Coles colored the sound exactly the way I wanted it to. The tambourine now sounded thick and chunky, and I recorded Willy playing the tam-bourine on a chorus of the song for him to listen to.

Willy hated my tambourine sound.

"I'm looking for something a little more jangly," he said.

"Really?" I replied, "I think a thick and chunky sound is far more appropriate for this tune."

"Don't get me wrong, I like the thick and chunky sound *very* much," Willy said, "but I think the thick and chunky tambourine is a bit much for this song. It needs to jangle."

So Willy and I went around the tambourine discussion for about twenty minutes, playing each other examples of recordings with tambourines that would support each of our claims. If dis-cussing a tambourine sound for twenty minutes seems excessive,

I can assure you it's not. Both of our points were valid, and my job is not to kiss Willy's ass and agree with everything he does for the sake of speed. If Willy weren't interested in engaging in discussion over the tambourine, he would have said so.

Finally, Willy agreed with my assessment, and we recorded the tambourine on the song. When Willy came back in and we listened down, the sound had grown on him, and he was completely digging on it. I, on the other hand, had grown to hate it.

"I think you were right," I said. "Jangly would be better for this song."

"No way, man! I love the thick and chunky sound," he replied. So we went around that for about five minutes until I had convinced Willy to lay down a jangly tambourine, and we could compare.

In the end, we kept both tambourines on tape. Not because we were putting off a decision, but because both Willy and I liked the chunk and the jangle together.

The rest of the day was fairly uneventful. We recorded some guitars. The only other item of note was that Willy wanted me to play Wurli (Wurlitzer electric piano) on a couple of the songs early next week. I play on albums all the time, and I love doing it, so that was fine by me. I made a CD of the roughs for myself, and I'm going to work out some parts over the weekend.

Now, if we could just find someone to sing the album, then we could keep the band out of the studio for the rest of the record.

But that would be asking too much.

– Mixerman

DAY 35

Makin' Records

POSTED: SEPTEMBER 17, 4:14 A.M. — WEEK 8

If only we had the drums for more than seven songs, we'd be finished with this record in just a couple of weeks' time. Lance's bass parts groove like a motherfucker, and he managed to make Dumb Ass's feel a relative nonissue. Willy's guitar parts were rarely anything short of genius. The doubles may seem like no-brainers, but there's a huge difference between playing the right chords at the right time and playing them with a feel. I probably harp on this all the time, but Jesus, this is music, and I shouldn't even have to say it.

All I can say is, there has *got* to be a resurgence of great bands with great songs. It's not because I'm old. I'm not. It's not as if I'm longing for yesterday's sound. As much as I like the way vinyl records sound better than CDs, I can get a bigger sound on CDs because they don't have the same limitations of keeping a needle implanted in a grove. I think, aside from the sound of vinyl records, what I like most about them is their limitation on running time.

Too often CDs have over an hour of music, and rarely do bands or artists have over sixty minutes of *great* material on any given album. Personally, I think it greatly weakens an album to include subpar songs. I like to put an album on and listen to it in its entirety. But if I find myself hitting the skip button, it greatly reduces my enjoyment of the album.

It's weird, because I don't find myself hitting the skip button when I watch a movie. I watch every scene, even if I've watched the movie many times before. That's because in a movie, every scene has a very specific reason for being there. Most moviemakers don't put scenes in movies that don't have some purpose. Why should an album be any different? Every song should have a purpose that relates to the other songs in the collection. I'm not saying that every album needs to be some sort of concept that tells a story. But clearly, when I listen to a sixteen-song CD, there are songs that just do not belong. If a record doesn't help the collection as a whole, then it shouldn't even make the album.

Unfortunately, I can often buy a DVD of a movie that costs over $100 million to make for less money than I can buy a CD that costs only $150,000 to make. That is, unless I buy my CDs at Best Buy—and I can't for the life of me figure out why *anyone* would buy his/her popular CDs anywhere but Best Buy. As much as I dislike that chain, they sell CDs for eleven or twelve dollars, which is considerably cheaper than a "real" record store. Supposedly, they take a loss on the CDs because they want you to buy slightly higher-ticket items such as digital cameras or computers.

Bitch Slap has seven songs that, once completed, would put us three songs short of a finished album. Unfortunately, we didn't necessarily record the best collection of songs first. The order in which we recorded songs was based more on the similarity in drum setups than on what songs would be best on the record. Out of a collection of demos, it can be nearly impossible to tell which records are going to come out the best. That's because the recording of a song does not live without a production— even if that production is nothing more than an instrument and a voice. Oftentimes, the production must be completed in order to determine whether it fits in the collection or not. That's why we originally planned to record seventeen songs and choose the best ones from those.

We are now on our thirty-fifth day on this project, and we only have seven songs in various stages of completion. At our present rate of work, aside from vocals, Willy, Lance, and I would have these productions completed by the end of the week. That is, were we to work the normal twelve-hour day. Today we worked fifteen.

We kicked serious ass today. Lance's bass parts were completed on seven of the songs. Willy wanted me to lay down some keyboard parts on several of the songs, so that's what we did. I don't really play that much anymore, so I wasn't going to be playing anything that required serious chops. I was merely trying to fill a role or give a song a slightly different feeling. I don't believe in adding a part for adding's sake. If I can't come up with a great part, then I won't lay anything down.

Most Bitch Slap songs are not in need of keyboards, but I ended up laying down a part on two of the songs, and then I played a countermelody with my Roland Jupiter 8. I also put an 808 kik drum in one of the songs, which is a hip-hop kik drum. The 808 sounds like a surge of low end that sustains and then dissipates over the course of a few beats.

We're entering the more interesting phase of making a record, because any part that is laid down now must be held to the following scrutiny: Does the part make the record better or worse? That's not always an instantaneous decision. Sometimes it's important to let a part age for a moment before you know whether it really does what you want.

Personally, I try to evaluate new parts by how they make me feel. For instance, today Willy laid down a guitar line that completely changed how the record made me feel. The part was great, worked with the scratch vocals, and worked with the instrumentation. But it didn't make me feel right. I expressed to Willy how the new part made me feel, and he agreed and came up with another part.

It's very difficult to engineer an album and simultaneously be aware of how things feel. They are two completely different brain processes. But after a while, you learn how to switch rather quickly between the two.

Anyway, nothing incredibly eventful went on today. After a fifteen-hour day, I can't believe I wrote even this much. Apparently Bitch Slap will be back in the studio Thursday. It's Willy's intention to have all of these tracks finished by then, barring the vocals. I wonder what the hell Bitch Slap is going to think of all this. It's one thing to blindly say, "Yeah, yeah, do what you want while we're on our cruise." It's another to come back and find that other people have made a good portion of your record without you. Personally, if I were they, I'd be nothing short of happy and elated, because the entire world is going to think they're a good band. Well, that is, the entire world except for us.

We know better.

– Mixerman

DAY 36

Marathon Man

POSTED: SEPTEMBER 18, 5:18 A.M.

Today was another fifteen-hour day, and I'm thoroughly exhausted from only four hours' sleep last night. To make matters worse, I think I'm coming down with a cold, which can be catastrophic on a session. For starters, there is no fresh air, just air-conditioning filters. So if I get sick, everyone gets sick. If the singer Johnny Breathe-Right becomes Johnny Clogged, we're fucked for what could be weeks in the vocal department. A cold certainly wouldn't help my cause, either. A cold can make it impossible to accurately judge sounds.

Willy is determined to finish these seven tracks before the band returns, and I can't say that I blame him. As much as fifteen-hour days are typically too long to be effective, it could save us a tremendous amount of grief later. So that's what we did. And while something very interesting occurred today, it will have to wait until tomorrow's entry.

How's that for a midweek cliffhanger?

– Mixerman

The Possible Repercussions of Percussion

POSTED: SEPTEMBER 19, 3:39 A.M.

I have no idea why, but Harmon's girlfriend, Virginia Skanky, (of the Huntington Beach Skankys) visited the studio yesterday. She wasn't the type of girl that I'd want to even stand behind in line at the grocery store, let alone allow into the Womb. It seems Harmon Neenot conveniently forgot to tell Virginia that he was going on a cruise. She was looking for him and was pissed that he wasn't returning her calls. She certainly acted brave when Harmon wasn't around.

"Where the fuck is Harmon?" she said to me out of the blue after barging into the Womb.

Good to see you, too, I thought to myself. She just stood there with her hands on her hips, obviously in no mood to exchange niceties. I decided it would be best to answer her question rather than pursue a Mr. Manners seminar with her.

"He's on a cruise. He didn't tell you?"

"A *cruise*? Bullshit!"

Then, upon looking at everyone else in the room who wasn't

laughing, and, with Lance nodding his head in confirmation, she must have realized that I wasn't kidding.

"That asshole!"

She entered into a long drawn-out tirade, calling Harmon every slur in the book, including ones that I didn't think necessarily applied to him. Just when I thought I'd heard every curse known to man, a scene that was beginning to become mildly humorous soured as Virginia broke down into sobs. I realized she was in desperate need of comfort, but I couldn't help but feel awkward at the fact that as much as she needed a hug was as much as I really didn't wish to hug her. Not because I disliked her—certainly I didn't know her well enough for that—but rather because I found her so distasteful. Still, she *was* distressed, and it was only right for me to try to offer up some comfort. But just as I began to approach the generally repulsive nymph, Lance swooped in to be her savior.

As much as I would have liked to believe that Lance was the kind of assistant that would fall on a sword for me, I'm pretty sure that he just happened to like tattoo-laden, oily-haired, and cheaply made-up girls. Lance began to treat her like a queen. He brought her coffee and muffins, and he even sat with her in the back of the room on the couch. I tried desperately to conjure up some sort of compassion for the girl, as I knew how abusive Harmon was to her, but all I could think of was how much her perfume made me want to puke.

Willy walked in to see Lance sitting on the couch with Virginia and then gave his wide-eyed "what the hell's going on?" look that I've grown so accustomed to seeing on this session. Lance and

Virginia were too wrapped up in what they were doing to notice Willy, so I pointed to the door, and Willy and I left the Womb.

"What the hell is going on?" Willy asked as we walked down the hall toward the kitchen for what I assumed was a pre-session muffin break. I briefed Willy. I was sure that Lance would get Virginia out of here as soon as he could.

After about an hour of listening to sniffles behind us and having Willy do nothing about it, I decided that I'd take matters into my own hands and I kindly asked her to leave. The most important part of "Womb removal" is the presentation.

"Perhaps you'd be more comfortable in the lounge," I said, feeling pretty good about my use of diplomacy.

From what I can tell, she must have thought I said, "Get the fuck out of the room, Bitch," because she instantly began sobbing again. Willy smacked his forehead so hard, I swear he had a red mark there for the rest of the day. We were trying to make a record here, and we had an unwanted Womb guest sobbing in the back of the room.

After we got Virginia sufficiently calmed down, Willy and I went back to work. I had several ideas of how to get rid of her, but I was fearful to even try, as we couldn't afford to lose another twenty minutes trying to calm down our unwanted Womb guest.

At one point, we were discussing the possibilities of percussion on several of the tracks, but in our conversation, we had discovered a slight problem with the plan. Aside from perhaps a simple tambourine part, like the one Willy laid down the other day, none of us could play percussion very well. That is, until Virginia spoke up.

"I can play percussion," she said.

At that moment, I was reminded why we don't typically allow visitors in the Womb. This was not the time or place to be auditioning percussion players.

"I play all the percussion parts on my band's demos," she said.

Willy and I sat there awkwardly exchanging apprehensive glances, still not buying the concept that Harmon Neenot's girlfriend was somehow a globally skilled percussion player.

"I can tell you I'm a hell of a lot better than that piece-of-shit excuse for a drummer they have!" she exclaimed.

That was good enough for Willy, who instantly went to his percussion bag and pulled out a tambourine and a shaker. He also grabbed his djembe on his way back into the control room.

"Here," he said. "Play these."

I rolled tape, and, to our amazement, she began to play the tambourine with remarkable feel and time. Then she put down the tambourine and played the shaker with equal skill. She could even play the damn djembe, which is nothing short of remarkable to me. Whereas this session is consistently cursed with the presence of the actual band, it is nothing short of blessed without them.

"Well, what the hell are we waiting for?" I yelled in excitement, as if I were Mickey, the grisly trainer in the first two *Rocky* movies.

The process of laying down percussion parts can be very tricky business. It doesn't *have* to be—it just can be. That's because a tambourine or a shaker can easily destroy the beauty of a track. Of course, the goal is to enhance the track, not destroy it, so one must examine exactly how a percussion part affects the song before accepting it as a keeper. It's not uncommon to try various rhythmic patterns with various percussion instruments, and even with varieties of the same percussion instruments. It's kind of like trying to find the piece of the puzzle that actually improves the song.

I find that for some reason artists, and sometimes producers, are almost compelled to lay down some sort of percussion on a rock song, regardless of whether it's needed or not. I don't agree with this sort of thinking. I like using percussion to enhance the lift of a song. It can be very effective for this. Percussion can also be very effective for enhancing the groove or even disguising a less-than-stellar groove. And while many of Dumb Ass's parts were fixed in a computer, they still didn't groove hard. That must come from the player. Certainly, Lance's bass parts drastically improved the groove of the songs, but adding percussion could further disguise any lack of groove in Cotton's drums.

Personally, I usually don't like laying down percussion parts until after the singer has laid down a vocal, *unless* the percussion parts happen to be integral to the pulse of the song. The shakers in the Rolling Stones' "Sympathy for the Devil" would be a good example of this. But, we didn't have a singer, and we certainly didn't want to give Dumb Ass the opportunity to play the parts. Besides, Willy wanted to record percussion. So we recorded percussion.

Virginia not only played the percussion instruments well, she came up with great parts that enhanced the song. A great performance of a tambourine part that destroys the quality of a production is counter to the process of making a great record. Fortunately for us, Virginia had a keen ear for where percussion was best suited. Willy and I just let her do her thing, simply amazed that this greasy angel had dropped into the Womb to play percussion for us. Yes, the pathetic creature was growing on me. If only she'd change that perfume!

We laid down the percussion parts on every song. After we completed that process, Virginia went back to hanging on the couch, which was fine by us. Lance kept her company, which, at one point, was starting to piss me off because he wasn't doing his fucking job. Willy wisely informed Virginia that we would call her for the next set of percussion parts. I guess she got the hint, because she didn't show up today.

Today we finished up recording another song, and then I made rough mixes of all seven productions to play for the band tomorrow. Only one rough mix actually contained an Yore guitar. Not because his guitar playing was bad, but because Willy's guitars were more consistent with the productions, as Willy wasn't married to one distinctive amp. The irony here floors me. For the only instrumentalist in the band who's made the majority of the cuts, the one person who was not replaced is not only the worst player in the band but the one person who, from what I can tell, was never intended to make the cut at all—Dumb Ass.

In the past three days, Willy, Lance, and I have basically completed seven productions, except for the most important part. The vocals. Of course, there were two songs with vocals. There was Harmon's impression of a dying seal. And then there was the vocal Johnny Opera did with Willy. But neither of these vocals were to Willy's liking. So much so, that he actually erased them from tape. A bold move if there ever was one.

Willy warned me that tomorrow would be a zoo in the Womb. The band, Marv, Jeramiah, Shortypants, and various record executives would all be joining us to listen to our tracks. If all goes according to plan, we will begin laying vocals on these productions as Jeramiah works with Cotton to find a drummer that is acceptable to all parties.

I can't help but wonder how the band is going to react when they hear the great tracks that Willy has put together. The tracks are miles beyond what I had ever expected them to mature into. But then I also never suspected the band would be on a cruise for the overdubbing process. Still, the repercussions of the band hearing tracks that none of them played on was far less interesting to me than the thought which was constantly and incessantly nagging at me since we recorded Virginia yesterday.

What would Harmon do when he found out his girlfriend recorded the percussion?

Setting aside my focus on what I can only term as the sideshow, I am hopeful that our most recent efforts on this album will provide the blueprint for the recording process on the next set of songs.

Record drums. Send band on cruise.

– Mixerman

DAY 38—PART 1

The Badly Timed Discovery

POSTED SEPTEMBER 20, 4:12 A.M.

On occasions like today, I always dress a touch better than the usual T-shirt and jeans. Today I wore a nice shirt and jeans and my Blundstone boots, which are imported from Australia. My father-in-law absolutely adores my pair of Blundstones and says that they are just like Romeos from back in the day. They were hand-delivered to me by an artist who was touring in Australia several years back, and at the time, they weren't being imported into the US. Now I see them all the time in stores, so if you go to purchase a pair for yourself, tell 'em Mixerman sent you, for I am hopeful that the company will send me a free pair for my father-in-law. But I digress before I've even started.

Today we were to be visited by the Mooks, or the Suits, or whatever the hell you want to call adults who attempt to make decisions on records that they can't possibly relate to. The visitation of Mooks to a session such as this one is a bittersweet event. The "sweet" being that the producer or the studio will spring for a fantastic spread of wine, beer, cheese, fruit, antipasto, and some kind of wraps or sandwiches. Unfortunately, you have to eat this food and drink this wine with Mooks, and therein lies the "bitter" part of the equation. These little shindigs are rebilled to the record company, which ultimately will be paid back with Bitch Slap royalties, further putting the band in debt. Of course, everyone pretends that it is a gift from the studio or the producer.

The plan for today was simple. At 4 P.M., there would be a small listening party in which we would play the tracks we had completed while Bitch Slap was on its cruise. This will be the first time in my career that I have attended a listening party of tracks that did *not* have a vocal on them. Like, who gives a shit what the instrumental came out like? If Johnny Frogthroat doesn't deliver a compelling vocal, the song is shot to hell. The vocal is money. It's like the come shot in a porno movie. There is nothing more important than the vocal on songs like these. The idea of record company execs coming to hear tracks that have no vocals was preposterous to me. Regardless, preposterous or not, this was the plan.

My job today was nothing more than to be present, be personable, and hang out as everyone listened to the tracks and oohed and ahhed over them as if they were somehow destined to be hits. Then, after each track was played, enormous billows of smoke would be blown up the band's asses by the Mooks, who would proceed to drink a bunch of wine, eat a bunch of cheese, and leave wondering why the hell we were making an instrumental record.

When I arrived, I found Lance in the Womb wearing a black-collared shirt buttoned up to his neck, which I promptly unbuttoned for him, as he looked like a dork. He was obviously nervous, and I encouraged him to try to relax. That didn't make a bit of difference, so I grabbed a fatty from Willy's stash. Fatties were strewn about the control room like little misplaced and forgotten prizes. I gave Lance one of the misplaced fatties and told him to smoke it outside, which he did.

Shortly after that, Jeramiah Weasel arrived.

"Are the tracks hot? Am I gonna love it?" he asked.

No, they suck, and you're going to hate it, is what I wanted to say, but then I remembered that my job today was to be personable, as opposed to acting like a sarcastic asshole, no matter how deserving Jeramiah was for asking such a stupid fucking question.

"Hot. You're gonna love it!" I replied as enthusiastically as I could.

"I heard you laid down some bitchin' keys," he complimented.

"Cool, thanks," I replied with a smile, as I started to wonder if I was being too hard on him, lumping him in with the Mooks.

Fortunately, Willy walked in, since I had already run out of things to talk about with Jeramiah. Willy hugged Jeramiah and then me, and then he turned around, slightly confused. Just then Marv Ellis walked in.

"Oh, there you are," Willy said.

Marv shook hands with me, and the three of them headed to the spread to get something to eat. I tagged along. Shortypants was there, bellying up to the grub station. He was joined by two strangers, who I discovered through introductions were the band's publisher and the label's head of marketing. As I shook the marketing Mook's hand, I was beginning to find this scene remarkably humorous. Why the hell would the head of marketing be at an instrumental listening party halfway through the album? This was ludicrous.

The band arrived in the same stretch limo that took them away for their cruise. As each member of Bitch Slap stepped out of the car, I couldn't help but start chuckling. These guys looked like Latin lovers who had just spent a weekend in a tanning booth. I figured I could cross off Alaska as the possible cruise destination. Johnny Smarmy was looking particularly odd, with his super-bright bleached white teeth contrasted with his ultra-dark complexion.

The therapy sessions must have done them good, because it seemed as if they were friendly to one another again. Or perhaps it was having a bunch of days off, as that always helps renew one's spirits.

Once everyone had gotten their fill of food and drink, the entire party shifted to the Womb. Lance was there waiting to play the songs. Willy had given Lance an order to play the songs, and without much fanfare, that's what he did.

Jeramiah was bopping like a fourteen-year-old at his first big rock show as the music blared from the large monitors. While I usually find the big monitors in a control room to be totally useless for any kind of critical listening, they do seem to impress the A&R Mooks.

I generally work on the little speakers posted on the meter bridge of the console, but when the A&R Mook wants to hear the song(s), the big speakers are very handy for turning the event into the "big rock show." Though OSHA isn't too keen on long exposures to 100-plus dB, no one from OSHA happened to be in the Womb at this particular moment. Besides, I had my ER1s in, which are formfitted, filtered ear plugs that reduce the level of the music by 25 dB without drastically altering the balance of frequency response.

Marv sat in front of the console along with the head of marketing and Harmon Neenot. Johnny Rockin' was standing between the couch and the catch-all counter, along with Dumb Ass and Paulie Yore. I always try to stand in a spot where I can see everyone in the room but won't necessarily be noticed myself. I like to watch everyone's reactions during playback, as it tells me a lot about the person.

Marv was performing body movements to the first song that were nothing short of stylistically unsuitable for the music. Far be it from me to criticize someone for how he or she physically reacts to music, but Marv was moving his body in a way that I would describe as "slinky." They were the kinds of movements that I would expect to see if we were listening to an R&B song. "Slinky" was *not* the body movement I typically see for a pseudo-punk, everyman-type song. This was the sort of song that one bops one's head to and raises one's fists. Further confusing the issue, Marv would, without warning, make this bold sort of spastic, jerky move, as if he were being stung by bees, and then immediately return to slinky. Consequently, I tried not to watch him, as I was afraid that I was going to go into laughing fits.

Johnny was bopping super hard to the music with Jeramiah, and they were high-fiving each other constantly, which was making me want to puke. Harmon Neenot and Paulie Yore weren't moving at all, and they both wore scowls on their faces that I could see in the reflection in the glass. Shortypants was as deadpan as could be, and I doubt he could have given two shits about the music.

After the first song finished, Marv looked over to Willy with a big smile.

"Oh, *man!*" exclaimed Marv. "Willy, that was great! I can't wait to hear the vocal on that track."

On Willy's suggestion, Johnny Crooner began to sing the songs live as they played down so that Marv and the marketing Mook could hear what the vocal would be like. Lance played the next two songs, which were the songs that we had already successfully fooled Harmon with. Then Lance played the fourth song. This was the song that Lance had taken some serious liberties with in his bass parts. It was also the moment of truth, for thus far in the playback Harmon did not seem to be anywhere close to enjoying himself.

As this new and improved version of the production played, demonstrating techniques in bass yet unrealized by Harmon; containing guitar tones currently unheralded by Yore; and presenting all manner of miscellaneous, unapproved instrumentation, played with skill miles beyond the capabilities of anyone actually *in* Bitch Slap; I had that awful sinking feeling that one usually acquires moments before everything goes awry. Harmon and Yore were obviously getting far more than they had bargained for.

Before the playback of this particular song had even made it to the first chorus, Harmon unceremoniously stood up from his chair at the console. Without a word, or even a nonverbal suggestion, he strode deliberately to the back of the room and, with his right index finger extended, pressed upon the stop button. The music halted abruptly.

"Where the fuck did that bass part come from? I didn't play that shit!" Harmon exclaimed. "You guys had someone come in and play fucking bass on my song?"

The vibe in the room suddenly became extremely heavy. Willy shot a horrified look over to Shortypants. I instantly knew what had happened. The agreement that Willy had made for using a session bass player was obviously made with Shortypants, but somehow this was never relayed to Harmon. It was a blunder, or perhaps a miscommunication of epic proportions. Either way, the result would be the same.

"And where the hell are my parts?" Yore piped in.

Uy-yuy-yuy! This was turning into a nightmare, and fast. Marv Ellis decided to step in.

"Look, guys, it sounds fantastic! You're going to be stars. Girls are going to just walk up and give you blow jobs. So it's been enhanced a little. So what? Look at the big picture," he said.

Then Willy spoke. "I'm sorry, Harmon, I thought you knew that this is what we'd be doing. You're an incredibly great and strong songwriter, but we really need some extra-special bass parts for your music to stand out. Lance is an excellent bass player—"

"Lance? LANCE?" Harmon screamed. "You've got to be fucking kidding me! Our assistant played the bass on our record?"

Whoops! I am hopeful that the editors of the *New England Journal of Medicine* don't read this diary, for I would hate to be the one to supply irrefutable evidence that excessive fatty smoking makes it difficult to concentrate on such things as not telling the bass player that the assistant on the album replaced all his parts.

The room went silent for what I would guess was about sixty seconds, but seemed nothing short of an eternity. Then Harmon spoke again, and his words were nothing short of profound to me.

To be continued . . .

– Mixerman

DAY 38—PART DEUX

Meeting of the Ages

POSTED: SEPTEMBER 23, 3:51 A.M.

This is fucking bullshit, man!" Harmon said.

Just then, Fingaz, who was now an hour late for the festivities, which I no longer feel is an appropriate word for our little get-together, walked into the room. He had a plate full of food in one hand, an imported German beer in the other, and he was dressed in his parka with the hood up. His mouth was half-stuffed with food, yet he still felt comfortable enough to attempt expressing himself verbally.

"Hey! What's up, Yo!" he exclaimed (I think), oblivious to the tensions that weighed upon the room. Harmon got up and walked out of the Womb.

"What'd I say?" Fingaz asked like he was some sort of comedian.

Yore, ignoring Fingaz, asked Willy again what the hell happened to his guitar parts.

"They're still on tape," Willy replied calmly, as he proceeded to roll a fatty, not caring at all that there were Suits in the room.

Willy began to explain that he wanted Yore to hear what the songs would sound like with a more modern guitar sound. The fact of the matter was, Yore wanted to use the VOX AC30 and *only* a VOX AC30 on every song, and Willy wanted to use the Marshall or Mesa Boogie sound on the majority of the album. This has been a point of contention since day one, but Willy just kept letting Yore lay down his parts.

Then Jeramiah interjected, "Yore, we want you guys to get played on the radio—the guitars that you recorded just don't sound modern. The album was beginning to sound like a classic rock album. We can't sell a classic rock album."

Marv got a wide-eyed scared look on his face. "We can't be making a classic rock album here! It'll never sell! Kids don't get classic rock. Radio won't play classic rock. We need a modern sound!"

I felt like I was listening to my own little tirade about this subject with the whole "modern" versus "classic rock" theme, somewhere around week four. Really, I wish I knew what the hell modern was! From what I've seen so far in my career, the most effective way to get a modern rock sound is by using thirty-five-year-old guitars and twenty-five-year-old amplifiers.

I suppose Paulie Yore didn't like what he was hearing from the three power players in the room, because he too left without a word. Fingaz was still by the door eating away and drinking his beer.

"Awright," he said again with a mouth full of food as Yore walked by. I understood Fingaz's "awright" to be some sort of a farewell, but he couldn't have picked a more inappropriate farewell, as things were far from all right.

Johnny grabbed Willy's shoulders from behind with both hands and told him the tracks were great, and he couldn't wait to sing on them. Then Johnny Outta-Here left the room. Meanwhile, Dumb Ass asked me quietly if those were his drum parts, to which I answered, "Of course!" and I encouraged him to go into the lounge for a while. He too exited the Womb.

Willy, who was remarkably under control considering the circumstances, turned to Shortypants and wanted to know how it happened that Harmon was never told of the replaced bass parts. The marketing Mook and the publisher, who had looked *very* uncomfortable for quite some time, decided that they should definitely exit stage left. They quietly shook Marv's and Jeramiah's hands and made a calm but swift exit from the room, followed by Fingaz, who looked in need of another beer. Poor Lance obviously didn't know what to do. He didn't dare exit the Womb to where the band might have been, for what I assume would have been a reasonable fear of being lynched. However, I can be reasonably sure he didn't want to stay in the Womb either. But stay he did. As did I.

Shortypants was quick to point out that Harmon would have reacted badly, regardless of whether he was given the bad news on the cruise or in the studio, which was probably true. But as Willy pointed out, at least Harmon would have had a few days to cool down over it. Willy went on to say that if Shortypants were any fucking good at his job, he would have had this all straightened out before they got back. The way this was being handled was an absolute disaster. Nobody likes surprises while making a record, least of all bands that find out their parts were replaced while they were on their mid-session cruise.

Shortypants then proceeded to launch into Willy for using archaic methods of making an album—a theme with which he seems inexplicably obsessed.

"You're the only guy in the world making fucking records on analog tape!" Shortypants yelled in his normally gruff manner.

This is absolutely not true! There are still an enormous number of records made on two-inch tape, but I certainly wasn't going to step into the shitstorm with that particular statistic.

"Just record the band to fucking Alsihad and edit them for Christ's sake! Don't you listen to the fucking radio?" Shortypants exploded.

Willy sat up in his chair and looked more sober than I have ever seen him, perhaps because he had been holding a fatty the entire meeting, as opposed to smoking it. I wish to God I had a mini tape recorder with me in order to capture Willy's response, as it was classic! Go figure, I'm in a recording studio, and I can't record a conversation for reference later. Still, I think I have it pretty well memorized, as I played it over and over in my head on my drive home.

"I'll tell you what, Shortypants: You can take Alsihad and shove it up your ass, okay? I've done extensive editing on this project. You know the dude in the parka that makes you so fucking uncomfortable? What was it you called him again? Yeah, him! He edits the hell out of your shitty fucking drummer, who's clearly demonstrated his exceptional lack of coordination by tripping over a mere ribbon of gaffer tape and falling and breaking his wrist. Your bass player couldn't find a groove in a fifty-year-old career hooker, and your guitar player, oh, Jesus *God*, your guitar player! The only member of the band that has even an iota of proficiency on his instrument is the most miserably uninspiring, unenthusiastic, apathetic excuse of a human being in the history of the world, and he has no clear understanding of artistic merit or the benefits of texture in a production!"

I had *never* seen this side of Willy. I love when arguments go into the mode of one person's monologue versus another's, as opposed to people irrationally talking over one another. It was as if they were standing toe-to-toe and delivering blows to each other like in a *Rocky* movie. I was so pleased to know that Willy could stand up for himself without the use of a fatty! I almost laughed aloud on the hooker line, but I held it in because I didn't want to get booted. This was better than *any* of the Bitch Slap fights that I've been privy to thus far.

Marv interjected, "I think Willy's a very capable producer. If he doesn't want to use Alsihad, then he shouldn't have to use it. Look, Shorty (can he call him Shorty?), we want to keep your artists happy, so you tell us what they want and we'll supply it for them."

"I think what my band wants is to play on their own album," Shortypants replied.

Willy nearly exploded. "Well I think your band needs a full-on fucking reality check. If they could play, they would be playing on the record. If they only had a little vibe to them, then we could possibly let them suck and it'd be cool, but they don't even have that! They're a shitty little band from the Midwest with great music that needs to be performed, not just slapped together in Alsihad."

Marv decided to step up to the plate again and told Shortypants that this wasn't a band at all, it was an artist with a backup band, a backup band that could easily be replaced if they don't get their shit together. He even compared Johnny to Jim Morrison. I haven't seen Johnny perform live, and come to think of it, I haven't seen Jim Morrison live either, so I certainly couldn't vouch for this bold comparison, but it might explain the reason Marv was so willing to throw money away on this band. Then Marv finally showed everyone in the room exactly why he was the president of a label, because you don't get to his position without having a firm grasp on the true art of persuasion.

"Look, if playing on their own album is what's going to make them happy, then I'm sure Willy can accommodate your request. I just don't want to see this record fall by the wayside, that's all. I'd hate to see that for the label, I'd hate to see that for the band, and most of all I'd hate to see that for you."

Shortypants was visibly pissed as he dragged on a newly lit Lucky Strike. He, like everyone else in the room, knew exactly what Marv was suggesting. Either the band complies with Willy, or the band will be shelved, which is worse than being dropped, because being shelved keeps the band under contract and unable to record with any other labels. Marv sat in his chair comfortably, with his fingertips on each hand touching their mates on the other hand, forming a sort of three-dimensional triangle. He was staring at Shortypants as if to say, "I can fuck you, and you can't do shit to me."

I thought this was an interesting play. First, Marv was telling Shortypants that he wanted to keep the band happy. Then Marv basically said that the band was irrelevant to him, and he'd be perfectly comfortable with replacing them. Then he topped it off with the veiled threat of shelving the band indefinitely. I couldn't help but wonder which Marv wanted most—a happy band, a replaced band, or a shelved band?

"Why the hell did you sign this band, anyway? You say they're great songwriters, yet you've rejected over a hundred songs from these guys. Why don't you just let them go?" Shortypants asked.

"I'm sure you're going to figure it out, Shortypants," Marv said as he stood up and grabbed his coat. "You always do," Marv said, as if he were running for governor of California, which quite honestly, I wish he were. Perhaps then he could just "shelve" the deficit or "replace" the children that don't do well in school.

Marv put on his jacket and proceeded to leave the room. On his way out, he put his hand on Willy's shoulder without saying a word to him, and then, in what I found to be an odd maneuver, he deliberately veered off the path to the exit, came to the back of the room, and shook my hand.

"And how are *you* doing?" he asked. With the amount of attention this guy gave me, I was starting to wonder if perhaps his "super hot" girlfriend was merely a beard, and I was going to be invited to his house for a "swim in the pool." I smiled and told him I was fine. Then Marv Ellis left the room with Jeramiah Weasel tagging close behind.

Willy turned to Shortypants.

"We're going to be auditioning drummers to play the rest of the album. Do you have a list of acceptable players?" Willy inquired.

"Auditioning drummers?" I blurted out. I don't know why I interrupted like that. I was so surprised by this turn of events that it just came out. Shortypants was looking at me as if I were his child who was only one word away from a whoopin'. Fortunately, we weren't related, so I wasn't too concerned by this prospect. Still, I got the message and refrained from blurting out anything else.

"I'll have a list by Monday. I've got to go find my fucking artist and his backup band before they're shelved," he replied sarcastically as he walked out of the Womb.

I remained in the back of the room, not saying a word. Willy sat in front of the console and fired up the fatty he'd been holding for what seemed to be an eternity. He passed it to me without saying a word, and seeing as I obviously wasn't going to have to work, I accepted the passing of the fatty.

I had so many questions in my head that I didn't even know where to begin. I was a bit reluctant to ask about my schedule, when Willy's whole evening had been ruined. I sat there holding my breath in order to experience the maximum effect of the fatty, strategizing as to the best way to commence a dialogue. There's nothing worse than having everything blow up in your face, and then to have people running up to you saying, "Me, me, me! What about me?" I certainly didn't want to come off in that manner, even though that's precisely how I felt. After a moment, I realized that I needed to start our little chat, not by complaining about how this news affected me, but by commiserating with Willy. I needed to let him know that I understood what he was going through.

"Well, that sucked," I said as I exhaled.

"Yep," Willy replied. "Fuck 'em."

"How long will drum auditions take?" I asked, and I immediately regretted such an idiotic question. I had started everything off so beautifully, but to follow up with that question was just beyond lame.

"Who the fuck knows? I think we'll take a few weeks off from recording the album. Once I find the right drummer, we have to rehearse him with the band. So you can have off for a little while," he replied.

This was bad. I'm not going to pretend that I'd be all broken up if this project went down the tubes. But I certainly wasn't digging the concept of waiting around for three weeks to find out at the end of that time span that we wouldn't be continuing the album. There certainly are no guarantees that everything won't self-destruct—that is, if it hasn't already. I could be out of work for a lot longer than just three weeks if that happened. It's not like records grow on trees and you go out and pick one. It can take months of courting and maneuvering your schedule to be available for a particular session.

I suppose Willy must know me like a book by now, because he addressed my concerns without a word from me. "I'll make sure you're paid for your time off. It won't be full pay, but I want you back on this project when this piece of shit gets back together. Just keep yourself available in case I want to record a drummer as part of the audition," Willy said.

Bonus! I felt so un-fucking-believably joyful from those words, I started to well up. I desperately needed a break from this project. Apparently, Willy and Marv had anticipated this particular situation and made prior arrangements to keep me on board. I was being temporarily released from prison with *pay*, albeit reduced pay. I was going to be able to spend time with my family again. I was going to get some rest. I wouldn't have to deal with these assholes with their incredible disdain for themselves and their own record. I wouldn't have to deal with retards who act like retards, whiny-voiced bass players, depressed guitar players, or megalomaniacal singers. I was temporarily *free*!

While I realize that these statements are a good indication that I probably shouldn't be on this session at *all* anymore, quite honestly, I've felt the same way on sessions that I've absolutely adored. It's a casualty of working ten to twelve hours a day for weeks on end with the same people on the same music. After a while, one just needs a break, and this was certainly one of those times, particularly given the trials and tribulations that I'd gone through on this session.

As I packed up my bag and put away my reference CDs, Willy and I hugged. He said he'd call me over the weekend or at the beginning of the week and keep me updated, and then he split.

To be continued.

– Mixerman

The Revealing

POSTED: SEPTEMBER 24, 3:22 A.M.

O nce I had finished collecting my belongings, I, too, exited the Womb. The moment I cracked the door, I could hear the tell-tale signs of a Bitch Slap discussion group session. They were obviously getting the bad news from Shortypants, and I didn't want to be anywhere near the vicinity of the fallout zone, so I marched right by the lounge without so much as a peek for fear of making some kind of eye contact and being somehow roped into the conversation.

When I arrived at the front desk, I had the opportunity to exchange niceties with Magnolia, who was getting ready to leave for the weekend herself. The argument had escalated to the point that it could now be clearly heard at the front desk, which was a considerable distance from Bitch Slap's lounge. Magnolia, who loved to pry, was curious as to what was going on.

"Oh, you know, the usual band shit," I replied with a smile. "See you in a few weeks."

Magnolia began freaking out on me.

"A few weeks?" she blurted. She sounded just like I did when I found out about drum auditions. I realized that I had made a serious blunder. I had no idea what arrangements had been made between Willy and Magnolia, regarding how long we were to be booked. Now she was probably freaking out because she'd be out a three-week booking. Magnolia continued before I could even respond.

"We've got another project starting in there in *two* weeks," she continued.

I hadn't really thought about that. Bitch Slap was only supposed to be a six- to eight-week affair. Of *course* Magnolia had booked the room. Why wouldn't she?

Then Magnolia pointed out that Bitch Slap was booked for another two weeks. I told her that I just assumed that they would be auditioning drummers in the studio, since Willy wanted me to be available to record them at a moment's notice. Magnolia let out a sigh of relief, but the fact of the matter was, I didn't know this for sure.

I told Magnolia that I really had no idea what was going on, and that I had been given a temporary hiatus. She would have to speak with Willy to get accurate and up-to-date information, as I worked on a need-to-know basis. Seeing as Willy's car was still in the lot, I figured he must have been participating in the melee down the hall, and I told her that he would likely be exiting the complex soon. Magnolia and I hugged. I told Magnolia to call me if the session left, so that I could have cartage come and pick up my gear.

Although the studios in the area tend to be decently stocked with compressors and such, I carry my own array of processors that I'm partial to. Unfortunately, the equipment needs to be trucked to and from the studio when I'm done with it. The cartage bills on moving my gear for one session can be more than a piece of gear itself. Fortunately, the record companies don't put up a squawk about cartage.

As I was leaving the lot, I noticed that the limo was gone. It was no longer blocking the exit to the lot, which I thought was odd, considering the band was arguing in the lounge. But it really wasn't any of my concern, so I didn't give this much thought beyond that.

As I was driving home, I got a call on my cell phone. It was Willy, who was asking me if I knew where Harmon had gone. I didn't, because I just figured he was with them, but when I thought about it, I didn't hear Harmon's voice coming from the lounge. Apparently, Harmon and the limo driver had taken off for some unknown location, and neither the driver nor Harmon could be reached for comment. I told Willy that I couldn't help.

I think I got more phone calls over this weekend than I have in two months' time. Phone call after phone call came in. I got multiple calls from Shortypants, Fingaz, Lance, Willy, Shortypants' secretary, Yore, Dumb Ass, Jeramiah—even Virginia Skanky called me, and I'd love to know how the fuck *she* got my number. Each call was stranger than the last. My Saturday was starting to turn into some kind of David Lynch movie.

It appears that Harmon and the limo had fallen off the face of the earth. Everyone involved on this project was searching for Harmon. They checked airports, hotels, and Virginia Skanky's pad (that sounds bad!). They checked Harmon's usual hangouts, and everywhere anyone could think of that Harmon might have gone, but to no avail. Harmon Neenot was nowhere to be found.

On Sunday afternoon, as I was enjoying my kid's soccer game, I got a call on my cell phone. It's rare for me to even remove my cell from my car these days. It's even rarer for me to carry my cell on family day, but these were unusual circumstances.

"It's Lance—I've got to tell you what's happened!" And tell me he did.

It seemed that Harmon had somehow managed to "leave" the limo driver at a diner just off Pacific Coast Highway and was now wanted for grand theft auto. I couldn't help but wonder if the ditching occurred at Alice's Restaurant, but that was neither here nor there. Then Lance, who was incapable of staying on one subject long enough for me to digest the information, told me that Shortypants had called to check his availability to play bass for the drummer auditions, at least until Harmon could be located.

"Located or bailed out?" I questioned facetiously, but that garnered no reaction from Lance, unless you somehow consider ignoring a reaction.

"Can we hook up?" Lance asked abruptly. He was obviously troubled, but I wasn't prepared to give up my family day quite yet. More importantly, I wasn't prepared to deal with the wrath that would surely ensue were I to actually *attempt* an interruption of family day. So I told Lance to meet me at a bar close to my house at 10 P.M., since my wife would likely be going to bed by then anyway.

I arrived at the bar around 10:15. Lance was already there drinking a vodka and tonic, which I immediately inquired about and discovered, to my horror, that he was drinking the house well vodka. Lance looked extremely nervous, which is an unusual look in a bar, and he was beginning to draw attention to himself. I didn't bother torturing him by beating around the bush with unnecessary niceties and such—rather, I got right to the heart of the matter.

"So what's up?" I said moments before I ordered us a pair of Belvedere vodka martinis chilled up with olives. I wasn't going to sit there and drink rubbing alcohol with quinine and bubbles when we could be savoring the flavor of superior vodka. I felt it was my duty to educate the lad on the finer things in life.

I would have ordered Chopin vodka, but they didn't happen to have any at this particular establishment. Chopin and Belvedere are both made in Poland. Belvedere is made from rye and is distilled four times. Suffice it to say, it's very pure! Chopin is vodka made from the Podlasie potato. I'm not sure I've ever eaten a Podlasie potato, but I'm certain they're fabulous. Both Belvedere and Chopin are excellent vodkas, although Belvedere is not the critics' darling. But fuck the critics.

All my friends prefer Grey Goose, and I'm sure it's also excellent vodka, but it tastes odd to me. It's French, so I fear the French might inadvertently allow the occasional grape to get into the batch somehow, and that would just fuck up vodka to a fare-thee-well. I think Ketel One is great vodka too, and that's what I keep at the house. In fact, the large majority of this diary is written while drinking a Ketel One martini on the rocks. Skyy vodka is probably the best buy, as it's made in San Francisco, and there are no import tariffs to cover. It, too, goes through a quadruple distillation process. I've A/B'd Skyy and Belvedere, and the difference in quality is marginal, but the difference in price is quite vast.

Anyway, these are just a few tips to keep in mind next time you buy vodka. Of course, as usual, I digress.

Lance was speaking in circles. "Now that I'm playing bass for the drum auditions, and since my playing bass on the recordings is what led me to playing bass on the drum auditions, will I still have my assisting gig when Harmon comes back?"

I had to go over what he had just said in my head a few times and then finally I got it. Lance was worried about losing his assisting gig. I assured him that he would stay on as my assistant, as he was getting better at the job every day. I then raised my glass to toast him and took a swig of vodka martini.

"What about the diary?" he asked.

Let me tell you, vodka, even one as smooth as Belvedere, burns like a motherfucker, and can be excruciatingly painful when it's coming out of your nose. I quickly grabbed a bar napkin, and as much as I had blown my cover, I *still* pretended I didn't know what he was talking about.

"Diary?" I gurgled, "What diary?"

I felt like a complete idiot. Here I was writhing in pain, collecting ice-cold Belvedere drippings with a soiled cocktail napkin, trying to pretend I didn't know what the hell he was talking about!

"How many Wombs in L.A. had their glass broken out this month?" Lance asked, as he began to laugh at me. I was frozen with terror at hearing this description. Either that or I was frozen from frostbitten nasal passages—I wasn't quite sure which. I had to face reality. I was busted, and the only real question was, To what extent was I busted? Fortunately, Lance spared me and immediately eased my fears on that front.

"Don't worry, I haven't told anyone," he confided, leaning toward me.

He asked how I came up with the first name of Lance for him. I told him it was because he had a zit that I felt could have used some "lancing" in that first week. I probably should have told him that it was someone I knew in high school, but I didn't think of it at the time.

"So what about the diary?" he asked me again, ignoring my insensitivity toward his epidermal conditions. For the life of me, I couldn't understand why the fuck he kept asking me this question.

"I don't know. What about it?" I snapped. I was losing patience with Lance's repetition of that particular question. I just didn't understand what he wanted to know.

"What if I were to chronicle the drum auditions during your break?" he asked.

I didn't say a word to Lance as I ordered another round of vodka martinis. I just sat and thought about what had just been proposed to me, and Lance, being the smart lad he is, allowed me time to think without a word and without even the slightest amount of nonverbal pressure. At first I was against the concept. But the more I thought about it, the more I liked the idea. Not only would it keep the viewing public informed as to what was going on with the Bitch Slap session, it would keep *me* informed as well.

I was convinced when Lance began to use terminology like "the Womb" and the names I had given each member of Bitch Slap. He even gave me a little taste of an imaginary day, and I began looking forward to the concept of actually being able to *read* about

Bitch Slap, as opposed to writing about them. Writing about them was becoming nothing short of draining. It was bad enough spending countless hours with the jokers, but then having to relive my experiences through writing about them has been nothing short of exhausting. I certainly can't go to sleep the moment I get home. I'm usually up for a good two or three hours after I get home anyway, but writing this diary was more than I bargained for.

I wrote a chapter early on calling this diary my albatross. You can imagine what it is now! At first I thought writing this diary would be fun, and to some extent it has been. But it's also been an enormous amount of work, and to get a break from it would be as revitalizing as getting a break from the session itself. Still, I have every intention of finishing this diary until the end.

Finally, I came to a decision. Without saying a word, I wrote down an e-mail address on a cardboard coaster and gave it to Lance.

"It's kind of like magic," I said to Lance. "You type out your thoughts, you e-mail them to the dude behind the curtain, and then your thoughts mysteriously appear on the website the next morning."

I can't say whether or not Lance will actually write his chronicles, or for how long. Hopefully, it'll all work out, and he'll be able to keep us all entertained as I get some work done around the house on my hiatus.

Lance and I had just about wrapped up our business, but we now had fresh drinks before us. So I figured this would be a good time to tell Lance about the rules.

"You're not allowed to go on any other sites to discuss your chronicles. You can never tell anyone that you're Lance. And I reserve the right to make up more rules as I see fit," I explained. "Most of all, you can never rename me in the story."

And we toasted to that.

– Mixerman

DAY 38—PART IV

Cancellations Suck
But Not as Much as Lance

NEVER POSTED:

The Lance Chronicles were abruptly canceled and were not included in this book because of copyright issues. I assure you that you are not missing anything, as the days were remarkably uneventful and poorly written.

Suffice it to say, Willy auditioned drummers, chose one, and we were to start recording again in just a few weeks.

– Mixerman

DAY 39

This Is Your Captain Speaking
Please Fasten Your Seat Belts

POSTED: NOVEMBER 16, 10:05 A.M.

NEW YORK CITY

I'm writing this journal entry at a cruising altitude of 35,000 feet, en route to New York City, where the Bitch Slap sessions will be resuming come Monday morning. I'm not quite sure exactly *why* we're recording in New York. The band, the producer, the label, and I all live in L.A., yet we are going to travel to the most expensive city in the Union to record Bitch Slap? The only person on this project who actually *lives* in NY is Fingaz, and he was more than content staying at the modestly priced Sportsman's Lodge in Studio City. Recording studios are considerably more expensive in New York, as are food, lodging, and equipment rentals. Hell, the sushi bills alone are going to put this album up over the million-dollar mark before January.

At the moment—and I stress the words "at the moment"—I'll be staying in a Midtown hotel that I've resided in once before and that, quite frankly, I abhor. The rooms are only slightly larger than a shoe box, and while my manager has convinced the label to upgrade me to a deluxe suite, I happen to know the deluxe suites are nothing more than French for "two shoe boxes connected." According to Ed Cherney, another engineer and great fan of this particular hotel, "The rooms were so small, I had to go into the hall to change my mind."

Apparently, I'm staying in Hotel Shoe Box because the ever-misguided label is trying to save money, as this project is costing them a fortune. I was so shocked to hear that the album was costing a fortune that I nearly fainted. Fortunately, I was sitting down. Of course, in the infinite wisdom that is so typical of the major label machine, they are flying the entire band and crew out to New York, putting us up in fairly expensive hotels (even Hotel Shoe Box isn't cheap), and paying an outrageous amount of money per day for a studio. I'm not sure whom they hired as their resident "money-saver" but so far this yet unnamed artisan has shown little-to-zero talent toward that particular job description.

Then, of course, there's our traveling personal assistant. Upon Willy's request, I hired an assistant, one who stays with the project as opposed to the studio. Unbeknownst to Willy, I ran a want ad on my forum, and I hired my assistant from those applicants. Our assistant will also need to stay in a hotel and will be paid a daily rate to pretty much do nothing all day, since the *studio* supplies an assistant. Of course, I'm always glad for the extra help considering the history of this project—even self-help.

You see, soon after my first eight-week stint recording Bitch Slap, I started to get the idea that I might be in need of certain self-improvement. Yes, given that I am the hero of this particular diary, I realize it may be difficult to bring yourself to admit that I might need some improvement. But let's try to be truly honest with ourselves. It's quite apparent that I was allowing Bitch Slap's blatant inadequacies as a band (and as human beings in general) to affect me negatively. So in an effort to combat this negativity, I sought out the help of a meditation guru, whom I prefer to call Dalai Llama.

I have begun a very intensive study with Dalai Llama on how to combat the negative effects of the blundering idiots surrounding me. So far, I'm happy to report, it's going quite well. Llama has been teaching me to employ the power of positive thinking, even in the most dismal of scenarios. To date, I haven't had the opportunity to test my techniques in the heat of battle, but I'm happy to report I'm optimistic.

It has been two months since I last worked on the Bitch Slap sessions. In that time I mixed an album for Bitch Slap's label, and I have produced an album in its entirety for another label. I was, however, present for one of the Los Angeles "audition" days, and I even documented the day and my thoughts on the auditions, but I've decided to scrap those writings, as I was rambling aimlessly, and I consider that particular day "old news." You see, according to Dalai Llama, I must continually move forward and resist the urge to focus on past events beyond their most profound lessons. Since I have no profound lessons from that particular day, my rantings have been deleted from my computer and subsequently forgotten.

I've been mostly absent from the goings-on since the inevitable meltdown. Therefore, you must understand that most of the information that I have regarding Bitch Slap is secondhand and sketchy at best. My knowledge of the events that transpired during my absence would not likely pass the legal scrutiny of the hearsay challenge, but then I'm not under oath here, so I'll share what I know.

I'll warn you now, that these reports sound like the fantasy of a raving lunatic. I promise you, I am neither a raving lunatic, nor is it a fantasy. I have actually considered leaving this information out because, quite frankly, it doesn't sound very credible. But I have decided that it is best if I report what truly happened, as I view my purpose here not as a storyteller, but as reporter of fact. So here are the facts.

Harmon, who had gone off the proverbial "deep end," managed to somehow hijack the "band" limousine all the way to Seattle, sans the driver of said limousine. He has since been recovered by a bounty hunter privately hired by the record company. Word has it that Harmon has been quietly "rehabilitated" by his most enabling sponsor, Marv Ellis and Co.; placed on potent prescription drugs under the care of a world-renowned psychiatrist (who apparently will be making frequent visits to NYC); and has been reestablished as the bass player for the band Bitch Slap. Since receiving this news, I have taken to actively and vigorously exercising my right middle finger in preparation for the outrageous amount of punch-ins I'll be performing during bass overdubs.

Oh, joy! I mean . . . Onnnnnngggggg.[56]

Lance, the once temporary bass player for the band Bitch Slap, met some chick during the New York drummer auditions and apparently got her pregnant. Under normal circumstances this would be horrifying news (for him, not for me—I don't particularly like the little twerp, since he wrote a bunch of crap about me in his diaries), save for the fact that the woman he impregnated is the daughter of an international dignitary. Most impressively,

Lance accomplished this feat concurrent with a visitation by Virginia Skanky (of the Huntington Beach Skankys). Ah, to be young again.

Now, I'm not quite clear on whether Lance managed to sleep with the tart in the presence or the absence of Virginia. Considering Lance's taste in obviously loose, skanky women, I can only assume the dignitary's daughter was nothing more than a tart, regardless of her position in life. But perhaps I'm wrong. Perhaps the dignitary's daughter is a very fine girl who isn't the least bit angry at her father for his constant unavailability throughout her childhood. Perhaps she feels no hatred toward her father whatsoever, as she fucks strange men in an unprotected manner during the ovulation stage of her cycle. Strange men—or should I say boys—who have little to no capacity to father themselves, let alone a child.

Ahem.

Oooonnnnnnnnggggggg!

I'm hoping to acquire the particulars on this wonderful bit of gossip from Willy one of these days soon. Post-fatty, of course.

Dumb Ass, who has now been permanently replaced as the drummer of the band, has managed to convince the band and the label that Bitch Slap needs a keyboard player. Apparently, Cotton is close to having his cast removed from his wrist and will be available for such duties in the near future. I don't believe the guy even knows how to play keyboards, so I can only assume he's taking lessons.

Why they keep Dumb Ass around is absolutely one of the great mysteries of life to me. No matter from what angle you view it, Dumb Ass is a pain in the ass. He's only mildly entertaining in a purely annoying sort of way. He has poor rhythm, (which, contrary to contemporary wisdom, is an important part of keyboard playing), and he has proven himself to have a severe lack of musicality. As if that's not enough, the entire band and crew hate him! If you really think about it, *you* probably hate him. I would have bet anything that once the band got a new drummer it would be curtains for Dumb Ass. I mean, they were so fucking close! What made them keep this loser? I'm missing something here, and it's now my mission to find out what.

The band has been rehearsing with the new drummer for over a month, and the plan is to record the album in its entirety before the end of January . . .

. . . from scratch.

If you read those last two words and heard an odd sort of *plunk* sound afterwards, that was your jaw hitting the floor. Pick it up.

While, for the most part, I'm over it, the magnitude of starting completely over again is nothing short of staggering to me. I'm confident that you, the reader, will feel similarly. And far be it for me to allow the reader of this journal to draw the glaringly obvious connection of this particular development on his or her own. So I'll spell things out for you.

Yes, somehow, in the course of eight weeks, in what has easily been the most heinously miserable time I have ever spent recording an album, with the most wretched, ungrateful, myopic group of dimwits and egotistical snobs to have ever graced the earth, I have somehow managed to be a party to the accomplishment of nothing. Nothing, that is, other than the blatant and most

343

egregious wasting of money and time. To make matters worse, I have not, to my satisfaction, gained one single viable relationship that could somehow, in some small way, make all the misery and squalor worthwhile. Spending my time with Bitch Slap has been about as enriching to my soul as a repeat episode of *SpongeBob*.[57] Of course, thanks to Dalai Llama, I now recognize that I must move forward from this revelation and accept that my purpose here is somehow greater than to be Bitch Slap's personal bitch.

Apparently, the replacement drummer will be one of three candidates whom I happened to record an audition of in L.A. If the drummer is who I think it is, I must say, I was quite impressed by his skills behind the kit. Under normal circumstances, I'd be confident that we could easily accomplish the goal that has been set forth to complete the album before the end of January. But in my short tenure as Bitch Slap's recordist, I have grown accustomed to the fact that these sessions are never "under normal circumstances." My every instinct says we will not come remotely close to that goal. Still, I must remain optimistic.

As I fly and write this journal entry, I have an obese woman on my right, who I would say suffers from severe apnea, and a slightly odoriferous man to my left, as I sit in the middle seat of a full plane that is barely adequate in leg room for a quadriplegic, let alone a man six feet ten inches tall. Regardless of the poor circumstances in which I attempt to type this entry, I can't help but chuckle in a most uncomfortable way at the fact that I will be recording this bunch of losers again. Don't get me wrong: They're a swell bunch of losers, so long as they aren't in the same room as one another—more importantly, so long as they're not playing musical instruments and so long as they're not actually talking.

While I'm truly intrigued, I'm partly concerned with the dynamic changes that will occur with the addition of a new band member to Bitch Slap. Through this concern, I have brought myself to two opposing ways of viewing the situation. On the one hand, Bitch Slap in its original configuration of Dumb Ass, Harmon Neenot, Paulie Yore, and Johnny LaLa are the devil I know.

On the other hand, the interpersonal relationships of Bitch Slap members are so poor, things couldn't possibly get worse.

Now that's positive thinking.

– Mixerman

Good Studio Hunting Day

POSTED: NOVEMBER 19, 10:58 A.M.

It was a beautiful day in New York City this morning, particularly if you enjoy obscenely cold wind whipping across your face as it travels down a concrete wind tunnel devoid of any direct sunlight. I grew up within an hour of New York, so I'm painfully aware that it's not even gotten that cold yet. Still, I'm starting to recall the original logic behind moving to Los Angeles. Nine times out of ten, the impetus for anyone who makes that particular cross-country move is the weather. My impetus was no exception.

On Saturday, my job was to look at studios in New York City. Since neither Willy nor I ever work in New York, we were not familiar with the rooms. Willy wanted me to find a room that would be good for us to do overdubs. Apparently, with our sudden pressing budget constraints, it has become necessary for me to search out an adequate overdub room for "not too much money," whatever the fuck that means. Compared to the cost of the tracking room in which we are currently scheduled, the L.A. Womb could be considered "not too much money," at $1,800 per day.

That's because we are scheduled for several weeks to be tracking in, by all accounts, the most expensive studio in New York City. From what I understand, the actual studio costs, which are quite hefty in their own right, can pale in comparison to the cost of fringe extras that don't technically come with the room. Even a glass of water is supposed to cost a fortune at this studio. In fact, the extraneous charges in this particular studio can be so outrageous that I can't help but wonder if there is a corkage fee for anyone who brings in his or her own water.

So there I was, trekking all over Manhattan on a Saturday, looking at recording studios that cost only slightly less than the L.A. Womb to try and save money for the project. Yet five band members, a producer, a personal assistant, and myself are all staying in hotels in Midtown Manhattan, all in an effort to cut costs!

Willy and the band spent the day in rehearsal, and I spent the day peeking in at seven studios. I probably walked for a total of three hours between studios and train stations. Jesus! I'm pathetically out of shape. By the time I finished looking at the last studio, my thighs were in such cramps, I couldn't actually walk without limping. My feet were blistered, and I was working on a matched pair of shin splints, both of which are absolutely killing me today. There were times that I would have *loved* to catch a cab, but for some inexplicable reason, they don't stop for me.

In addition to being out of shape, I didn't bring sneakers with me. I was actually planning to purchase sneakers in New York, as I wanted to replace mine anyway, but I didn't have time to do that on Good Studio Hunting Day. Consequently, I found myself walking throughout the city in my Australian-made Blundstone boots. I discussed these shoes earlier in this diary, and I'm happy to report that I still love them, because they are extremely comfortable. Unfortunately, they are *not* what one would term sensible power-walking shoes.

I had many conversations by cell phone with Willy on Saturday. Quite frankly, he was annoying the shit out of me for his inability to make up his mind. It was quite clear that he didn't want to work at any of the overdub rooms that I was visiting, regardless of their quality. He wanted to book the entire project at the super-expensive tracking studio.

After I soaked in a hot bath in an effort to relieve the cramping of my thighs, Willy made his way uptown from where he and the band had been rehearsing. Most thankfully, he didn't bring the band with him, and we went out to eat. Apparently, when Willy is in New York, he likes to eat steak. That was okay with me, because when I'm in New York, I like to drink eighteen-year-old Scotch—specifically The Macallan.

It was good to chat with Willy again, as I drank my eighteen-year-old Scotch and ate a salad that contained as much arterial clogging power as the steak that Willy was eating. (My kingdom for a lightly tossed tricolore salad, hold the cheese!) We talked about Lance and his upcoming wedding into royalty. Apparently, the daughter that Lance impregnated is like the princess of some country I've never heard of before. I doubt that even Alex Trebek has heard of *this* country, and from what I can tell, Alex knows everything. I guess there's a big hurry to get the wedding done, because the father doesn't want the daughter "showing" as she wears a white wedding dress symbolizing her pureness and virginity. Go figure.

From now on, Lance will be known as a prince, although, according to Willy, he will have no power and will never be able to rule in the country. I don't think he'll even be allowed *in* their country. Shit, I thought *my* life was interesting. Lance is the one who should be writing a diary! Or maybe not. Again, I seriously considered leaving this information out, because quite honestly, I don't believe it myself. It sounds a little far-fetched to me. But Willy assures me that it's all true.

As Willy cut into a steak the size of my laptop computer, he began expressing how pleased he was with the new drummer. Willy felt the drummer was strong in both his playing abilities and his look. That was all well and good, but we still had to contend with Harmon's shitty playing, Yore's lack of ingenuity regarding guitar sounds, and Dumb Ass's keyboard overdubs (I can't wait for that treat). But my inner voice, the one that Dalai Llama introduced to me, that I *used* to tell to "shut the fuck up," advised me to keep that particular bit of negative energy to myself.

Ong namo guru dev namo. Ong namo guru dev namo.

In the course of our dinner, Willy finally filled me in on what was going on. Apparently, the sessions were moved to New York so as to be directly overseen by a woman who was hired personally by Marv Ellis to be Bitch Slap's A&R rep. Her sole duty is the overseeing of this project. I have named her Penny Pincher, although I happen to know she didn't get to where she is by just pinching pennies. Jeramiah was no longer overseeing this project, although to date he still works for the company. Willy claimed to know little about Penny, save the fact that she used to be Marv's secretary and managed to move very quickly up the ranks of the company. Now Penny was in charge of Marv's pet project, and she has made things difficult for Willy right from the start. This should be interesting.

On Sunday, Willy and I ate in Little Italy. It's funny when you tell people that you're going to Little Italy, because the person you are revealing this information to invariably gets excited and immediately divulges what they have personally deemed to be the best restaurant in Little Italy. The limo driver from the airport was partial to Vincent's; my manger insisted we go to Umberto's; and the concierge at the hotel preferred Angeli's. Since Willy was buying, I let him pick. He picked Umberto's.

Our new personal assistant arrived late Sunday night. I've named him Rod. He met Willy and me for some drinks at a small local Irish pub as we watched the Lakers game via satellite.

Rod is totally cool. There's no doubt in my mind that Rod is going to work out fantastically. Sometimes I just get overcome by a good vibe from a person, and this was one of those times. He's totally into the job at hand, wholly prepared to pitch in and make our lives easier, and he *loves* the Lakers. What more could I possibly want in an assistant? I know of marriages that have been based on less. Most impressively of all—and I don't know this for sure—but I believe he actually had a tear in his eye when the Lakers lost to Houston last night.

Either that or he got some hot sauce in his eye.

– Mixerman

The Manifestation of a Womb

POSTED: NOVEMBER 19, 10:58 A.M. — WEEK 9

When Rod and I arrived at the studio today, we were greeted by a security guard.

"You are here for what session?" he asked.

"Bitch Slap," I replied.

"And your name?" he inquired.

"Mixerman," I said proudly.

"Who's he?" the security guard asked pointing toward my assistant.

"This is Rod. He's an assistant engineer on the session." I replied.

The security guard ran his finger slowly down his list in search of Rod's name.

"He's not on the list."

"Well, add him, dear Henry," I replied smartly with a smile.

"My name's not Henry," he retorted as he licked his index finger in order to turn a page on his "list."

We then went into this long circular dialogue about how the assistants work for the studio, and that Rod doesn't work for the studio, so how could he be the assistant. No matter what I said, he was confused. Finally I just asked him if he was going to let us pass or not.

"I need verification on him," he said as he picked up the phone and called "upstairs," looking at us suspiciously.

Upon verification, the guard pointed us toward the room that we would be working in. When I arrived at the control room, which was in dire need of some Wombification, I was greeted by the sight of a fully torn-apart console.

Motherfucker . . . I mean, Ong.

Standing before the carnage was a strange man. He was a tall man with super-long silver hair that went all the way down to his ass, a hooked nose, and a wartlike skin tag right smack in the middle of his forehead. My first thought was that the guy should have his skin tag permanently painted red, like a bull's-eye, but I kept that to myself, at least until I get to know him a little better.

The strange man was wearing biker boots, faded black jeans, a wallet with a chain on it, and a Mercenary Audio T-shirt.

"Do you know Fletcher?" I asked, referring to a friend of mine at Mercenary Audio.

"Fuckin'-A right I know Fletcher. He's like my brother. You?" replied my new biker brother—even though I don't ride bikes.

"Hell fucking yeah I do!" I replied with vigor and zeal, wanting to make a good impression by speaking in a manner that he might understand.

We kibitzed for a moment, exchanging our funny little Fletcher stories. He introduced himself as Harley. I introduced myself as Mixerman. Despite the discovery of a mutual friend and the certain bond that is created from such discovery, I was slightly dismayed over the fact that the entire console was ripped apart, mostly because this makes recording difficult at best.

"So what's wrong with the console?" I asked

"Well, we seem to have problem," he replied matter-of-factly.

Being the veteran I am of the recording process, I knew that even in New York, the console being torn apart and strewn about the room was a sure indication that there was a "problem." It was the specifics that I was in search of.

"What exactly is wrong?" I asked patiently.

"Well, if I knew that, I'd have fucking told you," he answered, with incredible amounts of tact and logic. Then he sort of went into an explanation that was way beyond my knowledge. Hell, he could have said the console had gotten unplugged, and he'd have been precariously close to going beyond my technical expertise, so why I even asked is beyond me. Somehow I think he sensed that, much as a horse can sense that I have no purpose being on its back.

Despite the circular nature of this conversation, and the obviously grumpy disposition of this individual, I couldn't help but like him. Perhaps I found his straightforwardness refreshing. Or perhaps, aside from his rough exterior and total lack of fashion sense, he was very similar to me.

I decided to take a slightly different tack.

"Do you know how long we'll be down for?" I asked.

"I'm sorry, I misplaced my crystal ball this morning," he replied with exaggerated feigned empathy.

"That's my line!" I replied.

"No, that's Fletcher's line," he responded without missing a beat, and he was right. "My best guess would be a few hours if you want the thing to sound right, and half an hour if you don't give a shit," he finished.

I chose the "few hours—good sound" option offered to me and left Harley to his job.

It's not like the console problem was a big deal, so long as it was fixed today, and I had no reason to believe it wouldn't be. The band wasn't even planning on coming until the evening. Today was setup day, and I was only planning to set up the room and the microphones. I could still do that regardless of the condition of the console. The only problem I was having was finding the assistant who actually went with the room. I felt like the little bird in the P. D. Eastman story *Are You My Mother?* as I walked around the complex asking, "Are you my assistant?"

"I am not your assistant! I am renting you my guitars."

"I am not your assistant! I am the drum tech."

"I am not your assistant! I am the runner for your session."

It took me twenty minutes before my assistant finally presented himself. Having Rod around is all well and good, but unfortunately, he doesn't have access to the mic locker or many of the other items that we would be in need of throughout the course of the day. Therefore, having an assistant who works for the studio is absolutely critical for working.

When I finally found the studio assistant, he seemed surprised that I was looking for him.

"Hi. I'm Lightning. Do you need some assistance?" he asked

"Are you my assistant?"

"Why yes, I am," he said with a big smile.

I asked him if he had received my setup, which was highly detailed and left nothing to the imagination. I had to-scale drawings of the room; a precise orderly list of the instruments and their respective microphones; where I wanted those microphones to come up on the console; and the processing gear (compressors and EQs) that were to be used for each chain. Yet nothing had been set up. This all seemed vaguely familiar to me, as my first session with Bitch Slap had started with an assistant who didn't believe in setting anything up until he felt like it. Of course, now he's a prince.

"Did you get my fax?" I asked Lightning.

"Yeah. I'm going to set the mics up now, but first I've got to go get them."

"Didn't you see the part of my letter where I asked that all the mics be set up before I arrived?" I asked, now imagining myself in my "happy place." Oooonnnnggg. Oooooooonnnnggggg.

"Well, yeah, but you can't work with the console apart, so I figured there wasn't a whole lot of urgency," he replied.

Indeed. I certainly couldn't argue with that logic.

So, having taken a lesson out of Willy's book, I delegated responsibility to my two assistants and exited stage left. My mission was far greater than the minutia of directing traffic for microphones and instruments. That's what Rod was there for. Nay, my purpose today was to be the Ambassador of Vibe. After all, if I'm going to spend several weeks in a room, I want it to be a place that I can seek refuge in. At the moment, it was a wasteland, lacking color, energy, scent, and warmth. This room was nothing more than a common control room, one which needed to be transformed into a Womb.

I spent the rest of the day in search of tapestries, pillows, candles, candle plates, candlesticks, candelabras, lava lamps, incense, and various other trinkets that make the Womb, the Womb. In total, I spent $800 on vibe materials, which I will rebill back to the label. Ultimately, this will be paid by Bitch Slap with record sales.

In the end, Willy didn't care much that the session was canceled. Apparently, he was hot on a couple of new songs that he was working on with the band. That gave Harley an opportunity to fix the console, and Lightning and Rod were able to set up the session. Franc, my feminine alter ego named after the character played by Martin Short in *Father of the Bride*, who has an eye for color and a flair for design, created the space that I would likely spend hundreds of hours in over the course of the next few weeks.

The Womb II.

– Mixerman

DAY 43

The Overrating of Melody and Lyrics

POSTED: NOVEMBER 20, 11:24 P.M.

Since Willy took me out for two dinners, I decided it was my turn to pick up the tab, so I took Willy and Rod out for breakfast. It seems the studio doesn't supply muffins, just a small bowl of fruit, but eating breakfast is critical to a good day's work. Our breakfast cost more than a typical dinner for three in L.A., but I'm growing accustomed to the fact that there's no need for any bills of less than $20 denomination in Midtown Manhattan, as I am basically working smack-dab in the middle of the biggest tourist trap in the world.

I have been assured by Harley, whom I spoke to last night, that the console will work without a hitch, and that the studio is completely set up and ready to go. Rod made sure that every mic was working, in its proper location, and ready to be placed. Rod is awesome! There's nothing like having an assistant who's done his own sessions, because that person understands fully how to be most helpful. Most assistants out of school know nothing other than some theory and, through no fault of their own, have no capacity to actually think ahead. Recent graduates have not actually been through the process, and they've not had to deal with the consequences of their own inadequacies.

Rod, on the other hand, knew the process well and could plan ahead in order to keep the session running smoothly. For instance, without my asking for it, Rod set up a noise gate for automatic muting of my talkback (TB) mics. He plugged a talkback mic at each person's station into the same wall input so that all the TB mics would be going to one mic pre, and then he patched them to tape to be recorded. I always record the TB mics, but I never told Rod this. How did he know?

Rod striped ten reels of tape with SMPTE (which is an audio tone that contains encoded time information; it sounds similar to a fax tone), and used the SMPTE as a way to open and close the talkback mics by keying a gate in duck mode. I'll explain for those who don't understand.

A gate is a device that works just as its name implies. It's a gateway for audio. If you put a gate on a signal, when the gate is open, you will hear that signal; when the gate is closed, you will not. A gate will open automatically at a certain level of sound called the threshold, allowing the signal to pass. They are often used to act as automatic mutes of sorts. One common use for them is on tom mics so as to eradicate the cymbal bleed on the tom tracks when the toms are tacit. In that scenario, when the tom is not being hit, the gate is closed, thus muting the cymbal leakage on the tom mics. When the tom is hit, the gate opens, allowing the tom hit to be heard.

One can set the threshold, or the level of signal that will force the gate open, how quickly the gate opens, how long the gate will open for, and in some cases, what frequency range will trigger the gate. Personally, I usually dislike using gates for toms, but that's just a personal preference. Sometimes gating is unavoidable, regardless of my personal preferences.

Many gates have another feature. They can open and close by what's called a "key." The key is a way to use a separate external signal to control the opening and closing of the gate. For instance, I can hold out whole notes on a synthesizer and make them sound like the synthesizer pulsing sixteenth notes by plugging a hi-hat into the key. The gate responds by opening and closing by virtue of the hi-hat's signal, but the gate affects the synthesizer. This creates the effect of the synthesizer pulsing. This is a classic example of how to use the key input on a gate.

Some gates have another function, which is called "ducking." Ducking is the opposite of gating. In gating, the gate opens when a certain threshold of signal is reached. In ducking, the gate closes, or ducks, when a certain threshold of signal is reached.

One of the problems with talkback (TB) mics is you have to constantly remember to open and close the channel. TB mics are the lines of communication between the band members who are isolated in a generally soundproof room and the crew in the Womb. We need the TB mics open to hear what the band is saying between takes, but we typically want the TB mics closed when the band is making a take, because if they're open, we're usually hearing too much room information in the monitoring blend. This can make it difficult to evaluate the quality of a take.

Rod fed the output of the SMPTE (simptee) tone that was on tape to the key of a gate and set the gate to duck. The gate was inserted on the playback of the TB mics. This way, when the tape is playing, the SMPTE tone keys the gate, the gate closes, and the talkback mics are muted. When the tape stops, the tone stops, the gate opens, and the TB mics are essentially unmuted. Rod, having done some sessions himself, understood the value of setting a gate to open and close the TB mics and took the liberty of thinking ahead and setting this up. This sort of assistant is invaluable to keeping a session running smoothly.

Rod also took the liberty of doing some A/B tests on the mics in order to find the best particular mic of each model that was available to us. He wasn't making judgments of what models I would use—I already made those initial decisions in my setup. He was picking the best specimen of the particular models I requested, as studios many times have multiples of the same microphones.

Mics are like instruments. There are mass-produced instruments that tend to be fairly consistent in their quality, and then there are the handmade instruments that have a wider variation of sound. For instance, you cannot find two Yamaha C7 pianos that sound or feel the same. Microphones are no different from instruments in this way.

While identical models of mics will have distinct similarities to them, they each will have their own sonic imprint. The differences between identical microphones can be staggering—especially when you start getting into very old microphones. Past environments, care, and maintenance of said microphones are key factors in how a microphone sounds.

A thirty-year-old microphone that was once a benchmark specimen of its model, if poorly maintained and cared for, can sound absolutely awful. Years of dust and smoke can wreak havoc on the capsule. There are techs that specialize solely in the refurbishing of old microphones, offering modifications that improve the mic, or the service of bringing the mic back to its original specs. Because of the individual nature of microphones and the large range of discrepancies possible between identical models, picking one is not quite as simple as picking a model number and just grabbing whatever one happens to be handy. At the same time, it's not necessarily beneficial to the session to be trying out ten C12s as the band waits for you find the best one. It's better to keep the session moving than to be assured you have the best microphone in the joint.

Rod did me the best favor he could have done. He found the lousy-sounding microphones, and he rejected them. This saves me time in trying to determine why something doesn't sound right.

After breakfast, Willy, Rod, and I headed for the studio. When we got there, we were once again stopped by the security guard.

"What session are you here for?" he asked.

"Bitch Slap." I replied.

"Names, please," he said as he looked down on his clipboard.

This was ridiculous. Was it going to be like this every day?

"Willy Show, Mixerman, and Rod," Willy replied.

"I don't have any Rod on my list," he replied.

"We went through all of this yesterday!" I said getting annoyed and breathing deeply through my nose as Dalai Llama had taught me.

"Well, that was yesterday; this is today. I'll call up and get some verification, if you like."

"Please," Willy said very patiently.

The security guard made his call and eventually allowed us to pass.

When we entered the Womb, I waited like a small child waiting for approval from his parent after coloring all over the walls. Willy had not seen the studio decorated yet, and this was, for all intents and purposes, the unveiling. I was grinning from ear to ear. Willy obviously couldn't believe his eyes.

"Wow! I love what you've done with the place," Willy said. "I could die in this room."

A tear came to my eye. This was exactly how I felt! I was filled with pride on my accomplishment of transforming a veritable vacuum of anti-vibe into an overflowing waterfall of warmth and beauty. Every square inch of the drab walls was covered with gorgeous unique tapestries. Icicle lights were dangling all along the borders of the ceiling to the wall. Handmade candles sat atop beautiful metal candle plates. Incense boxes stood ready for their ash collection abilities. Pillows and a blanket transformed a cold leather couch into an oasis for listening in absolute comfort. This was *now* a Womb—a place that I could die in, and from the sounds of it, Willy too.

"Thanks," I replied.

Everything was perfect. The love in the room was mind-boggling. We had a team that was able to conquer any obstacle. We had Rod, the superhuman assistant, who, like the great chess player Kasparov, was twenty-five moves ahead at all times. We had Willy, our fearless leader, who has been so patient in this process of making what would undoubtedly be a landmark album (ahem). There was me, who, regardless of my talents or lack thereof as a recordist and mixer, at the very least could stake the claim to decorating a room to perfection. I was floating in elation.

Then Bitch Slap walked in.

"What's with the Christmas lights?" Harmon complained with that ultra-repressive whiny voice as he entered the Womb. I hugged him, although I wanted to punch him.

"I like them," replied Johnny On-the-Spot, who was right behind him and was now hugging Willy.

"Well, I think they suck, and what's with all the faggy pillows on the couch?" Harmon continued as Johnny made his way to me for a hug. I couldn't help but see the humor in the fact that all these men were hugging, and Harmon was bitching about a couple of pillows being "faggy."

"Hey, I'm going to put these three lava lamps over by me," Johnny stated, as he pointed to what I called my Triad of Power. The Triad consisted of three lava lamps arranged in a triangle on a speaker stand behind the console.

"I gave you three lava lamps in your Apartment over there," I replied, pointing to his area in the room. As you may recall, I like to give the players their own little sections of the room with a comfortable chair, a nice wool rug, some candles, lights, whatever I can scrounge up.

"Yeah, but wouldn't it be rad for me to have six lava lamps in my Apartment?" he responded.

Yes, I'm sure it would be rad, you miserable selfish cunt, I thought to myself.

"Sure, be my guest," I said, choosing the more diplomatic route of giving the singer—and technically the client on this session— what he desires. I considered buying three more lava lamps, because I really loved having the Triad of Power right there in front of me. But I didn't bother sending the runner out, because if I set up a new Triad, Johnny would most assuredly want nine lava lamps in his Apartment.

Willy had already sparked up a fatty, as everyone was halfheart-edly introducing themselves to Rod and Lightning. After taking a long draw, Willy handed me the fatty, but I passed. I hadn't had a fatty since the last Bitch Slap session. I hadn't even thought about a fatty since then. I decided that I would resist the fatties for as long as I could.

The band was mingling about the room when the new drum-mer walked in. He was a handsome African-American man, with awesome shoulder-length dreadlocks. He stood about six feet tall, and he was obviously no stranger to the gym, as he was in excel-lent shape, with sharply cut muscles. He introduced himself.

"It's good to meet you. These guys speak quite highly of you," he said as he shook my hand with a not-too-firm, not-too-weak handshake.

"Likewise," I replied, foregoing my usual smart-ass response of "Indeed!" "I thought you were great during your auditions. I'm glad they picked you for the gig," I continued.

"Me too . . ." he said, and it would have been fine for him to have left it at that, but somehow, he felt the need to continue, ". . . I think."

That particular comment told me that our new drummer was an intuitive and smart dude. He obviously understood that on the surface of things, he's in a very good position playing for a band that has as much support as they do from their label. But underneath the surface, he must know there is something very, very wrong.

"I know what you mean," I said with a chuckle, hoping to let him know that I'm well aware of how fucked up the dynamic is with this band without fully giving away my position on the matter.

Not wanting to belabor the point, I suggested that we work on drum sounds, and he graciously went in to adjust and tune his drums. The guy could actually tune his own drums! Sadly, this is quite unusual in this day and age. The moment our new drummer was situated and ready to play, Rod was moving the mics in and around the drums.

We had drum sounds in less than ten minutes flat. It was the antithesis of working with Dumb Ass on drums. This guy played his drums with balance, tone, and feel. Quite honestly, I could have used one well-placed quality microphone, and I would have had a better sound than I ever got with Dumb Ass.

Willy entered the Womb and absolutely loved the drum sound, although he wasn't quite sure about the snare drum. But that was as easy to fix as changing out the snare drum.

As Rod and I were working on the drums, Lightning was working with Harmon to set up his bass rig. By the time we were done drums, I was able to work on the bass sound, which took considerably longer than the drums. I didn't particularly care for the bass amp that we had rented. It was an Ampeg-SVT combo with the standard 8 x 10 cabinet (a speaker cabinet with eight ten-inch woofers), but it wasn't a particularly good specimen. So I ordered another head and cab, and an Ampeg B15,[58] just in case.

We moved on to guitar sounds, which didn't take much time at all. Before I knew it, the band was making music, although we were only using the direct signal[59] of the bass, as the amps didn't arrive for hours. Unfortunately, when you order rental gear in Midtown Manhattan, you can expect to wait half a day before it arrives, as the traffic makes it impossible to get anything quickly. That's why so many couriers use bikes there. It's considerably faster to get around Manhattan on a bike than it is in a truck. There aren't many people who could cart a hundred-pound Ampeg head and a five-foot-tall SVT speaker cabinet on their backs while riding a bicycle. So we had to wait for a truck to get through Midtown Manhattan.

The new drummer was awesome. I mean, this guy kicked ass. Even Harmon played halfway decent when he played with the new drummer. Everything was fantastic. I was happy, the band was happy, and we were ready to record once the bass amps had arrived.

Everyone was super hot on the new song, which they had been writing since they arrived in New York. The band members wanted to start with that song, and Willy did nothing to dissuade them. Unfortunately, the song wasn't fully written, and they needed to finish it. They didn't have a melody they were sure of in the chorus. They didn't have the bridge fully ironed out, and they had very few lyrics. Even the form of the song was still up for discussion, which is no great surprise since the lyrics weren't done. Yes, I could see why they were so hot on this song.

The band spent the entire rest of the day trying to work out the song. Lightning, Rod, and I pretty much sat around for the remainder of the day. Sure, I would occasionally make adjustments and dial in the sound a bit more, but you can only do this so much before you start destroying what you have. So for the most part, I laid around in the Womb.

By the end of the day, we had recorded nothing, because for some inexplicable reason, this yet undeveloped song was *very* important and was going to be a sure-fire radio hit, so long as they came up with a great lyric and a great melody.

Oh, is that all?

– Mixerman

DAY 44

The Great Discovery

POSTED: NOVEMBER 21, 11:32 A.M.

The lack of pastries at the studio and, more importantly, the lack of chocolate muffins weighed heavily on my mind as I got ready this morning. The hotel pastries are subpar at best, as hotel pastries usually are. I've stopped at several bakeries in the past few days that have been good but certainly not exceptional, and none of them had chocolate muffins.

The chocolate muffins that I've grown accustomed to in L.A. come from a killer bakery, so I am, without a doubt, spoiled. But this is New York City, one of the culinary capitals of the world! To date, recommendations from locals have only taken me so far, as it seems I'm some sort of pastry snob. What else is new? As with most things in my life, finding the perfect bakery would likely require more kismet than ingenuity.

Understanding the ways of kismet, I decided to take a different route to the studio. As it turns out, it's the best decision I've made in quite some time. As I limped, fully in pain from my splints and clearly underdressed for fall in New York, I was stopped dead in my tracks by the most delightfully pleasing smell that has ever stimulated my olfactory senses.

I felt like Buddy Hackett in the movie *It's a Mad, Mad, Mad, Mad World* when he stopped dead in his tracks after running right under the palm trees that formed the big W that he and every other character in the movie was searching for. I stood there in the middle of the sidewalk, squatting with my arms out like a wrestler preparing to take down his opponent, sniffing frantically, trying to locate precisely where the smell was coming from.

Just as Buddy Hackett had done, I turned slowly and most deliberately around to see before me the most glorious bakery I've ever set eyes on—an authentic French bakery, jammed with people and filled with pastries. Without another thought, I entered.

Alas, this bakery, too, did not have the chocolate muffins I so adore. No, they had something better! They had freshly made chocolate croissants, and that is precisely what I ordered.

"One chocolate croissant and a large coffee, please," I said to the worker behind the counter.

As excited as a teenager who had just scored his first nudie magazine, I found myself a little table, brushed off the crumbs left by the inconsiderate little prick who sat there before me, quickly unwrapped my croissant, and took my first bite. I swear to you, it was by far the best croissant that I've ever had in my life. And my coffee! Oh, my coffee was easily the greatest cup of coffee I've had since I was in France.

This place was as authentically French as a French bakery can be, save the Latino workers behind the counter. In fact, were it not for the Latino workers, I'm thoroughly convinced that I would have actually been *in* France, and we would be discussing the fact that there is a direct portal to Paris located somewhere in Midtown Manhattan. Of course, this is far from being a C. S. Lewis novel, so I'll spare you that particular claim.

This bakery was too good to not share, even with Bitch Slap. I purchased a box of twenty croissants and headed toward the studio.

When I arrived, I was greeted by my favorite security guard, and for the briefest of moments I thought that I would be automatically permitted to pass. But I wasn't.

"Name, please," the security guard said.

"Mixerman?" I replied quizzically.

As he searched for my name, I opened up my box of croissants and placed them on his desk in front of him.

"Have a croissant," I said. "There are cheese, chocolate, apple, and plain ones. Take your pick, and take one for later," I continued.

"Well, I don't mind if I do! This is one of my favorite bakeries," said the security guard as he picked up two croissants—one chocolate, one cheese. He immediately took a bite from the cheese one, strewing crumbs everywhere in the process.

"You're not on the list," he said with his mouth full of cheese croissant. "Which studio are you working in?" he asked.

Were I a comic book character—and I'm beginning to wonder if I am—I'm quite confident that there would have been a black scribble hovering over my head at that particular moment. This is the third time I've come to the studio, I offer him a bribe, and he still has to make sure I'm on the list?

"So who's in charge of the list?" I asked.

"Well, that would be Violet" he replied, as he picked up the phone for verification.

Violet is the studio manager. She came down yesterday to meet and greet, and I've spoken to her on the phone on more than one occasion in order to deal with the details of preparing for the session, but it was apparent I'd need to spend some time with her.

When I finally got to the Womb, the band was already there, which I can remember happening only twice before this, and both times I happened to be late. Perhaps the move to New York was actually a good decision and would help the band be more focused. It's a pretty expensive way to focus, but I suppose the label has no shortage of money.

Willy and the band enjoyed the croissants so much that he immediately called Violet and asked her to come down to our room. When she arrived, he offered her a croissant, which she declined. I don't really blame her, because as delicious as croissants are is as messy as they are. When you bite into them, they flake all over the fucking place. The control room was covered with greasy little flakes of croissant. Violet is obviously an experienced woman in the ways of croissants, because there is really no way to eat these things gracefully.

Violet agreed to have the bakery deliver our croissants every morning. Apparently, you can have anything delivered in New York, and delivery is almost always free. They don't even build the delivery costs into the price! Not wanting there to be any errors, I asked Violet to make sure there were always at least five chocolate croissants in the box. She assured me that she would.

I took a moment to ask Violet about the list and the security guard. She promised me that she would make sure that we were all on the list from now on and apologized for the problems getting in. Personally, I'll believe it when I see it. I mean, if a chocolate croissant can't get you in without incident, then as far as I'm concerned, nothing will.

The band and Willy were still working on their lyrics and melodies for their new hit single, so I slipped out and went shopping for sneakers, but I couldn't find the ones I was looking for.

When I was in a small shop in Brentwood, California, I found a pair of Ecco walking shoes that looked like black athletic sneakers. Unfortunately they didn't have my size, and so I have been searching for a store that carries this particular shoe. The best news of all is that this model of shoe is just over $100, which is extremely inexpensive for Eccos. If you've never tried on a pair of Eccos, you're missing out, because they are the most technologically advanced shoes in the world where comfort is concerned. Stylistically, I feel they leave something to be desired. But they *are* the premier walking shoe. I found several little shops that carried Eccos, but none of them carried this particular shoe.

When I returned, the band and Willy seemed prepared to start recording the song. They were still at an impasse on the melody in the chorus, but they would record the song anyway. I have never quite understood the thinking behind recording a song that isn't completely written. It's quite common, and it's fraught with problems that cause the process to take twice as long. I can't understand why the hell we weren't recording the songs that are fully written and, I would assume, well rehearsed.

If you don't know the melody of the chorus, it's impossible to write countermelodies. Oftentimes, it's the top note in the guitar voicing that supplies the countermelody. What invariably happens is that a guitar part or a bass part is laid down, only to have to be reworked later because some note rubs with the melody. To be fair, sometimes having the basic parts recorded makes it easier to finish the song, but this is best served by a demo, not a master.

Then, one must consider the fact that, without a lyric, one relinquishes the possibility of the use of prosody—that is, performing the music so as to take the lyric literally. The simplest example of this is having the music stop on the word "Stop" which happens in countless songs, such as "Stop . . . in the name of love" or even "You gotta stop . . . children, what's that sound, everybody look what's goin' round." In these two examples, the music stops on the word "stop." That is an example of prosody.

Despite my opinions on this subject, I wasn't running the show. That would be Willy Show. So we recorded the song a few times, and the band came in to listen before getting into a two-hour debate on the form of the song. How you debate the form of a song that doesn't have a clear content, a clear melody, and a clear direction in general is beyond me. But that's what happened, and this is precisely my point.

Normally, the band would come in and be debating the merits of the sounds or the arrangements. These guys weren't listening to that aspect of the recording at all. That was irrelevant, because they were still focusing on the song itself.

We recorded the song three more times. Willy felt it was too fast, and they had a twenty-minute debate about *that*! Call me crazy, but one of the biggest factors that I use in determining a tempo is how it sings. Sometimes the track will sound great at one tempo, but the singer can't get the words out. Without lyrics, how the hell do we know how the song sings?

By the time the day was done, we had seven reels of this song with different forms and different tempos. Tomorrow we will sort through the twenty-one takes and figure out where to go from there—the humor of which does not escape me.

No longer did we have to deal with the painstaking recording of twenty-one takes just to get enough material to put together a mediocre drum take. The new drummer put an end to that nonsense. So what do we do? Fuck around recording a song that isn't even remotely ready to be recorded, and record twenty-one takes of that!

Let me just set the record straight here. I understand that this is a creative process, and that sometimes it's important to take a detour in the course of this process. I get that the band is excited about the song, and this sort of enthusiasm is valuable to a session, particularly this one. But the band spent two fucking years writing hundreds of songs, *none* of which are actually recorded after forty-some days of recording. I mean, shouldn't we be trying to record the album?

As I type this, I can't resist asking myself the question that all men ask when they are involved in a debacle of epic proportions. It's the question that the greatest philosophers in the history of the world ultimately ask themselves, and it's the question the simplest of men have asked themselves. Most definitely, it's the question that I have been asking myself on many occasions since this project started. It's a question that is simultaneously the most egotistical question one could ask oneself and the most unassuming question one could ask oneself.

Is it just me?

– Mixerman

DAY 45

Penny Pincher

POSTED: NOVEMBER 23, 12:33 A.M.

I'm sick to death of ordering pastrami sandwiches and getting a pound of meat on two slices of rye bread. Whatever happened to balance? Making a great sandwich is an art form. It requires quality ingredients and *balance*. Really, putting together a great sandwich is no different from putting together a great mix.

A great sandwich should have the highest-quality meat, cheese, bread, salad, and condiments. Skimping on any one ingredient will most assuredly ruin the sandwich. The lettuce should add the necessary crispness to the sandwich. The tomato should add the necessary sweetness, and the onion the prerequisite spiciness to the sandwich. If the meat is fatty, then one should use mustard for spice. If the meat is lean, one should use mayonnaise for fat. It's all about balance.

Now, while I don't like lettuce and tomato on my pastrami—they only do *that* in California—at least put some fucking onion and mustard on the thing! And if I can't pick the sandwich up and stick it in my mouth, then it's no longer a sandwich. It's your sliced meat packaged in my rye bread. I digress before I've even begun, only because I'm trying to eat one of these behemoth sandwiches as I type this.

This morning I went through the usual trials and tribulations of getting past the security guard, who is now getting a name for the purposes of this diary. He will, from this point forward, be referred to as Al Zeimer, and for good reason! I swear to God, this guy doesn't recognize me from one day to the next. Case in point: I asked my good friend Al Zeimer if he enjoyed the croissants I gave him yesterday, and he looked at me confused, as if he had no idea what I was talking about.

Al is an older black dude, whose hair is very short and mostly gray. He has a fairly small build, and I could easily just walk right by him, as he'd certainly not be able to stop me. But I always stop, since the whole ritual is becoming more comical than annoying.

Al Zeimer actually has to look up the extension in his phone directory in order to make his "verification." I watch him do it every day. He opens up his little phone book, and he runs his finger down the list until he comes to Violet's name, and then he methodically runs his finger across the page to Violet's extension, picks up the phone, and dials said extension to ask her if the guy who's been coming here for four days now is allowed in the studio. With the way this studio compiles its list of daily clients, you have to imagine that Al is calling that particular extension twenty times a day, yet he's *still* looking it up?

When I got to the Womb, the band, Willy, and my two assistants were already there. New York must be like some sort of alternate universe, because the fact that I'm consistently getting there after the others is very odd to me. We set our start time for 2 P.M. today, and when I looked at my watch it said 2 P.M. It used to be that if I arrived right on time, I was an hour early, but not anymore. I prefer to arrive before the band, so that I can listen to some things on my own and take care of any problems that might have occurred the day before.

Fortunately for me, I have Rod, who takes care of everything on his own. Apparently, he shows up to the session an hour early every day, and I have no reason to doubt him. I've never had an assistant as good as Rod. I want to hire the guy permanently in L.A., but unfortunately he's from Ohio, and he doesn't have any plans to move.

Then there's Lightning. Frankly, there's not too much to tell you about him. I mean, he's a nice guy, I like him a lot, but I don't think he knows much. Sometimes I'll ask him a question, and he'll give me a blank stare, much like my main man Al Zeimer does. I don't really even have to deal with Lightning much, as Rod has taken over the duties of directing him, which I'm very grateful for, because I've been *very* busy, what with having to re-plenish candles, fluff pillows, and the general resting that comes from waiting for a band to write a song.

The band, which, if I didn't know better, had been full of love for each other for the past two days, was beginning to revert back to its old ways. Today, rather than starting right away, the band had one of their classic two-hour meetings about writer's royalty splits. This was a very common theme among them. They are so concerned with the fair and equitable divvying of Monopoly money that they spend inordinate amounts of time and energy doing so with the impetus of making sure that one person doesn't come out ahead of the others. I have watched Harmon turn down great lyrical ideas from Yore with absolutely no explanation as to why, other than "not liking it." I can assure you that Harmon turns down all lyrical ideas, because he doesn't want to give up a percentage of the song to Yore, or anyone else for that matter.

The writer's royalty is where the big money is in this business. If you're in a band and you write nothing, you can sell millions of records and be broke, particularly on a project like this one. Even if this record is hugely successful, the band will not likely ever recoup the money that it cost to make the album. But the label has to pay the writer's share, regardless of what they shelled out to make the record. Therefore, the only people who will make any kind of money from this album are the ones who wrote the songs.

Once a song has been written and recorded, anyone may then record the same song. If any song on this album becomes a hit, even years later, or if the song is used in a commercial, it is the writer of that song who will make the money.

Rather than coming up with an across-the-board equitable split, which would be the easiest solution for this neurotic bunch of numb-nuts to do, they prefer to spend half their days negotiating with each other as to exactly who should get what percentage of what song. And it gets pretty deep.

I've overheard arguments among Bitch Slap as to who wrote what *word* in a song, with computations coming down to dividing the total number of words by the number of words contributed by a particular band member. That result was then *divided by two* because the lyric was only half of the song with the melody being the other half. Unless, of course, there was a particular guitar line or melodic countermelody that drove the song (like the guitar riff in the Rolling Stones' "Satisfaction," for instance), in which case an entirely new formula had to be negotiated in order to figure out the splits.

I've even overheard Dumb Ass claim that he came up with a particular note in a melody, and, therefore, should get one percent of the writer's royalties. Were I a judgmental person, I would call this group petty; but quite honestly, petty doesn't begin to describe the depths of their communal disease.

These discussions are usually held before we start out the day, and I can always tell when one of their classic meetings has taken place, because they don't really talk to each other, except to get in some snide, sarcastic quip.

Today, Bitch Slap obviously arrived early for one such meeting, and Willy got dragged into the fray, as he has been actively participating in the writing of this new song. This might explain Willy's lack of focus on the job at hand, which was supposed to be the recording of a group of preselected songs, for what would one day be deemed the greatest album of all time!

Since the band was still in a meeting, and I really didn't have much to do, I decided to go outside and eat one of my sandwiches. As I walked out, I realized that not only was it too cold, but there was no place to sit, and it smelled like a combination of exhaust and trash outside. I decided to reenter to find someplace else to eat, but as I turned toward the turnstile, a very aggressive woman pushed her way in front of me and walked into the building. At the time, I didn't think much of it, because this was New York and that's par for the course here.

As I entered the building, I watched the strange woman walk straight past Al's desk without so much as a hesitation as she announced herself and walked right into the complex.

"Penny Pincher, Bitch Slap," she announced.

I've never seen anybody walk as quickly as Ms. Pincher. I had to run just to keep up with her. She turned around to see who was following her. It was me.

If I had to describe her in one fragmented sentence, that description would have to be "well put-together." She wasn't classically beautiful, whatever the hell that is. I just know she isn't that. To be quite honest, I found her somewhat repulsive, but in a slutty way that was inexplicably sexy—if you can imagine that.

Penny knew her way around this studio, because she walked straight into the Womb.

"I'm looking for Willy Show," I heard her say sternly to Rod. "Get him for me."

"May I tell him who's calling?" Rod asked as I smacked my forehead with my hand and grimaced in pain. One thing I know from my years of doing sessions—you do *not* ask who's calling when it's the A&R person on the project. She must have heard the smack, because she turned around to look at me.

"This is none other than Penny Pincher," I said, half smiling, half wincing. "I'm Mixerman," I continued as I extended my hand, hoping to take her mind off the faux pas that had just occurred.

Then, like a light switch, she became quite charming.

"Ah, yes, Mixerman. So glad to finally meet you. Marv absolutely adores you," she said as she took my hand to shake it.

"Indeed," I replied.

Without hesitation, Penny opened a bag that she was holding and handed me a packet. "I understand you don't like your hotel, which is fine by me. You'll be staying in an apartment from now on. You can share it with your assistant," she said without batting an eye.

"Oh, your manager seems to think that I should pay for your weekend plane tickets. I'll pay for three of them, coach, and only two-week advance purchases, so you might want to get your travel agent on it immediately," she continued. "Now, where's Willy?"

I found her monologue to be nothing short of staggering. I didn't know how to respond to this woman. She just told me that I would be sharing an apartment, that I would have to fly coach, and that I would have to wait two weeks to see my family, unless I were so inclined to pay the $1,500 it would likely cost to fly out on less notice. Don't get me wrong—I usually fly coach, when I'm paying for my own ticket. But on a project such as this, where so much money is being spent, plane fares back are usually at the very least business class. I suppose I was being a bit transparent in my thought process; either that or the woman's clairvoyant.

"Look, this project is already over budget, and you probably are only halfway through the tracking by now. We all have to make sacrifices," she explained.

Ah, yes, she pulled out the old "we" bit and spoke of making sacrifices, as if she were participating in such sacrifices. Who does she think she's fooling with that bullshit? Yes, *we* all have to make sacrifices. She doesn't have to make any fucking sacrifices!

Willy came out from the lounge, where I imagine he had been negotiating with Bitch Slap over who was to be paid for a particular note in a chorus that wasn't finished. He looked quite surprised to see Penny.

"Hey, Penny," he said with a huge smile that I could tell was completely fake.

"Willy, I need to speak with you about a few things." So Willy and Penny left the Womb. They returned a few minutes later, and Penny was about to leave, when she asked if she could listen to something.

Willy pulled out the classic response to such a request. "Well, we could, but they aren't ready yet. We need to do a little more work on the tracks before they're even presentable," he fibbed.

"I see," Penny replied. "I suppose I'll accept that answer for the moment. You all have until the end of the weekend to find apartments to your satisfaction. If you go over the limit, it comes out of *your* pocket," she finished, and then she headed out the door.

"Oh, one other thing," she said as she handed me a business card. "From now on, you'll be dealing with Leslie Atard on these matters. If you have any questions, call her at my office."

We couldn't get shit done for several hours after that visit—not that we were being unusually productive in the first place. Surprise visits from A&R representatives are usually exceptionally traumatic to the flow of a session. There are some Mooks that can get away with such unannounced visits, but Penny Pincher was obviously not one of them. The Mooks that *can* make a surprise visit without blowing the vibe typically would never do such a thing and typically aren't even Mooks.

One positive *did* come out of Penny Pincher's visit, though. Harmon and Yore wrote a hilariously poignant, not-so-flattering song about her (without mentioning her by name), and in a matter of minutes. The band worked out their parts, the form, and an arrangement without much hassle, and we recorded it. I dare say it's the best song Bitch Slap's ever recorded.

But then, how difficult was that?

— Mixerman

DAY 46

One Down, Sixteen to Go

POSTED: NOVEMBER 24, 11:37 A.M.

Friday was the best day I've ever had recording Bitch Slap. Our communal run-in with Ms. Penny Pincher, the most extraordinary combination of high-powered executive and dirty little whore, inspired Harmon to write a brilliant song—the details of which I cannot reveal. Suffice it to say, the song is catchy, intelligent, funny, and, best of all, finished.

Yes, we finally completed a song. After a week of dicking around, we managed to finish a song in a little over twelve hours. If we continue on at the current rate of one song per week, we'll be ready to mix in seventeen weeks. If we actually stop fucking around and treat every song like we did this one, we'll be done in seventeen days. Of course, if you consider the fact that we started four months ago, well then we'll be done in about five years. Still, I'm encouraged.

For the first time, these guys looked as if they were actually enjoying themselves. While they still had their deficiencies, it worked, because they weren't trying to be something else. They weren't trying to write a song to be a hit. They were just trying to be Bitch Slap—nothing more, nothing less.

Harmon's bass parts required only a few fixes, and we were done in about ten minutes, as opposed to the usual two hours of tedious punching. Finding the right guitar/amp combination was, for once, an enjoyable experience rather than the usual teeth-pulling affair. Yore only drank half a bottle of Maker's Mark, as opposed to his usual full fifth, and he actually invited Willy to write and lay down a guitar part.

Dumb Ass, who, as I suspected, doesn't have a clue how to play the keyboards short of perhaps an abbreviated version of "Chopsticks," asked me to lay down a part for him. He wanted me to keep it simple enough for him to learn to play live, which seemed like a reasonable request.

I couldn't help but chuckle to myself that if this band ever hit it big, Dumb Ass would be like the Edge of keyboard players. The Edge is U2's self-taught guitar player, who could barely play when they made their first hit album. But then I woke up and once again came to terms with the fact that this band hasn't a chance in hell of making it big! Whatever the hell "making it big" means. You only hear that term in shitty fucking movies about the music business, so why the hell am I using that term here?

We all participated in the laying down of percussion by forming what could only be described as a drum circle. It was a blast, and the percussion came out great. The lead vocal was done in three takes, which Willy and I compiled into one take and in less than half an hour. We even got ourselves into a pretty cool and fruitful Science Experiment.

Friday's session was how a session should run. It was fun, it was creative, it was guttural, it was fast, and we were all proud of the end results. I even did a quick mix of the song, although I really have no idea if that mix will stand or not. Rough mixes[60] can have a certain magic to them, but I won't know whether I captured that magic, until I've had a moment away from the song.

Everybody was pretty high on our day's accomplishments—that is until Willy asked Rod to burn a CD and have it messengered to Ms. Penny Pincher. The band and I exchanged looks of absolute horror. At first Willy didn't catch on (that's why they call it dope), and then he too contracted a similar look of horror. It was quite apparent to me that we were all asking ourselves the same question. I chose to say it aloud.

"How do you play a disparaging song about your new A&R rep to your new A&R rep?" I asked.

"You don't," Willy sighed.

– Mixerman

DAY 47

Amscray

POSTED: NOVEMBER 27, 9:09 A.M. — WEEK 10

Penny Pincher is like the Joseph Stalin of A&R men . . . er . . . you know what I mean. I was at dinner with Willy on Sunday, just before we watched the Lakers-Bucks game, and she called Willy on his cell phone for the gazillionth time that day. The moment he picked up the phone, you could hear her relentless squawking, and it didn't stop. Willy actually put the phone down on the table and turned it up full blast for close to five minutes without picking it up. She didn't stop talking. People at the tables around us were being entertained as we all listened to her ramble on and on endlessly. Finally, her monologue turned into, "Willy? Willy?" Willy feigned a dropped call by simply hanging up on her.

When she called again, Willy held the phone up for both of us to hear.

"Hello? Willy?" I could hear the very tiny distorted voice of Penny.

"Oh, hello, Penny, was that you who called earlier?"

"WHAT?? You didn't hear any of that?"

"Hello? Penny? You're breaking up. Hello?" Willy said, and then he hit the end button again.

Apparently, she's been up Willy's ass the entire weekend. Willy has refused to play her anything, and she's threatened to call Marv. Like that's a threat! Let me see if I can imagine that particular threat. "If you don't play me some music, I'm going to call your best friend." Oooh, I'll bet Willy was shaking in his boots.

In an earlier call, which I also happened to be privy to, Penny tried to tell Willy that we were to work the whole week, including Thanksgiving. Apparently, she had negotiated a half-rate at our insanely overpriced studio for the full Thanksgiving weekend. Willy's response was classic.

"I happen to know that Mixerman will charge four times his normal rate to stay in New York over the Thanksgiving weekend, so it doesn't sound like a bargain to me at all."

I'd probably have stayed for three times the rate, but what the hell. Then Willy surprised us both with his next statement.

"As if that weren't enough, our new drummer is Jewish and has no intention of missing the first couple of days of Hanukkah with *his* family," Willy continued. "From my limited experiences as a producer, it's very difficult to track a band when the drummer isn't there."

She went ape shit from those statements. I could hear Penny screaming at the top of her lungs, distorting the speaker because Willy had it turned up so loud. I've never heard so many curse words come out of a woman's mouth before. It was a remarkable diatribe of epic proportions. At first it was all rather harmless, until she began to spew some rather disturbing and disparaging remarks that I'd rather not get too detailed about here. Suffice it to say, Willy had to pull out Sammy Davis Jr. as an example, and the conversation ended abruptly.

As Willy and I watched the Lakers without saying a word to each other, he had obviously come to an abrupt conclusion, as he smacked his palm down on the bar.

"We're outta here," Willy said as he picked up his phone to make a call. Kobe Bryant made a spectacular dunk from the weak side. Had I not been so engrossed in the game and had I actually believed we were going home, I might have gotten excited.

"Marv? Willy."

Marv's voice didn't cut like Penny's did, and Willy obviously had the phone at a reasonable volume and next to his ear this time, so I couldn't hear the other end of the conversation.

"We need to pack it up for the week. Do me a favor and tell Penny to set it up, please. She's being a royal pain in my balls, and I can't make a record like this."

Then there were a lot of "uh-huhs" and "yeahs" and "sures" followed by a complex series of grunts of many different varieties.

"Really? Well, didn't you give her any cuddle time?" Willy said next.

This conversation had gone somewhere that I didn't want to be a part of. I got up and went to the other end of the bar. Willy came over when he had finished the conversation.

"What'd he say?" I asked Willy as he approached.

Willy acted like Marv momentarily, "Sure, sure! Whatever you need, Willy. I just want hits, bring me hits!"

I literally jumped out of my chair in exuberance. I wasn't going to have to spend my Thanksgiving holiday working in New York!

"Tomorrow afternoon, Marv's calling Penny and Shortypants, and between the two of them, they'll take care of all our arrangements," Willy said.

"I told him about the song. He's very excited to hear it," Willy stated as he sucked down the last of his drink and pulled out his wallet to pay the tab.

Ah, yes. The song. After a week of struggling to write a hit, Bitch Slap had written their "hit" in thirty minutes and recorded it to completion in twelve hours' time. Of course, I've said this before: It's preposterous to call a song a hit before it's *actually* a hit. One day, I would love to make a documentary where I follow a song on its way to becoming a hit. The hurdles and obstacles a song must overcome before becoming a hit are numerous and huge, and a song can get hung up anywhere in the process, beginning with the band, and continuing through the producer, the mixer, the mastering engineer, the accountants, the executive department, the A&R department, the promotion department, the radio department, the marketing department, Program Directors, MTV, and Clear Channel. All this happens before anyone in the public gets a chance to even react to the song. Still, the song was surely a hit.

So the entire crew and band flew home on Monday, with the intention of starting up again the following Monday. It was a great flight, because Marv, who is hands down the greatest label president of all time, knew just how to keep people happy.

He flew us all home first class.

– Mixerman

DAY 48

Bitch Slap or Bust

POSTED: DECEMBER 3, 9:15 A.M.

I don't believe for one moment that Willy had any intention of setting foot in New York City again, so long as he was recording Bitch Slap, that is. Who could honestly blame him? Who knew that out of a city of eleven million people it only took *one* to make life there so unbearable? He couldn't get out of there fast enough. Neither could I.

Willy must have been very busy lobbying for our return to work in L.A., because I actually got a call from Shortypants on Thanksgiving. Shorty (can I call him Shorty?) didn't even bother with niceties or kibitzing and got right to the crux of the matter. What a surprise.

"I want to know what possible fucking advantage there could be to recording in New York."

Why, hello, Shortypants, and how are you? I thought to myself.

It was an interesting question. One that I felt would have been better asked *before* we all got on planes to go there—that is to say, the band and the entire crew save one. Still, I was being asked a legitimate question, and he was obviously looking for some sort of list, so that's what I gave him.

"None," I replied dryly.

I guess I can be fairly persuasive when I want to be, because Willy called me shortly afterwards to powwow about studios, just in case somehow he was unable to get back into his usual room. Apparently, this was a distinct possibility. So on Friday, I called Ellis at Studio Referral Service,[61] which is a company that basically finds which studios are available at what price range in town, as they all tend to check in with him. After about a half hour of research, Ellis called me back to tell me what studios were available within the specifications that I had given him. Normally, one of those specifications would have been price, but in this particular case we didn't discuss price. That's because the beautiful Ms. Penny Pincher would do the hard-nosed negotiating, and she would likely end up costing the band $300 to $500 per day too much! You see, studios don't give people like Penny Pincher good deals.

For starters, she doesn't have a clue how to ask for a deal. Oh, sure, studios will give her what she *thinks* is a good deal, but the reality of the matter is, she's clueless. The studio will quote her $2,500, she'll bitch, and they'll come down $300. Before you know it, Bitch Slap will be paying $2,200 for a $2,000-a-day room that they were paying $1,800 a day for just two months ago.

Regardless of the pointless gyrations that go with negotiating on a blank check, Ellis gave me the lowdown on which rooms could potentially be made available for the next couple of months. The list was short, very short, considering our requirements and the short notice.

Personally, I choose rooms for a wide variety of reasons—the nearby restaurants, the sound of the recording room, my general comfort there, the console, the mic selection, my mood, and even the service are just a few of the considerations when choosing a room. All of these are important. Still, it's the people at the studio who make the experience enjoyable. If I'm stuck in the control room for hours on end with Bitch Slap, I certainly don't want to take the opportunity to escape their pleasant company only to be confronted with yet *more* despicable and useless people.

The quality of the people in a studio is a direct reflection of the traffic manager. If the traffic manager is cool, the staff will generally be cool. If the traffic manager is aloof, the staff will generally be aloof. If the traffic manager has a good sense of humor, the staff will have a good sense of humor. There will be a test on this later, so do pay attention.

One of my favorite rooms is run by Connie Carrot, and she happens to be a good friend of mine. Connie runs a tight ship. Her staff, particularly the runners, will go way above and beyond the call of duty for a client. I've called Connie Carrot's studio and asked the runners to do a run for me while I was working at another studio, and they've done it. Can you imagine that? "Hey, this is Mixerman, could you pick me up some Starbucks and bring it to me at this other studio that I'm working at?" Now, I've only done that once, late at night, and I'm quite sure I couldn't get away with that very often or if they happened to be busy. But if you're a record maker and you want to see how good a client the studio considers you, try that one—then you'll know.

Probably the most compelling reason for choosing a room is the room itself. The room plays an enormous role in recording, and it is probably the most underrated aspect of same. I could put the identical drum set with the identical drummer on the same day in two different rooms, and the difference in drum sound will be staggering. The room is absolutely critical to the recording, since the microphones are picking up the sound waves as they are excited within the room. Makes sense, right? So if the drums sound like shit in the room, they're generally going to sound like shit on the microphones.

Setting aside the overall subjective quality of a room's sound, there is also the decay time of a room to consider. For a rock recording, one generally wants a room that has some decay time to it—we call this "live." A room that has no decay time to it whatsoever is called "dead." If you've ever walked into an apartment or house with no carpeting or furniture in it, then you have likely experienced a live room. Size and building materials are the biggest factors in how live a room sounds.

The building materials are referred to as the "treatment" of the room. An enormous room made completely of concrete will have an enormous decay time. A parking garage would be a good example of this. A smallish room with carpeting on the floors, walls, and ceilings will have almost no decay time. Typically, rooms are treated with more than one building material so as to have a certain sound to it. Rooms that have wood floors sound different from rooms with tile floors. Acoustical tile on the walls will react differently from carpeting.

There are so many variables that go into creating a good-sounding acoustical space that I couldn't possibly even scratch the surface in this diary. Suffice it to say, even acoustical experts don't have it figured out yet. You see, there is a certain hit-or-miss aspect to the designing of a room, regardless of one's expertise in acoustical spaces. It is impossible to predict how good a room will actually sound until the room is actually completed, making planning for such activities a bit sketchy at best. Acoustics are far too complex for one to predict a result with absolute certainty, especially given the typical limitations on space. Although the goal of any great room designer is to achieve a "magical" recording space, the results rarely hit the mark. But then, isn't that always the way with "magical"?

Connie Carrot certainly had a "magical" room—a room that I've recorded countless records in. But sometimes, one must make compromises in one category for the sake of another category. It was Willy's feeling that the control room wasn't big enough for Bitch Slap, which to me was an advantage, as it might keep the members of Bitch Slap *out* of the control room. But this was Willy's Show, and Willy was desirous to work at the other room on the short list, which was no surprise to me, for this was Willy's room—the room where it all began.

Yes, the L.A. Womb had become miraculously available to us, most assuredly due to Willy's tremendous pull with Magnolia. I assure you, twelve hours of Penny Pincher's berating couldn't match one of Willy's tiny little "could you do me a favor" requests. I'm quite sure that Magnolia will jump through any number of hazardous hoops in order to keep Willy in the Womb.

I can certainly understand why Willy likes working at the Womb. Magnolia is friends with Willy, just as I am friends with Connie, and she makes sure that he's comfortable. I'd even be willing to bet that Willy could call from another studio and get coffee delivered to him, which is now my barometer for one's importance as a client.

The Womb also happens to be a place where the band is comfortable working, and believe me, it's always advantageous to have the band and the producer comfortable. Hell, I can't think of a more comfortable Womb anywhere, so I'm certainly all for it.

So starting Wednesday, I am to set up to record Bitch Slap, yet again. I still don't know who will assist me in this setup. Regardless, I have been assured by Willy that this is the last time I'll have to do a full day's setup on these sessions. I have accepted those terms wholeheartedly.

For this time, it's Bitch Slap or bust.

– Mixerman

Super Freak

POSTED: DECEMBER 6, 11:36 P.M.

Apparently, Willy had made the executive decision to fly Rod to Los Angeles. When I arrived today, and to my pleasant surprise, my superhuman assistant, who had traveled with us to New York, was standing by the entrance of the complex. He was on the patio with coffee and muffin at the ready, prepared to do whatever it took to get the job done today. I thanked Rod as I accepted my muffin and coffee. Then I noticed that Rod had a strange and pained look on his face.

"I think I met the Wegro," he whispered to me, as if he'd seen a ghost.

"Yes, well, we probably shouldn't refer to Fingaz as the Wegro," I informed him. "Besides," I continued with a mouthful of muffin, "what do you mean, you *think* you met the Wegro? You can't *miss* the Wegro!"

I knew just at that moment this was going to be a bad timing day, because as I finished my statement Fingaz appeared.

"Don't be talkin' no racist booshit, Yo. I be omnipotent," Fingaz admonished.

I figured he meant omnipresent, but there was no point in correcting him. I'm pretty sure he already knew this.

Fingaz was still wearing his blue parka, and it smelled considerably better than the last time I saw him. Figuring he must have cleaned the foul-smelling garment, I decided it was probably safe to give him a hug.

"Aw, shit! I missed youz, Yo!" I said in a language he could understand as I offered an embrace. He accepted.

It was nice to see Fingaz again, although the irony of this certainly did not escape me. We had been in New York, Fingaz's hometown, and he hadn't been on the session. He hadn't even visited! Albeit, we were there for a very short time. Still, here we are in L.A., and Fingaz is on the payroll from day one. I couldn't help but wonder why the hell Fingaz was even here. It's not like this drummer needed a tremendous amount of editing. On "Penny Pincher Song" I did only five edits. It took me all of twenty minutes. We needed Fingaz for that?

Upon the completion of our hugging ritual and the formal introduction of Fingaz to Rod, I felt the foreign presence of a stranger. Behind me stood an exceptionally large, overly tan stranger, with bulging and defined muscles, which had muscles of their own. His hair was perfectly coifed in an annoying sort of way, as not a single strand was out of place. To make matters worse, his hair was slightly thicker in the front, causing his hair to precede him. His teeth were pure white, and were so obnoxiously bright that I was fortunate to be wearing sunglasses at the time, for

I could have easily burned out a retina were I unprotected. The stranger offered his hand, which I apprehensively accepted for fear that he might crush it, which he nearly did.

"Welcome!" the stranger said to me as he shook my hand so exuberantly that he nearly tore off my limb. "My name's Thor, and I'll be your assistant."

Ah, yes. The assistant. Of course! The studio will always supply an assistant, regardless of the fact that we're carrying our own. Now we had two assistants, one as big as a house.

"You're Mixerman! I'm a big fan of your work!" he said.

At that moment, for some inexplicable reason, I took an instant liking to the lad.

So after exchanging niceties, we set forth to the tracking room. As I entered the room, I remembered exactly why I have such disdain for setup. Before me stood a mountain of cases in all varieties of shapes and sizes. They were piled indiscriminately in the middle of the room, and they covered a large percentage of the floor space. We were back where we started.

"I figured I'd put all the cases in here, and then we could sort through them!" Thor said eagerly.

A worse decision could not have been made. Among the stack were my racks; Willy's racks; Willy's road cases for his guitars, amps, and percussion; drum cases galore containing three full drum kits and twenty snare drums individually cased; Yore's guitars individually cased; Harmon's basses with their respective amplifiers individually cased; and Willy's Alsihad rig that we never use. It was a sight to behold—if you're young, stupid, and built like Arnold Schwarzenegger, that is!

I stood there with Rod, just staring at the mountain of gear before us.

"Welp! Let's dig in then!" yelped Thor, who began manhandling cases as large as oxen with undeniable ease. He was flicking them around like they were the little plastic squares in one of those slide puzzles. You know, the ones that you have only one blank space in which to reorganize the squares to form a picture.

It took us about three hours to sort through everything. I went through the cases and determined which were which, and told Thor where to carry them. Some cases belonged in the Womb, some in the shitter-turned–editing room, and the rest in the tracking room. Rod began to set up the Apartments where the players would perform, and I became my usual keeper of the vibe.

Fingaz was very unhappy about his position in the shitter again, and I promised him that I would do something extra special to the room, but really, how special can you make a shitter? The commode was the main hurdle to overcome. How does one make a commode beautiful? Covering it completely is certainly not beautiful. Covering only the tank seems to work well, but the ugliest part of the toilet still shows.

I struggled with this for close to half an hour until Thor came in with three packages of cut flowers from the grocery store.

"I took the liberty of ordering these for you," Thor said, as he lifted the toilet seat and began arranging the flowers in the commode. He gracefully folded the tapestry and covered the tank and seat. He delicately arranged the flowers in the bowl until the bowl was completely filled with a fall blend of flowers that they sell at the grocery store. When he was through, the bowl, which was once an ordinary vessel used to capture and dispose of feces, was miraculously transformed into the most beautiful porcelain vase I had ever set eyes upon. It was a sight to behold! A tear came to my eye.

"I'm allergic to flowers, Yo!" Fingaz said, poking his head in the door.

"You're shitting me," I replied, at the time not quite realizing the humor in that particular choice of words.

But Fingaz was vastly more allergic to flowers than I, as he began to sneeze ten times in a row without stopping.

"Get that shit outta' here, Yo!" Fingaz screamed as he ran from the room.

Thor, without hesitation or remorse, removed the flowers and threw them out. I decided that my efforts to make an ordinary toilet somehow look like an *objet d'art* were wasted. Disgusted, I did what I should have done in the first place—I haphazardly covered the toilet with my least favorite tapestry in my final last-ditch efforts to salvage vibe in the shitter.

Dejected, I returned to the Womb. Thor was at the console instructing Rod to scratch mics. Before a session starts, it's typical to literally scratch the microphones to make sure that you have the right mics labeled in the right positions. This prevents the "right drum overhead" mic from being in the "left drum over-head" position on the console, which is an easy mistake to make. Particularly considering some people envision the microphones from standing in front of the drums (called audience perspective), and some envision the microphones from behind the drums (called player's perspective). Since I often pan the left and right overheads to their respective positions in the stereo field, it's good to be certain which mic is which.

After a long day, we finally had the room completely set up. The mics were scratched, and it was time to go home. I put on my coat and picked up my bag, and I turned to walk out of the Womb as I had done so many times before. Unfortunately, my path was blocked. It was Penny Pincher, standing well inside the entrance of the Womb, in her usual four-inch stiletto heels. She was glaring at me, quite obviously beside herself with anger. How she'd entered the room in this state without my being aware of her presence was beyond me, for her anger was all-consuming and filled the room like a noxious gas.

"Give me the song," she said feigning calm.

"The song?" I replied.

"Don't play fucking dumb with ME, you shit. Give me the fucking song. The one about ME, asshole!" she shrieked.

"I don't know what you're talking about, Penny. Perhaps we should call Willy," I suggested as I made my way to the phone.

"*You!*" She yelled at Rod. "Get me all the tapes and CDs for the band. *Now!*"

Both Rod and Thor stood there not knowing what to do. I stared at them and then gave a slight shake of the head. Penny was obviously watching as well.

"FUCK YOU! You're not going to be working tomorrow, you FUCK!" She bellowed at me.

My heart was racing—not because I was in fear of getting fired; she really didn't have that authority, and she'd probably be doing me a favor if she did. The weight of the negative energy in the room was enough to crush an elephant. Being slightly smaller than an elephant, I was feeling the pressure quite severely.

Penny began frantically searching the room. She had completely lost it as she tossed through the large piles of CDs in the back of the room. The CD wasn't in the room, and the multitrack tapes contained only the basic tracks. The song in its multitrack form was on the Radar, and she wasn't going to figure that out in this particular state. Even if she had, she wouldn't know how to get the Radar to pass audio, let alone turn it on.

Penny was beginning to throw my own personal belongings around the room in her search. As I watched her, a calm came over me. Rather than the prudent act of either giving her the CD, which was in my car, or even giving her a fake CD, I felt compelled to escalate the situation.

"We don't have the CD, and there are no copies, but I can tell you where it is," I said.

"Where is it then?" she asked as she whipped around glaring at me, eyes glowing with rage.

I paused for a moment, for I had set her up. I wanted not to say it—I *really* wanted not to say it.

But I couldn't help myself.

"It's in Marv's car. Apparently he loves it," I said calmly.

That did it! She ran toward me with a clipboard, which she threw at my head as I ducked out of the way. The clipboard hit my Crane Song STC-8, which thankfully is built like a tank and came out unscathed. Then she grabbed the next available projectile, a Bob's Big Boy bobblehead doll. I moved toward the console for cover. She hurled the bobblehead doll toward me as she screamed. It also missed me but had made an obvious dent in one of the mains'[62] woofers. The bobblehead doll, I'm thankful to say, came out unscathed.

"You miserable shit! You think you can go writing whatever you want on the Internet? 'Dirty little whore'? 'The Joseph Stalin of A&R men'?"

She was clearly losing it.

"How can you be so fucking stupid to think that this wouldn't be discovered? You *know* that we've been reading this diary, and you write that bullshit about me?"

"I wrote that over a week ago—you're just discovering it now?"

"Well, I didn't actually think you would be so brazen as to write shit about ME!!!!" she screamed.

She was right. I have known for some time that the label was reading the diary. I knew for certain when the audio placebos used to dupe Jeramiah Weasel were abruptly removed. I knew Jeramiah's cold treatment of me was a clear indication that he had read of his own duping. In fact, I wrote that entry in order to prove to myself that the label was reading the diary. I knew by how Marv Ellis would go out of his way to acknowledge me. I knew because friends of mine in the music business were sending me links to my own diary. I knew because Lance had discovered it.

Penny was now hyperventilating, and her hair was literally standing on end. Her eyes were bright with rage, and her hands were visibly shaking.

"You should have been fired the moment we discovered it! Marv and his stupid fucking ideas! He thought it would make great PR."

I couldn't help but wonder how an online journal in which a band is depicted as talentless, petty, generally unlikable imbeciles could make for "great PR." But then, I just make records, I don't sell them. So I have to assume Marv had a plan, and I have a pretty good guess as to what that plan might have been.

I suppose Marv felt that if he could sell 50,000 to 75,000 CDs in a short period from the strength of this diary, that could act as a sort of catapult for a wider audience. It is a common business plan to penetrate a niche market in order to jump-start sales in the mainstream market. Certainly, my depicting the band negatively would only serve to make my audience more curious. Marv was obviously banking on this.

What I couldn't understand was how the hell the label kept the band from reading the diary. I can tell you by how they've acted throughout, there's absolutely no possibility whatsoever that the band has been reading these entries. I can only guess the band just never discovered it.

And what of Willy? Willy *had* to have known about this diary. Perhaps he had enough self-control not to read it. Perhaps he agreed with my observations. Or perhaps, as with most things, he just didn't give a shit. I don't know. All of this is speculation on my part, as I'm certainly not going to ask Willy or the band if they've been reading my brutally forthright personal accounts of the idiocy surrounding me.

"Now GIVE ME THE FUCKING SONG!!!!" Penny screamed at the top of her lungs in hysterics as she picked up a metal two-inch flange used to hold a reel of tape and hurled it toward me like a Frisbee. Had it hit me, it could have knocked me out cold, as they are not, by any stretch of the imagination, light.

Thor, who had finally seen enough, and whose duty it was to protect the interests of the studio, not to mention me, grabbed Penny from behind and around her waist, picked her up, and physically removed her from the room. She was pitching and screaming, and although she wore dangerous weapons upon her feet, she was no match for the brute strength of Thor. He carried her out into the middle of the parking lot, placed her ass down on the pavement, ran into the building, and locked the door. I have seen freak-outs in sessions before, but not quite to this magnitude, and certainly *never* by an A&R executive!

Thor, Rod, Fingaz, and I stood in the lobby, motionless, gazing through our own reflections at the scene before us. She remained precisely where Thor had placed her, smack in the middle of the parking lot, like an escapee from the insane asylum. She was screaming obscenities at me from the courtyard, many of which made absolutely no sense. Had I called the police at the height of her hysteria, she would have surely been taken away in a strait-jacket, but I wouldn't have done that. Her aspersions dissipated in a frequency not unlike the popping of microwave popcorn. All told, the freak-out lasted no more than five minutes. To me, it seemed like an eternity.

She had run out of steam. No longer could she protest from her seat upon the pavement. She was dejected and unusually di-sheveled. Her shoes were on the other side of the parking lot, where she had managed to throw them in her rage. One of the heels lay there, cast aside, as it had broken off during the trauma. Without even attempting to tidy herself, she retrieved her shoes. With nary a glance toward her observers, she got into her car and drove out of the automatic gate. It closed behind her.

On my way home, I called Willy and described to him, in great detail, Penny's hysterical episode. I didn't bother to mention anything about the diary. What would be the point? If he knew about the diary, then he would know why she freaked. He wasn't surprised that she knew about the song, so I can only assume he knew where she found out about it. Willy assured me that we would work everything out and that he would call me tomorrow. I'm not sure what there was to work out. I certainly couldn't document these sessions any further. I certainly couldn't work with Penny Pincher any longer.

As I sit here reflecting on Penny's epic freak-out, writing what is quite obviously one of my last entries documenting these sessions, I can't help but chuckle to myself. For in recent days, I have been criticized by some online readers for my use of the term "Bitch Slap" as it relates to this diary. Although Penny's temporary loss of sanity was regrettable, there was certainly something positive that came out of it. Penny had unwittingly supplied new meaning and validity to the term "Bitch Slap."

For that, at least, I am grateful.

– Mixerman

DAY 50

The Waiting Game

POSTED: DECEMBER 10, 8:57 P.M.

It seems Ms. Penny Pincher's antics have had widespread effects. For starters, my superhuman assistant Rod left straightaway for his hometown in Ohio. He had had quite enough of life on a high-budget session. I tried to explain to him that not all the sessions were this bad, but he wasn't interested. I can't say that I blame him.

Willy called me on Saturday and briefed me. Apparently, Willy gave Marv an ultimatum: Either Penny goes or he goes. At first blush, this wouldn't seem like a very difficult decision on Marv's part. Certainly he wasn't going to fire his most trusted friend from a job of such importance to him. But one would have to be very naïve as to the extent of Ms. Penny Pincher's relationship with Marv to think that. I'm having trouble coming right out and saying it, so perhaps I should try to explain what has been explained to me by my Dalai Llama.

If a married "working man" is with another woman, the indiscretion is typically highly secretive and is usually considered cheating. If a married executive is with another woman, the indiscretion is kept behind lightly closed doors, is widely discussed among the minions, and is considered an affair. If a married tycoon is with another woman, it's generally out in the open and is considered outside interests.

Let's put it this way: Marv has outside interests.

I'm sure we all have a fairly solid understanding of the power contained in outside interests in the world of high finance. Willy certainly understood this well enough. Regardless, until the terms of Willy's ultimatum were met, we were on hiatus.

I spoke to Harmon on the phone, which I held about a foot off my ear, as his voice was so irritating. Harmon seemed to relate well to my story about Penny's freak-out, since he went through similar experiences on a monthly basis with Virginia. This, of course, brought Harmon onto the subject of Virginia, which, in my opinion, was the real reason for the call.

"Hey, speaking of Virginia," Harmon said, taking the rather obvious and well-thought-out opening to arrive at the *true* purpose of our phone conversation, "do you think she fucked Lance?"

"I would have no way of actually knowing this unless I happened to be there," I replied with as much logic and tact as I could muster.

"Were you?" Harmon responded.

"What?"

"Were you there?"

"Of *course* I wasn't there! Jesus, Harmon, I think you need to schedule an appointment with your shrink!"

Harmon concurred.

I spoke with Fingaz, who has been sitting in his hotel room all day, racking up hours on the Pay Nintendo at $5.95 per hour.

He called me on Friday, challenging me to a Mario Kart race with him, which I passed on. His invitation quickly transformed to begging, which was pathetic and didn't sway me. I told Fingaz he should take up golf or some kind of outdoor activity, but then he pointed out that "they don't let no Wegros play golf."

Not thinking, I told Fingaz that Wegros are not generally considered a suppressed or prejudiced-against people. Holy shit! The guy launched in on me, telling me how hard it is for him to get a cab in New York City, how his "peoples" had to ride in the back of the bus only forty years ago, how nine out of ten Wegros are in prison because of the Man, yadda, yadda, yadda. I just didn't have the heart to tell him that he's *white*! I also hadn't the inclination to stay on the phone for an hour, so I commiserated and pretended another call was coming in.

That's about all the stories that I have for you at the moment. I suppose where matters of Bitch Slap are concerned, it's the waiting game. Not that I actually expect to be recording Bitch Slap again. It's quite apparent that this session has run its course—surely where my involvement is concerned. Since I have little of substance to offer on a daily basis, and since I'm sure you all have better things to do than to continually read about how I manage to avoid cleaning my socks, I'll get back to you as soon as I know something.

Until then . . .

. . . Enjoy,

– Mixerman

The Final Entry

It has been nearly two months since Penny Pincher threw her fit of epic proportions outside the complex containing the Womb, although in the context of this diary it shall seem far more immediate. Willy Show's ultimatum had been under review by Marv for what seemed like an eternity, although by the time he had made a decision, I was already working on another session. I have been under no pretense that either Willy or I would be working on this album again. Willy made the play of someone who wanted off without actually quitting. Ultimately, Marv made the only choice he could: He let Willy go from the project.

This result was a no-brainer where the displaying of talents in clairvoyant abilities is concerned. What I'm quite certain, however, no person foresaw, was the immediate hiring of Willy's replacement, Penny Pincher. I can assure you, the depths of Penny's lack of qualifications to be Bitch Slap's A&R man pale in comparison to her lack of qualification to be their producer. She knows absolutely nothing about making a record, which, sadly, in and of itself, doesn't necessarily disqualify her.

What she lacks more than anything is the skill to keep this not so merry band of idiots together long enough to record a first take. Of course, in her defense, the person who does have that skill should likely be a candidate for the Nobel Peace Prize, if for no other reason than the impossibility of the task.

Marv wasn't too concerned with Penny's lack of qualifications, as he was negotiating hard with my manager to keep me on the project, for the obvious reason that it's always best to have someone in the Womb who actually knows what the fuck he's doing. I wasn't too interested in the proposals, although I was curious just how far Marv would go.

In the end, none of that mattered, because Marv had recently been fired from his job as president of the label. Of course, the media was told that Marv resigned. Regardless, Marv was supplied a gazillion dollars with which to start his own label. A very nice severance package . . . er, I mean resignation present, indeed!

Firings of old presidents and hirings of new ones usually result in many more firings down the line and a drastic weeding of acts from the roster. If the new president drops an act that cost the label two million dollars, that act is considered one of the old president's failures. Rather than spend more money toward what is deemed a losing effort, it is better for the new regime to cut its losses by dropping the bands with little to no chance of offering large profits. It is especially important to drop those bands that have cost the label too much money, as these costs would surely be inherited by the new president. Sometimes the weeding process can take months, but as you can well imagine, it only took the new regime two days to drop Bitch Slap.

Being dropped from a major label is a traumatic event that, for most new bands, would most assuredly end their record-making career. But Bitch Slap isn't like most bands. Within hours of being dropped, they were given another two million dollars in advance money and another contract, by none other than Marv Ellis himself. He, much like his successor at the parent label, also had a clean slate where spending on Bitch Slap was concerned.

Penny Pincher, knowing where and how her bread is buttered, also resigned and Marv, knowing same, immediately hired her to work for his new label. I know all this because Marv called me personally and expressed his desire for me to record Bitch Slap once he's gotten the label up and running—a process that could take months. I would record them and Penny Pincher would produce them. I found this nothing short of amusing, given the fact that the last time I saw Penny, she was flinging objects at me and yelling at the top of her lungs every bad word in the book.

If I've learned nothing else in this business, I've learned this: One should never actually turn down a gig, but rather either make oneself too expensive or too unavailable. I told Marv to give me a call when he was ready to start recording, although I'm quite certain that I'll be in the middle of a long project when that call comes in. I'm sure I'll recommend a couple of engineers who I really don't like very much, as I would never offer up a friend for such a gig.

Fingaz remained in his hotel for more than a month after Bitch Slap was dropped. Apparently, no one told him that the sessions were over despite the fact that he was submitting weekly invoices. As is typical with major labels, they allow invoices to age. In many cases, invoices are not even reviewed by major labels until they are over thirty days old. I suspect that was the case here. I'm sure Fingaz is going to have a hell of a time collecting on that!

The band, as far as I know, has taken a hiatus, until such time as Marv is ready to fund the recording of their first album. Yes, you read that correctly—the funding of their first album. This would make everything previous to that demos—very expensive demos. Counting up large advances to the band, Willy Show's fees, studio costs, my fees, Fingaz's fees, tape supplies, hard drives, couriers, rentals, sushi dinners, non-sushi dinners, film crews, cruises, psychiatrists, limousines, travel, hotel rooms, and a week in the most expensive studio in the world, I would put the costs of these particular Bitch Slap demos in the vicinity of $3.5 million. I'm going to go out on a limb here, but that has to be some sort of world record.

In the meantime, this diary is over as abruptly as it began, for there is no purpose in continuing it. As is typical in life and atypical in most creative salable mediums, there are rarely tidy little endings that seem to make sense . . . although, if you ask me—and you don't really have to ask—I hardly find this particular ending to be a surprise.

The fact of the matter is, this project was on course toward implosion two years before Bitch Slap set foot in the studio. And while it's not entirely over for Bitch Slap, since they have been picked up again by Marv and his new label venture, they are all but dead. By dead I mean they don't have a chance. If I were to have been perfectly honest with myself at the beginning of this project, I would have known they didn't have a chance—even then.

And despite the bickering, the pettiness, the disdain, the assholishness, the stupidity, and the all-around lack of goodwill that goes on in the day-to-day interactions of Bitch Slap, I can't help but feel sorry for them—for it is the industry that is truly to blame for this debacle.

It is the industry that taught them that they don't need to become proficient at their instruments to get a record deal; that's what computers are for. It is the industry that taught them to spend their last dollar chasing Monopoly money. It is the industry that taught them it's not about the music, it's about a hit, and whoever writes the hit makes the money. It is the industry that taught them that making music isn't about fun, it's about business. It is the industry that taught each of them to be a selfish asshole, for one rarely gets ahead in this business without such a trait. Although, in fairness, it seems that one rarely gets ahead in any industry without such a trait.

As for me, I think that I will make some changes in my life. While I recognize my obligation to my family to provide income, I also have an obligation to both myself and my family to supply happiness. Herein lies the universal truth of this diary. No matter what you choose to do in life, regardless of your dedication to excellence or your commitment to your own sanity, you will always be at the mercy of the idiots who surround you. No matter how much you love your work, there will always be others trying to make it a chore, for they are of the ilk that believe work should actually be work. And if I may personally serve as a lesson for anything whatsoever, let it be this—choose those who surround you carefully, for it has been well established that you will always become a product of your own environment.

I will continue to mix and produce for a living, although I've resigned myself to no longer offer my services as a recordist, for a multitude of reasons both personal and professional that I will not go into here. It seems my next session will be a mixing session with Willy Show, and while I'm sure that the mixing with Willy will be nothing short of fascinating, I have no intention of documenting those events. If for no other reason, it is a term of our working together. As an alternative, I have chosen to relegate myself to the more pedestrian practice of vegging out in front of the television when I come home from work.

To be perfectly honest, I will probably never document another session—certainly not in real time. For I have determined that my writings actually have a direct influence on those around me, much like the scientific principle that says a watched molecule will always react differently from an unwatched one.

I suppose I could provide you with further insights and thoughts on major labels and their ways of doing business. But quite honestly, I think this book sums that up. The big question is the following: Will this diary ultimately serve as a snapshot of how things once were in the record business, or shall it serve as a timeless exposé on how things have been for many years in the record-making business?

While I ask this question for you, the reader, to ponder and to possibly invoke thought, and while I should probably leave this diary at that, I am somehow inexplicably compelled to answer

417

my own question with a well-known and oft-overused phrase, which I am quite certain predates my own existence, let alone this question.

The more things change, the more they remain the same.

– Mixerman

Notes

1. *isolation booth* (*iso booth*): A smaller recording room attached to the main room and used to isolate an instrument or singer from said main room. Iso booths usually have heavy sliding glass doors for high visibility. It is not uncommon for a studio to have several iso booths surrounding one main room.

2. *mic* (abbr. pl. *mics*): Short for microphone. The more common abbreviation would be mike, but I don't like that.

3. *A/C strips*: Electrical strips that allow you to plug in multiple electronic devices into one outlet in order to obtain electricity.

4. *kit* (abbr. *drum kit*): Drum set.

5. *dog shit*: Digested waste as expelled by a canine. It is not uncommon to refer to sounds with references to other senses. Generally, if the descriptive word being used is negative to one sense, it's a negative description as it relates to our perception of sound. Since dog shit doesn't smell very good, you can logically assume that something that sounds like dog shit doesn't sound very good.

6. *head and cab*: The head is the amplifier and the cab is an ab-breviation for "cabinet," which is short for "speaker cabinet." Some amplifiers house both the speakers and the amplifier in one assembly, and that's called a "combo."

7. *rig*: General terminology used to describe the players instru-ment and/or amplifier.

8. *baffles*: Large separators that we use in the studio to block off sound. They are usually quite heavy, stand eight feet tall, sometimes have a window, and are preferably on casters. This allows me to section off a room without completely isolating the players from each other.

9. *PA system*: Short for "public address system." This allows me to amplify instruments in the room.

10. *kik* (abbr. *kick*): Bass drum on a drum set that is played with the foot. It's written "kik" out of habit, mostly because it's fast-er for me to write in the studio. I could have spelled it long for this diary if I really wanted to, but it's my diary, so I didn't.

11. *source*: The source is the instrument and player that you are recording. It is the source of the sound.

12. *"tube" equipment*: Gear that uses vacuum tubes as opposed to transistors. Tube gear should be shut off at night so as to not burn the tubes out.

13. *two-inch tape*: Refers to analog multitrack recording tape, which is two inches in width. I can record a little more than fifteen minutes of twenty-four tracks of music on one reel of two-inch tape. If you slow down the tape machine speed, you can get thirty minutes of recording time per reel, but there can be tape hiss issues. The machine that plays this tape is often called a two-inch machine.

14. *hat* (abbr. *hi-hat*): Two cymbals clasped together that a drummer typically uses to supply an eighth- or sixteenth-note pulse.
15. *mix*: The process that occurs after recording in which the instruments are blended and then rerecorded down to two tracks—left and right.
16. *discography* (pl. *discographies*): This is basically a résumé of records that one has worked on.
17. *A&R reps* (abbr. *artists and repertoire representatives*): The A&R department deals with signing artists, and oversees the making of the product.
18. *Red Bull*: An energy drink that contains high amounts of taurine, glucose, and caffeine. I have no idea what taurine is, but a friend of mine jokes that it's derived from bull testicles. He's full of shit, but that's pretty funny.
19. *sample* (pl. *samples*): A sample is basically a very short recording. Many hip-hop records use samples of famous songs to help create a new song. Rock records use samples of instruments like snare drums or kik drums. These samples are used to replace the actual instrument so as to provide a very consistent sound.
20. *low end*: The lower part of the audible frequency range. From 30 Hz to 150 Hz.
21. *bright*: Having an excess of high frequencies.
22. *loud*: Having little to no dynamic range, which is then brought up to maximum level on your CD by a mastering engineer. You might find that you need to turn up the volume of older CDs as compared to newer CDs. That's because newer CDs are loud.

23. *A/B-ing*: Comparing. Listening to A, then listening to B and making a judgment.

24. *clik track* (abbr. *click track*): This is basically a metronome that is pumped through the players' headphones. This allows them to stay at a certain tempo throughout the song.

25. *production reels*: Reels that contain valuable recorded information that might be needed for masters at a later time.

26. *multitrack*: A recording machine that is capable of recording many individual tracks.

27. trigger: A trigger is a device that will replace the source with samples by acting as a trigger mechanism. If I am using a kik sample, and I send the original recorded kik into the trigger, when the trigger device receives a certain threshold of level, the trigger will play the sample.

28. *Radar*: A hard drive–based digital multitrack recorder. It operates much like a tape machine, but has many of the benefits of a digital recorder, such as undo, and non-destructive editing. http://recordingtheworld.com

29. *mutes*: On/off switches on the console that can allow or disallow the passage of audio on an individual channel, or even on the console as a whole.

30. *mistriggers*: Triggers that miss or go off at the wrong time. This happens often with drums because there is usually more information going into a mic than just its designated source. For instance, the kik drum mic will primarily pick up the kik drum, but it will also pick up some snare drum and cymbals. This information can cause mistriggers.

31. *gating*: Using a gate. A gate is a device that works just as its name implies. It's a gateway for audio. If you put a gate on a

signal, when the gate is open you will hear that signal; when the gate is closed you won't. A gate will open automatically at a certain level of sound (called the threshold), allowing the signal to pass.

32. *slave*: When locking two machines using SMPTE time code, the second machine is called the slave because it's following the first machine. Once I fill up twenty-four tracks on a two-inch reel, I can reduce twenty-four tracks down to eight tracks (for example) by mixing them down to stereo pairs and rerecording them onto the slave. If there are twelve tracks of drums, I can mix them down to a stereo pair of drums. Because the slave locks to the master, I can ultimately play both the slave and the master, and have up to forty-eight tracks by virtue of using two machines. It's fine to mix by locking machines, but it's best to record on one machine, as there is a lag time for the machines to lock.

33. *punch*: When playing the tape, I can put the multitrack machine into and out of record at any time. This is called punching. If I have recorded a bass part, and there is a mistake on the third measure, I can punch in to the third measure, and punch out of the fourth measure, thereby recording the bass on only the third measure, and leaving the rest of the recording intact. In this case I used the term "punch-fest," which, if translated literally, would mean "a festival of punches." Trust me when I tell you this: No one actually *wants* to go to a festival of punches.

34. *neti pot*: A clay pot for cleaning out sinuses by pouring a homemade saline solution (warm water and pure kosher sea salt) through one nostril, and allowing the solution to flow

through your sinuses and out the other nostril. There is a technique to this, and I recommend highly that you buy and use a neti pot. I use mine daily.

35. *overdub*: To record on top of preexisting tracks. The initial recording, the one that occurs with the entire band, is called "tracking." After tracking a song we are then overdubbing. The overdub sessions can be the lion's share of the recording process, particularly when drums are the only instrument kept from tracking.

36. *pop screen*: The consonant sounds made from the letters *p* and *b* make what's called a plosive. On a closely placed microphone, a plosive is exaggerated greatly with a severe burst of low end, which can sound like a pop. A pop screen is mounted in front of a singer's mic so as to reduce a plosive's blast of air towards the microphone.

37. *throne*: Drum stool.

38. *mixers*: People who primarily mix records. This term can also refer to the device used for mixing records.

39. *mastering engineer*: The engineer who prepares the stereo master for its final presentation medium. These days that would be a CD. If a production has been to a mastering engineer, then the resulting CD would be called a mastered CD.

40. *Dangerous Mixers*: A brand of high-quality mixers that I highly recommend. http://dangerousmusic.com

41. *Paul McCartney*: The bass player for the Beatles, a pleasant little foursome from the '60s.

42. *mic pre* (abbr. *microphone preamplifier*): Used to amplify a microphone for recording.

43. *Full Sail*: A well-known recording school in the US, supply-ing yet more hopeful recording engineers to an already satu-rated job market.

44. *Ed Cherney*: A highly respected Los Angeles recordist/mixer/ producer and all-around good guy. http://edcherney.com

45. *ghost*: A singer or player hired to record for a player in the band, but receiving no credit for doing so. It's as if they were never even there.

46. *bussed* (past tense of *bus*): A bus is a path in which an audio signal can be sent. To bus is to send audio down the path of a bus. It is a way to route audio. Look, it took me close to a year to understand what the hell a bus or bussing was, and I was doing it on a daily basis. Do you really think I can explain it to you here?

47. *Art Bell*: A late-night radio talk show host. His show deals with UFOs, conspiracy theories, supernatural events, and anything weird. I sometimes listen to his show on my drive home from the studio. He has guests who will often make outrageous claims that make me yell, "Bullshit!" Art will fre-quently reply, "Indeed." For some reason this just slays me.

48. *sample replacements*: Samples that replace an organic source, like a kik drum or a snare drum.

49. *monitor mix*: The mix that is being heard at any given time during the tracking or overdubbing process.

50. *stereo bus*: The path in which multiple channels of audio are summed to a stereo left and right. I can put equalizers and compressors on the stereo bus in order to affect all instru-ments at once.

51. *cue mix*: The mix that is being fed to the headphones.

52. *cans*: Slang for "headphones."

53. *Bias Beach*: This is kind of a wonky joke, one that I'm not particularly proud of. But "bias" is a technical term having to do with recording to magnetic tape, and in this case would refer to the erasure of a track. Bias Beach is some magical place where all the erased parts go. Forever.

54. *loop*: A sample that plays over and over again.

55. *scratch*: A part that will most likely not be kept. For example, a vocal that is sung with the drums playing in the same room will typically be considered a scratch vocal. Sometimes a scratch track becomes a keeper. When this happens, everyone makes sure you know about it. I suppose they're proud.

56. *ong*: Same function as the more commonly heard "ohm." Used as a focusing chant in kundalini yoga. I'll bet you didn't believe that I meditated or did yoga. Well, you were wrong. "Ong namo guru dev namo" is also a chant used for a specific meditation.

57. *SpongeBob*: A cartoon on Nickelodeon, which at the time of writing this diary I thought was mindless. But I have persistent children, and have since come to fully appreciate and enjoy the show. I suppose I've grown.

58. *Ampeg B15*: A classic old tube bass amplifier and cabinet, all in one. They sound great.

59. *direct signal*: This is the signal that is generated directly from the bass without going through an amplifier.

60. *rough mixes*: Mixes that are made quickly, and are rough in nature in order to give an idea of where the production is at. Sometimes rough mixes become final mixes, and that always makes for a good story.

61. *Studio Referral Service*: This company, located in Los Angeles, can help you find a studio that fits your needs just about anywhere in the US. They will also help you negotiate a good rate. Ask for Ellis. And no, not *Marv* Ellis! http://studioreferral.com

62. *mains*: The enormous speakers that are built into the wall of a studio.